The Seaforth Highlanders

Other Titles by Paul Chrystal and in print with Pen & Sword Books

A History of Chocolate in York (2012)

Roman Military Disasters: Dark Days and Lost Legions (2015)

Women at War in the Classical World (2017)

Leeds's Military Legacy (2017)

Emperors of Rome: The Monsters – From Tiberius to Theodora, AD 14–548 (2018)

British Army of the Rhine: The BAOR, 1945–1993 (2018)

Rome: Republic into Empire – The Civil Wars of the First Century BCE (2019)

War in Roman Myth and Legend (2020)

War in Greek Mythology (2020)

A Historical Guide to Roman York (2021)

The History of Sweets (2021)

The History of the World in 100 Pandemics, Plagues and Epidemics (2021)

Rowntree's – The Early History (2021)

Factory Girls: The Working Lives of Women and Children (2022)

Bioterrorism and Biological Warfare: Disease as a Weapon of War (2023)

Gunners from the Sky: 1st Air Landing Light Regiment in Italy and at Arnhem, 1942–44 (2024)

Women at Work in World Wars I and II: Factories, Farms and the Military and Civil Services (2024)

World-Changing Women: 150 Women who Rewrote the Histories of Ancient Egypt, Israel, Greece and Rome (2024)

The Book in the Ancient World: How the Wisdom of the Ages Was Preserved (2025)

The Seaforth Highlanders

Aiding the King, 1881–1961

Paul Chrystal

Pen & Sword
MILITARY

First published in Great Britain in 2025 by
Pen & Sword Military
An imprint of Pen & Sword Books Limited
Yorkshire – Philadelphia

ISBN 978 1 39905 200 9

A CIP catalogue record for this book is available from the British Library.

Typeset by Mac Style
Printed in the UK by CPI Group (UK) Ltd, Croydon, CR0 4YY.

FSC www.fsc.org MIX Paper | Supporting responsible forestry FSC® C013604

The Publisher's authorised representative in the EU for product safety is Authorised Rep Compliance Ltd., Ground Floor, 71 Lower Baggot Street, Dublin D02 P593, Ireland.
www.arccompliance.com

For a complete list of Pen & Sword titles please contact

PEN & SWORD BOOKS LIMITED
47 Church Street, Barnsley, South Yorkshire, S70 2AS, England
E-mail: enquiries@pen-and-sword.co.uk
Website: www.pen-and-sword.co.uk
or
PEN AND SWORD BOOKS
1950 Lawrence Road, Havertown, PA 19083, USA
E-mail: uspen-and-sword@casematepublishers.com
Website: www.penandswordbooks.com

Contents

About the Author

Paul **Chrystal** attended the universities of Hull and Southampton where he studied classics (BA Hons and MPhil) and the Sorbonne, Paris; for the next 35 years he worked in medical publishing sales.

More recently he has been history advisor to various Yorkshire visitor attractions, writing features for national newspapers, and broadcasting on radio, including Radio 4's 'PM' programme and on the BBC World Service.

He has contributed to many history and archaeology magazines, and TV and radio programmes, and is the author of over 160 books published on a wide range of subjects, including military history and conflict.

He is past editor of *York History*, journal of the York Archaeological & York Architectural Society, and of *Yorkshire Archaeological Journal*. His books have been translated into Chinese and Japanese.

Acknowledgements

Huge thanks go to Angela C. and Helen S., Sergeant Eric Priest's granddaughters and my cousins, who provided personal information, photographs and documents. Unwittingly, in doing so they also gave important details about the Seaforth Highlanders generally. Without their help and thoughtfulness, and their anecdotes, this book would have been deficient in many ways.

I must acknowledge the wonderfully detailed and informative website – https://web.archive.org/web/20220928094629/https://www.britishmilitaryhistory.co.uk/ established and maintained by Robert Palmer. It has been a great help in researching my book.

Two excellent books, *Seaforth Highlanders* by Colonel John Sym and *Queen's Own Highlanders (Seaforth and Camerons): An Illustrated History* by Angus Fairee have also proved invaluable as standard works on the regiment. Thanks also to Philip Sidnell at Pen and Sword who, with his usual perceptiveness, saw the need for this book. Richard Doherty, editor, also at Pen & Sword, pointed out inconsistencies, inaccuracies and various other deficiencies, making the book a better work all round. What remains is all down to me.

The Museum of the Royal Regiment of Scotland Archive at Edinburgh Castle was particularly helpful. Finally, I must thank the archivists at the Highlanders Museum at Fort George, Ardersier, Inverness, and particularly Neil Thompson-Burton, Volunteer Researcher there, for the fantastic job he has done hunting down Sergeant Eric Priest and filling in some yawning gaps relating to my uncle Eric's long journey with the Regiment.

Introduction

Compared with some other regiments, comparatively little has been written about or published on the Seaforth Highlanders, even though the regiment has fought in many of Britain's theatres of war – from Egypt, Sudan to the Cape, from Burma and India, from North Africa to Normandy, from Italy to Salonika, from Palestine and Aden to Madagascar.[1]

This book tells the story of the regiment's various battalions as they fought their way through trenches, mud and deserts, mountains and jungles to emerge as a tenacious and brave body of men in the finest tradition of fighting Scottish regiments.

They acquitted themselves well in the Second Boer War and in the First World War, in which their fighting included the Battle of le Cateau in 1914, the Ypres salient giving them their introduction to chemical warfare in 1915, witnessing the dawn of tank warfare at Beaumont Hammel in 1916, Arras and Passchendaele in 1917 and, finally, advancing into Picardy in 1918.

During the Second World War, the 2nd Battalion of the regiment, albeit the reconstituted incarnation after St Valéry, fought valiantly in North Africa, Sicily, Italy, Madagascar, Operation OVERLORD and, finally, in the invasion of Germany in 1945. Before all that, though, they were part of 152 Brigade in 51st (Highland) Division with the British Expeditionary Force (BEF), fighting a ferocious last stand which sadly culminated in the ignominious surrender and capture at Saint-Valéry-en-Caux during the desperate Battle of France in June 1940 when the eyes of the world were transfixed on the evacuation from Dunkirk. The men of the Seaforth deserve better than that and it is hoped, perhaps naively, that this book will go a small way to avert the gaze and refocus on St Valéry.

The 1st Battalion acquitted itself in the hellish Burma Campaign of 1942–1945, not least at the Battle of Kohima which saved India from the Japanese.

The Seaforth Highlanders is a much-needed book, filling a gap in our military history which enables us to benefit from a more accurate and complete record of the regiment and the theatres of war in which its various battalions fought.

Unlike other books on the regiment, this book is as much about context and background as it is about dates, battles and places. So, for example, other writers baldly state that 'in 1805 the 72nd fought at the Battle of Cape Town'; I state likewise, but in addition reveal why the regiment was in Cape Town in the first place, giving the historical, political, military and, where appropriate, the social context of their presence in some detail. Who would deny that this gives a more complete, comprehensive and educative picture of the events under discussion? I explain, for example, the whys and wherefores surrounding, in no particular order:

- The Battle of Jersey.
- The Arab Revolt in Palestine.
- The International Occupation of Crete.
- The Walcheren Campaign and Walcheren Fever.
- What was going on in Java, Brunei and Belize to involve the Seaforth?
- The religious and cultural significance of the cartridge in India.
- Atrocities in India.
- The devastating role of cholera and other crowd diseases in the military.
- Khaki: bright crimson turns to dust.
- The pivotal role of the East India Company.
- Headhunting in Sudan and Malaya.
- The strategic importance of Madagascar in the Second World War and its (unfulfilled) role in the Holocaust.
- Irish Partition, and the Troubles from 1969.
- The Calton Riots, the Lancashire Riots.
- The 1921 Miners' Strike and the Defence Force.
- Torture on the North West Frontier.
- Atrocities and war crimes in the Malayan Emergency.
- The Burma campaign: Kohima and Imphal.

All of these and many more incidents involved one battalion or another of the Seaforth Highlanders or their antecedents. All and more are discussed within their historical, political and military contexts to explain why there was conflict, who was involved, its outcome, resolution and legacy.

The Seaforth Highlanders is one of the world-famous Scottish regiments with its roots in the regiments raised originally from clans and communities of the Highlands and Islands in the late seventeenth century.

The Regiment was officially formed in 1881 during the reign of Queen Victoria when the 72nd (Duke of Albany's Own Highlanders) Regiment of Foot and the 78th (Highlanders) (Ross-shire Buffs) Regiment of Foot, which became the 1st and 2nd battalions of the new regiment, amalgamated as part of the Childers Reforms; Hugh Childers was the Secretary of State for War.[2] The regiment acquired its name from Kenneth Mackenzie, 1st Earl of Seaforth, and his cousin Francis Mackenzie, 1st Baron Seaforth, who, respectively, initially raised the 72nd[3] and 78th[4] Regiments. Originally named Seaforth Highlanders (Ross-shire Buffs), on 22 November 1881 Queen Victoria approved the regiment's title as Seaforth Highlanders (Ross-shire Buffs, The Duke of Albany's).[5]

During the eighty-eight years from its formation to its disappearance as an individual regiment, the 78th saw service in a dozen foreign countries and accumulated an enviable array of battle honours. Eight officers and men were awarded Britain's highest military honour, the Victoria Cross.

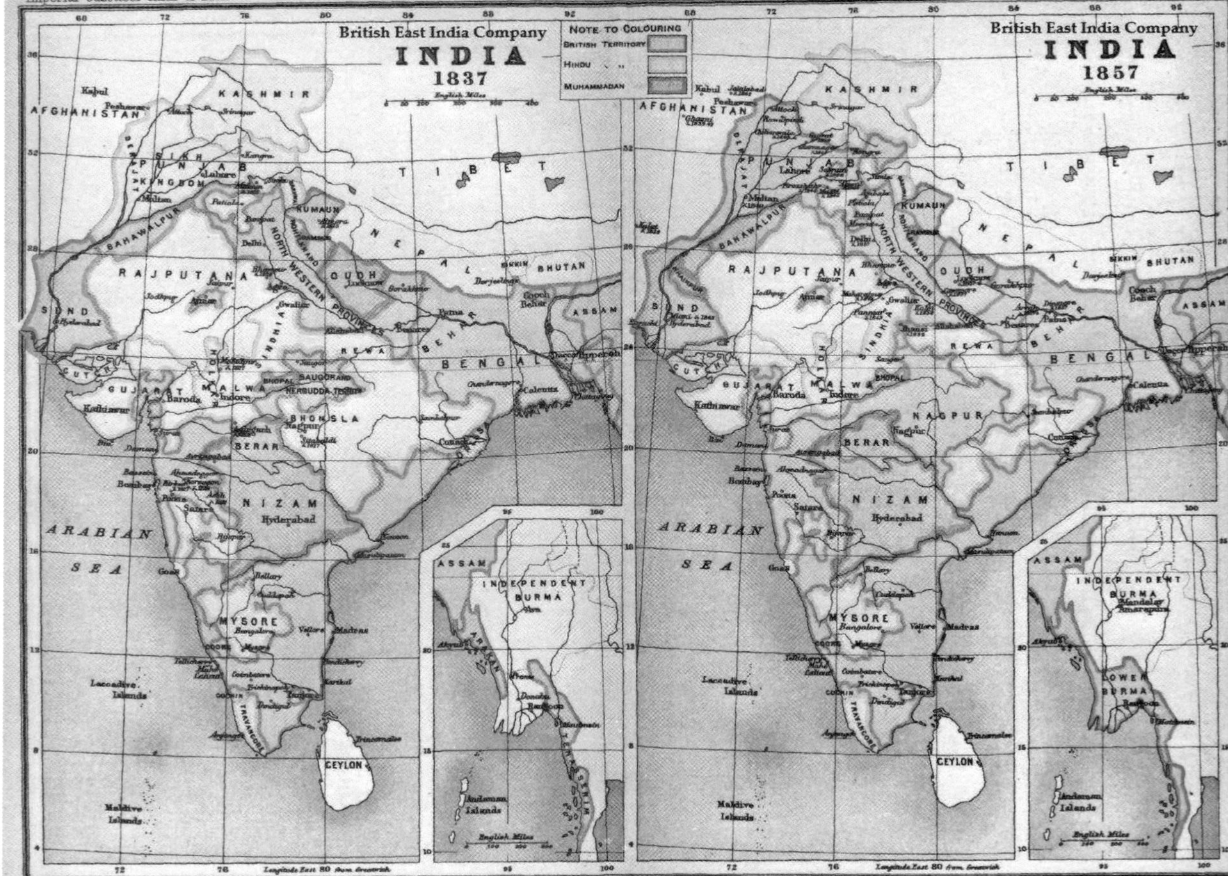
British East India Company
INDIA
1837
British East India Company
INDIA
1857
NOTE TO COLOURING
BRITISH TERRITORY
HINDU
MUHAMMADAN
English Miles
AFGHANISTAN
KASHMIR
PUNJAB
TIBET
NEPAL
BHUTAN
RAJPUTANA
SIND
KUMAUN
OUDH
NORTH WESTERN PROVINCES
REWA
BENGAL
BEHAR
ASSAM
GUJARAT
MALWA
BHONSLA
NAGPUR
BERAR
NIZAM
Hyderabad
MYSORE
TRAVANCORE
CEYLON
ARABIAN SEA
Laccadive Islands
Maldive Islands
INDEPENDENT BURMA
LOWER BURMA
Andaman Islands
Longitude East 80 from Greenwich

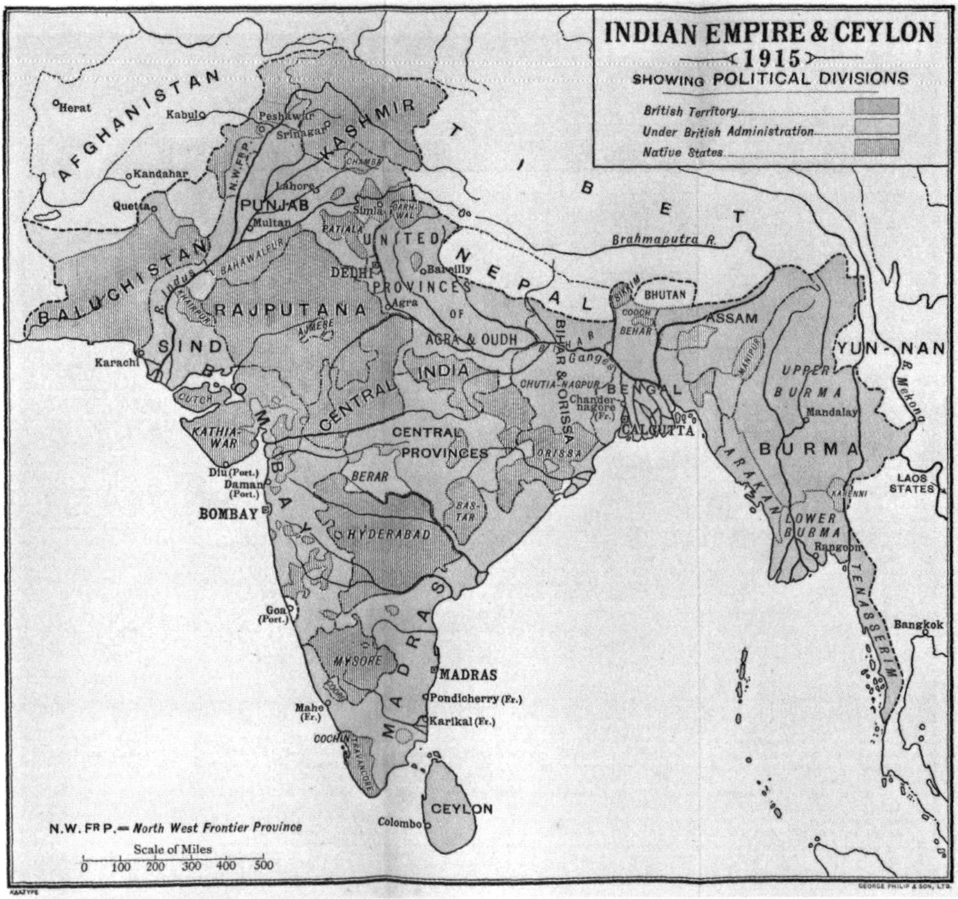
INDIAN EMPIRE & CEYLON
1915
SHOWING POLITICAL DIVISIONS
British Territory
Under British Administration
Native States
AFGHANISTAN
Herat
Kabul
Kandahar
Quetta
BALUCHISTAN
N.W. FR P.
Peshawar
Srinagar
KASHMIR
CHAMBA
TIBET
Lahore
PUNJAB
Multan
Simla
PATIALA
BAHAWALPUR
R. Indus
KHAIRPUR
RAJPUTANA
AJMERE
DELHI
UNITED PROVINCES OF AGRA & OUDH
Bareilly
Agra
NEPAL
Brahmaputra R.
SIKKIM
BHUTAN
COOCH BEHAR
ASSAM
MANIPUR
BIHAR & ORISSA
Ganges
CHUTIA-NAGPUR
BENGAL
Chandernagore (Fr.)
CALCUTTA
SIND
Karachi
CUTCH
KATHIAWAR
BOMBAY
CENTRAL INDIA
CENTRAL PROVINCES
BERAR
BASTAR
ORISSA
Diu (Port.)
Daman (Port.)
HYDERABAD
Goa (Port.)
MYSORE
COORG
MADRAS
Pondicherry (Fr.)
Karikal (Fr.)
Mahe (Fr.)
COCHIN
TRAVANCORE
CEYLON
Colombo
YUN-NAN
R. Mekong
UPPER BURMA
Mandalay
BURMA
ARAKAN
KARENNI
LOWER BURMA
Rangoon
TENASSERIM
LAOS STATES
Bangkok
N.W. FR P. = North West Frontier Province
Scale of Miles
0 100 200 300 400 500
GEORGE PHILIP & SON, LTD.

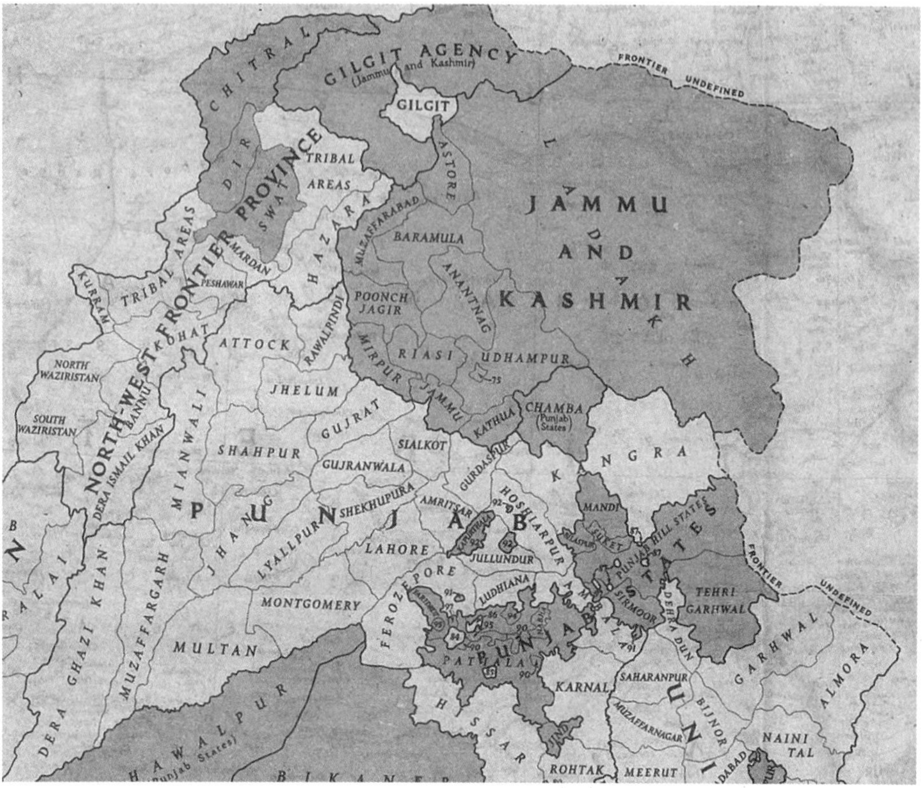

Map of Jammu and Kashmir produced in 1946 just before the independence of India and Pakistan.

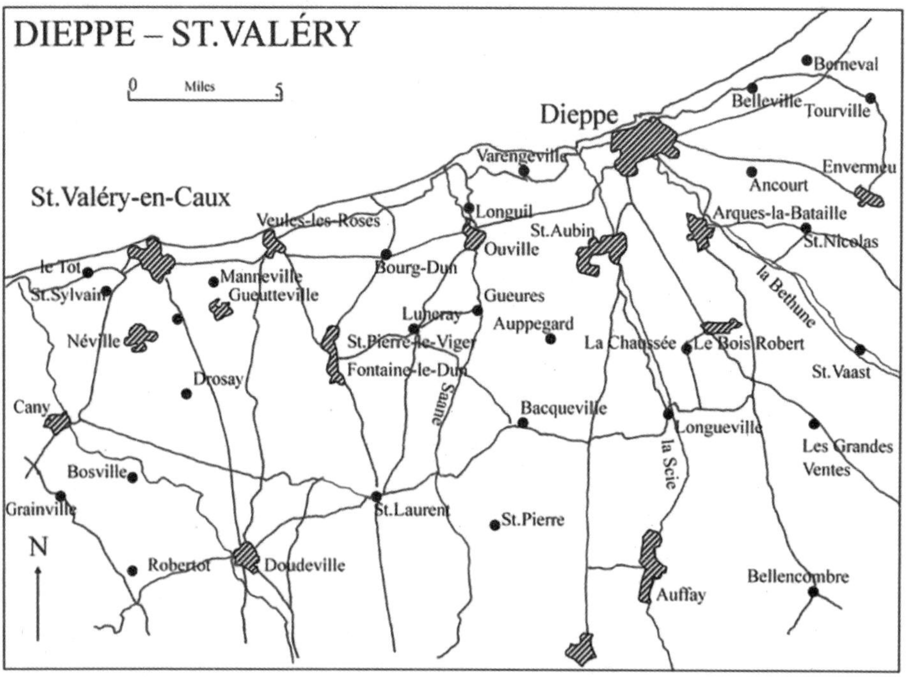

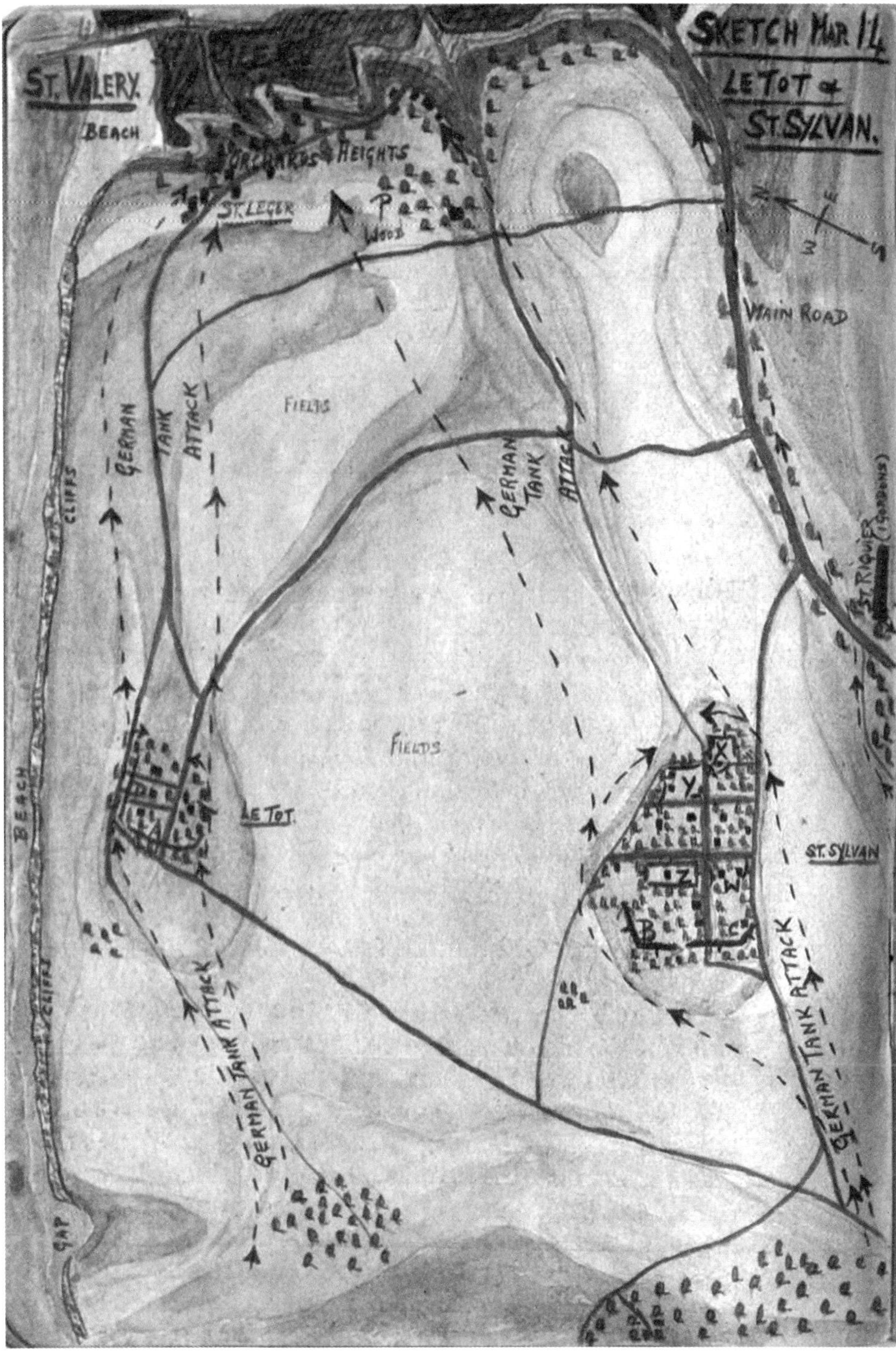
SKETCH MAP 14
LE TOT & ST. SYLVAN.
ST. VALERY.
BEACH
ORCHARDS & HEIGHTS
ST. LEGER
P
WOOD
MAIN ROAD
FIELDS
GERMAN TANK ATTACK
GERMAN TANK ATTACK
CLIFFS
FIELDS
ST. RIQUIER (GORDONS)
LE TOT
ST. SYLVAN
BEACH
GERMAN TANK ATTACK
GERMAN TANK ATTACK
CLIFFS
GAP

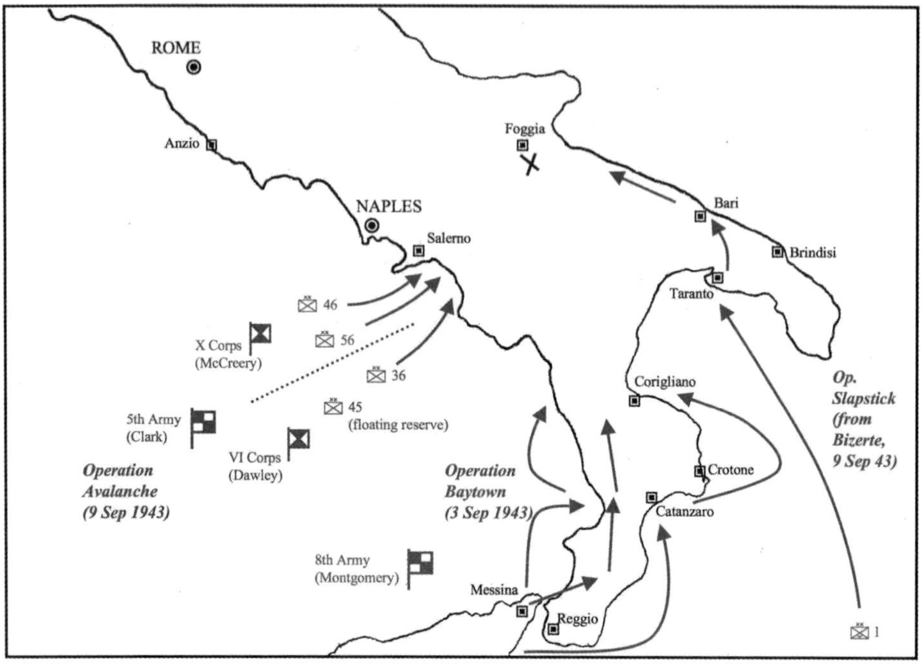

The Invasions of Italy, September 1943

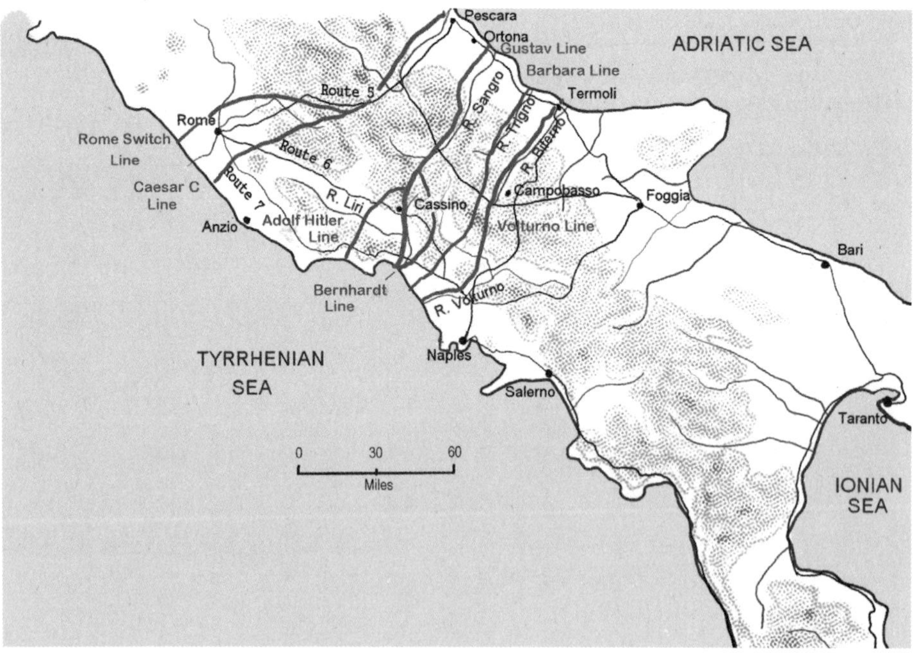

German defensive lines in Italy, 1943–1944. (*Stephen Kirrage via Wikimedia Commons/CC BY-SA 3.0*)

Chapter 1

Early Seaforth: The 78th (later 72nd) 1778–1793

The Seaforth Highlanders can trace their history back to 1778 but even before that the Mackenzies, or Clan Kenneth, held land in Kintail in the early fourteenth century and extended their influence throughout Ross-shire. In 1609 things were looking promising when Kenneth (the 13th Chief of the Clan) was elevated to the first Lord Mackenzie of Kintail (c.1569–1611). He won control of the Isle of Lewis in the Outer Hebrides from the Macleods of Lewis and successfully prosecuted a bloody feud with the Macdonells of Glengarry. Kenneth's son Colin became 1st Earl of Seaforth in 1623, taking his title from Loch Seaforth on the Isle of Lewis.

Members of the clan were also referred to as 'The Macraes', in recognition of the fact that many of the men of the regiment were members of Clan Macrae. Since a stag's antlers form the regiment's coat of arms, it was also known as 'Caber Feidh', Gaelic for stag's antlers. We learn that

> The 78th Highland Regiment of Foot were raised in 1793 by Colonel Francis Humberston Mackenzie and Lord Seaforth (Chief of the Clan Mackenzie) at Fort George, some 15 miles northeast of Inverness in the Scottish Highlands. ... initially a single-battalion regiment, a second battalion was added a year later, but they merged in 1796 while stationed in South Africa. In 1804, a second battalion was again raised. In 1817, the two battalions were merged and finally, in 1881, the 78th became the 2nd Battalion of the Seaforth Highlanders.[1]

The regimental march is 'Pibroch O' Donuil Dubh'; the tartan is Seaforth Mackenzie because the regiment was raised by the Head of Clan Mackenzie and most of the men of the regiment came from Clan Mackenzie lands in Ross-shire. The 78th wore red doublets, kilts, sporrans, feather bonnets and red-and-white-checkered hose. Since the regiment's collar and cuffs facings were buff, the 78th were also known as the Ross-shire Buffs. Regimental pipers wore green uniforms.

The regimental motto of the Ross-shire Buffs is *Cuidich'n Righ*, Gaelic for 'Help the king'. Legend has it that, in 1266, King Alexander III of Scotland was charged by a stag while out hunting. Colin of Kintail, then the Mackenzie Chief, galloped to the king's aid yelling 'Cuidich'n Righ' and, with sword in hand, chopped off the stag's head.

Keen to show his gratitude King Alexander bestowed upon the Mackenzies the motto 'Cuidich'n Righ' and the stag's head ('Cabar Feidh') as its clan crest. The 78th adopted the clan crest as its regimental badge and the eighteenth-century pipe tune *Cabar Feidh* as their regimental charge. 'Cabar Feidh' also became a regimental motto.

'Tulach Ard', after Tulach Ard, a mountain in the McKenzie heartland of Kintail, was the McKenzie clan's war cry. The signal for a clan gathering was a fire ablaze at the summit. The tune 'Tulloch-ard' is also known as 'Seaforth's gathering'.

The original 78th (Highland) Regiment was also known as Fraser's Highlanders, raised in Inverness in 1757 to fight in the Seven Years' War (known as the French and Indian War in the USA). The 78th was one of the first three Highland Regiments to see conflict in North America.

Raised by Lieutenant Colonel Simon Fraser of Lovat as the 2nd Highland Battalion, it embarked for Halifax, Nova Scotia in July 1757 to take part in the Seven Years' War, engaging in the Siege of Louisbourg later that month, the Battle of the Plains of Abraham in September 1759 and the Montreal Campaign in August 1760. During the war, the regiment suffered 103 soldiers killed and 383 wounded.

Disbanded in Quebec in December 1763, each man was offered a grant of land if he remained in Canada. Of those who accepted the offer, more than 300 joined the 84th Royal Highland Emigrants when it was raised in 1775.

A number of famous regiments have been raised from the Mackenzie clan, including the Highland Light Infantry (raised in 1777), the Seaforth Highlanders (as noted, raised in 1778), and the second battalion of the Seaforth Highlanders, known as the Ross-shire Buffs (raised in 1793). All those regiments wore the Mackenzie tartan. Born in 1754, Chief Francis Mackenzie, 1st Baron Seaforth, the last Lord Seaforth, raised a regiment for the British Army in 1778, the 72nd, and the clan produced another, the 78th, in 1793. Both had distinguished records fighting against Napoleon and were later amalgamated into the Queen's Own Highlanders.

Association with the Stuart kings cost the Clan Mackenzie dearly; when in 1715 William 'Dubh', the 5th Earl supported the Jacobite rising, he was disgraced and his lands forfeited. But pardon came in 1726 thanks to the support of General George Wade; fifteen years later the lost lands were recovered, but at the extortionate price of around £23,000. In 1745 there was another Jacobite rising after which measures were taken to ensure that this was going to be the last. Those measures included the deconstruction of the traditional clan system which ushered in existentialist and economic ruin and hardship for the clans. But there was a way out of this catastrophe: money could be raised by raising Highland infantry regiments. In 1771 Kenneth, Earl of Seaforth, seeing the commercial and social advantages for his destitute tenants, offered to raise a regiment for the king, George III.

Meanwhile, war in the American colonies had depleted the British Army and triggered a recruitment crisis. Any offer of a new regiment was, therefore, very attractive to the king. The 78th Regiment of (Highland) Foot, as it was first called, was raised in 1778 from men on the Seaforth and other Mackenzie estates. The Highlands had already been harvested of manpower by earlier recruitment campaigns by other regiments but the Earl tapped into the traditional loyalty of his clan and raised the forty-seven officers and 1,130 men needed to form the fledgling regiment. Most hailed from Ross-shire and Lewis (900 men) but there was a significant constituent of 300 lowlanders, and others from England and Ireland.

The regiment was embodied at Elgin in May 1778 and entered on the establishment of the British Army under the designation 'Seaforth's Highlanders' and numbered the 78th Regiment Foot.

Mutiny

Three months later, in August, the 78th found itself marching down to Leith for embarkation to India. Perhaps none of the recruiting officers had bothered to tell them that this strange and exotic faraway land was to be their first posting? Anyway, the soldiers soon got wind of this and 'began to show symptoms of dissatisfaction' in the words of *Sketches of The Character, Manners, and Present State of the Highlanders of Scotland – Seaforth Highlanders.* The soldiers had understood they were bound for the far more attractive sounding, less foreign, American colonies and took badly what they saw as duplicity. This led 400 or so of the men to march from Edinburgh Castle down the Canongate to the banks of the Forth. After 'a ludicrous altercation' with Seaforth and the rest of the regiment, the mutineers wheeled back to take a position of defiant protest on the highly symbolic Arthur's Seat, camping there for several days and in no mood to talk. There they were supplied with food and drink by the good people of Edinburgh, who supported them in their grievances. Meanwhile, those who had not mutinied boarded the transports bound for India. News of the mutiny was even picked up by the far distant London newspapers which included articles by James Boswell no less. As Royle tells us, 'cavalry was called out to surround the area but fortunately the senior officer in Scotland, Lieutenant General Sir James Oughton, was determined to avoid bloodshed. Not only did he understand the depth of feeling that had provoked the mutiny but he could see that the soldiers' action enjoyed widespread support'.[2] With Oughton reluctant to lose a whole regiment, after three days of hard negotiating a compromise was reached and he acceded to the mutineers' demands: the soldiers were pardoned and any charges of mutiny evaporated with a Court of Enquiry 'papering over the cracks'. The troops were again marched to Leith, led by the Earl of Seaforth, but bounties were paid and the immediate plan to send them to India was abandoned. The Channel Islands was the new destination where the 78th was assigned to repel the French invasion of Jersey.

Discipline

Despite it all, the 78th won for itself a reputation for sound discipline. Major General David Stewart in his famous *Sketches* assures us that 'amongst these men desertion was unknown and corporal punishment unnecessary'. It seems that 'the threat to report a man to his parents, or to have his name posted in his local parish church, was immensely potent, as it not only entailed disgrace, but ensured the culprit became an outcast, unable to return to his home.[3]

India and the East India Company, 1782–1798

The Earl of Seaforth eventually sailed with the Regiment to India in 1781 but died on the voyage out. With no male heir, his cousin, Colonel Thomas Mackenzie Humberston, succeeded him as Chief of Clan Mackenzie and Colonel of the 78th. The Regiment had embarked to assist the East India Company against the aggressions of the Sultan of Mysore during the Second Maratha War (1803–05) under the command of Arthur Wellesley, later Duke of Wellington, at the Battle of Assaye. Thomas died in Bombay in 1783 from wounds incurred in a sea fight against the Marathas and was succeeded by his brother Francis, MP for Ross-shire from 1784 to 1790.

No account of British military, economic or political involvement in India can be complete without acknowledgement of the role played by the East India Company in the sub-continent. The Company was a hugely powerful economic, commercial force with its own military capability which held sway in India from the early seventeenth century and dictated many aspects of life and activity there to some degree. The regiments that served in India were, indirectly and directly, influenced by the Company's presence there.

Meanwhile, in 1786, the 78th was renumbered the 72nd.

The Battle of Jersey 1781

On 1 May 1779, while the Anglo-French War of 1778–83 was raging, a French force under the command of the French-born Prince of Nassau-Siegen tried to land at St Ouen's Bay. Early that morning observers had spotted five large vessels and a multitude of boats some three leagues off the coast, proceeding at speed towards Jersey. The *London Gazette* of 4 May 1779 reported that guns on the French cutters and small craft supporting the landing fired grapeshot at the defenders on the coast.

The *London Gazette* continues its report:

> the defenders, the half regiment of 78th Seaforth Highlanders, and Jersey Militia, together with some field artillery that they dragged through the sand of the beaches, had by fast marching arrived in time to oppose the landing. The defenders were able to prevent any of the French forces landing, suffering only a few men wounded from a cannon burst. The French vessels withdrew, first holding off one league from the coast before departing Jersey waters completely.

The French were nothing if not persistent. In 1781 the Seaforth Highlanders surrounded a French raiding party which had landed on Jersey, taken St Helier and forced it to surrender on 6 January. As it turned out, this was something of a Pyrrhic victory: the French expedition lost nearly half its force, including its commander, soldier for hire Philippe Charles Félix Macquart, and Baron Philippe de Rullecourt, second-in-command to the Prince of Nassau-Siegen, who died of his wounds. His title 'Baron de Rullecourt' was self-bestowed; de Rullecourt was at once an adventurer and a colonel in the French Army. Louis XVI had promised de Rullecourt the rank of general and the Cordon Rouge as soon as he had control of St Helier.

On 5 January 1781 the French expedition set out from Granville, consisting of some 2,000 soldiers in four divisions. Then a storm blew up which scattered some of the ships with the result that only 1,200 initially made it to Jersey. As it happened Jersey still celebrated 6 January as 'Old Christmas Night', so the guard was down militarily and socially, and the French were able to land undetected. The 800 men of their first division landed at la Rocque, Grouville, on the south-east coast and passed close by the guards unnoticed. The *London Gazette* of 13 January 1781 tells how a French officer said that he had crept beneath the guards, but that the guards had not heard the French and were subsequently court martialled for having abandoned their posts to go drinking.

The French first division stayed there most of the night. The 400 men of the second division landed amongst rocks and were entirely destroyed. The initial British report was that a privateer and four transport vessels had been lost, together with 'upwards of 200 men'.

The boats that contained the third division, consisting of 600 men, separated from the rest of the fleet and were unable to connect with it. The fourth division, consisting of 200 men, landed early the next morning at la Rocque. The total of French troops landed on the island was therefore about 1,400.

According to Major General Porter, a French force of 700 men under the Baron de Rollecourt marched the four kilometres to St Helier,[1] arriving between 6.00 and 7.00am on January 6. When they entered the market, Royal Square, with its recently erected statue to King George II, they killed a sentry and surprised the guard, according to Henry Wimbush in *The Channel Islands*. The first division set up defensive positions in the market while most of the town was sleeping. At about 8.00am a French patrol surrounded Government House, then situated at le Manoir de la Motte on the east of the town. There they took the island's governor, Major Moses Corbet, by surprise. He was in bed.[2]

The baron's second-in-command, the exiled Indian prince Mir Sayyad, an ally of France in the Seven Years' War, advised him to ransack everything and to put the town to fire and to blood. Rullecourt now used Corbet as a bargaining chip in a bid to engineer a British surrender.

The French took Corbet to the Royal Court House in the market square where de Rullecourt convinced Corbet that thousands of French troops had already taken Jersey. Rullecourt threatened to burn the town and slaughter the inhabitants if Corbet did not sign a capitulation. Moreover, Corbet was advised to order the commander at Elizabeth Castle to surrender. Corbet replied that, as he was a prisoner, he had no authority and that anything he signed would 'be of no avail'. Rullecourt insisted and so Corbet, to avoid further harm to St Helier, and maybe to himself, signed.

As it happened, the French had already parleyed with the commander at Elizabeth Castle, Captain Mulcaster, who refused their request to surrender. When the French advanced towards the castle the troops there fired on them, killing two or three and causing them to withdraw. Porter tells us that Captain Aylward of the Invalids then arrived at the Castle and, being senior, assumed command. When the French delivered Corbet's written order to surrender, the castle's defenders signalled their stubborn refusal by firing on them.

Command now passed to the next most senior British commander, the 24-year-old Major Francis Peirson of the 95th (Yorkshire) Regiment, who commanded the troops at Saint Peter's Barracks. The British troops and militia assembled on the Mont ès Pendus, now Westmount, to the west of the town.

Peirson soon had 2,000 men at his disposal, with whom he resolved to descend the hill and attack into the town. The French, who were camped in the market, probably numbered 800–900 men.

According to Major General Porter, Major Peirson detached the 78th Seaforth Highlanders under Captain Lumsdaine and sent them to take possession of the Mont de la Ville hill, now the site of Fort Regent, to block any French retreat. Once Peirson believed that the 78th had reached their destination, he ordered his remaining troops to attack. The British were stopped at the edge of the town, where de Rullecourt sent Corbet to tell the British that, if they did not capitulate, the French would ransack the town within half an hour. The *London Gazette* reported that Peirson and Captain Campbell retorted that the French themselves had twenty minutes to surrender.

The five companies of the 83rd Regiment of Foot and elements of the East Regiment in Grouville to the east who were now covering the landing area also refused to surrender. When de Rullecourt received their answer he was heard to remark, 'Since they do not want to surrender, I have come to die.'

The attack began. The British forces in the Grande Rue, now Broad Street, included the 78th Seaforth Regiment, the Battalion of Saint Lawrence, the South-East Regiment, and the *Compagnies de Saint-Jean*. The 95th Regiment of Foot, with the rest of the militia, advanced down other roads.

The French resistance was short, the action lasting a quarter of an hour. The British positioned a howitzer directly opposite the market in the Grande Rue which, at each shot, 'cleaned all the surroundings of French'.

Major Peirson and the 95th Regiment advanced towards the Avenue du Marché where a musket ball to the heart killed Peirson; nevertheless, his troops rushed forward and continued the fight. When de Rullecourt fell wounded, many French soldiers gave up the fight, throwing down their weapons and fleeing. Others reached the houses in the market from where they continued to fire.

A guard of forty-five grenadiers of the 83rd Regiment, led by Captain Campbell, resisted 140 French soldiers until the arrival of elements of the East Regiment, whereupon the French were soundly defeated, suffering thirty dead or wounded, with seventy men taken prisoner. Seven grenadiers were killed during this action. The remaining French soldiers dispersed throughout the countryside to try to reach their boats but several were captured by local people.

The British took 600 prisoners; all were subsequently transported to England. The British losses were eleven dead and thirty-six wounded among the regular troops, and four dead and twenty-nine wounded from the militia. In addition, Captain Charlton of the Royal Artillery was wounded while in French custody. The French had seventy-eight killed and seventy-four wounded. Rullecourt was seriously wounded and died that night at the house of Dr Lerrier in Royal

Square, now the public house called The Peirson; he was buried in the grounds of the parish church of St Helier.

Captain Lumsdaine concluded, 'The face of the affairs being in a few hours thus changed, the enemy's vessels quit the Island, the troops that they had landed being drowned, killed, wounded or prisoners.'

The battle was the last attempt by French forces to take Jersey. John Singleton Copley's epic painting 'The Death of Major Peirson' imaginatively captures a version of the scene. Pierson was 24 when he died.[3]

This all happened during the American War of Independence (19 April 1775 to 3 September 1783); the French objective was to remove the threat they believed the island posed to French and American shipping. Jersey, fourteen miles off the French coast, was a base for privateers; Jersey privateers even operated off the coast of America. France was an ally of the newly created United States.

All adult males had for centuries been required by law to serve in the Jersey Militia which, in 1780, comprised some 3,000 men in five regiments, including artillery and dragoons.

British troops included:[4]

- 71st (Highland) Regiment of Foot (Fraser's Highlanders)
- 78th (Highland) Regiment of Foot (Seaforth Highlanders)
- 83rd Regiment of Foot (Royal Glasgow Volunteers)
- 95th Regiment of Foot (Reid's)
- 1st (North West) Regiment of Jersey Militia
- 3rd (East) Regiment of Jersey Militia
- 6th (South West) Regiment of Jersey Militia
- 700 Invalids (semi-retired reservists)

That amounts to a total force of about 6,250 troops available on Jersey. A naval force, the Jersey Squadron, was also based on the island, but was on an operation against the Dutch at the time of the invasion.

We learn from *Military Annals of the Highland Regiments: The Seaforth Highlanders*

> The intention of sending them to India having been postponed, they landed in Guernsey and Jersey in equal divisions, whence, at the end of March, they were removed to Portsmouth, where, on the 1st of May 1781, they embarked for the East Indies [India] amounting to 1,110 rank and file, all in high health, and well disciplined. But however hardy their constitutions, and however capable of active exertions on land, they did not withstand the diseases incident to a voyage of eleven months, in

> bad transports, and living on food so different from that to which they had been accustomed.

The 'bad transports' included 'a Newcastle collier fitted up as a transport'.

India 1781–1802

The Short History of the Seaforth Highlanders describes the voyage to India from Jersey via Portsmouth as 'a disastrous one … and [it] lasted over ten months. The Colonel died before St Helena was reached'. He was not alone: 'by the time the Battalion disembarked at Madras 247 men out of 1,100 had died of scurvy and of tropical diseases, and only 369 men could carry arms.' Fairrie describes it as 'one of the most melancholy episodes in the history of the regiment.[1] As noted, the Earl of Seaforth died off the coast of West Africa on 27 August 1781.

Sym describes the sorry affair as follows:[2]

> Shortly afterwards, the Regiment embarked for India, sailing in the 'June' fleet from Portsmouth on 4 June 1781. The voyage was a disastrous one … and lasted over ten months. On 3 July the *Nassau*, with Captain Thomas Fraser's Company of the 78th on board, lost her foretopmast and had all her booms and boats washed away in a gale. She became separated from the convoy and returned to Plymouth for repair. On 27 August the Colonel, the Earl of Seaforth, died and was buried at sea the next day, before St Helena was reached.

Provisioning left a lot to be desired, exacerbating the death toll and incapacitation of the troops: scurvy was not the only problem. Mouldy ships' biscuits and pork preserved in brine served only to bring on stomach upsets and increased the thirst of already thirsty soldiers forced to drink foul water.

When the 78th sailed in 1794 from Guernsey to occupy Zeeland Major General Stewart reveals that:

> Unpardonable neglect, the troops were put on board transports recently arrived from the West Indies with a number of prisoners, of whom many had died of fever in the passage. Without any inspection the same bedding was served out to the troops, who, as might have been anticipated, caught the infection.

Indeed, when the 2nd Battalion of the 78th was raised in 1804 and stationed in Kent, the sudden transition from a wholesome Scottish highland diet of barley, oats and vegetables to red meat caused much vomiting, boils and inflammations for up to two months.

The command of the regiment fell to Thomas Mackenzie Humberston, cousin of Lord Seaforth; Mackenzie, with only ten years' service before he took command, also succeeded to the estates but not to the coveted title. Wounded in the action against the Marathas, he died at sea aged only twenty-eight.

> The pressure of the service not admitting of delay, those who were able to march were moved up the country under the command of Major James Stuart, and joined the army under Sir Eyre Coote, in the beginning of May, at Chingleput. Many still being weak from the effects of the scurvy, and more liable to be affected by the heat on account of the impure state of their blood occasioned by the salt provisions, on which they had so long subsisted, they suffered extremely on this march. 'This regiment was composed of men sinewy and robust, which rendered them much more susceptible of the sun's violence than those of more slender habits.'

Colonel Munro's India

On 2 June they fought with the 72nd at the Battle of Arnee and although casualties were light with two rank and file killed and two wounded others were dying from the heat and exhaustion. As Sym says[3] 'the inevitable result of throwing unacclimatised Troops into action, soon after the privations of a long sea voyage'.

Over the next fifteen and a half years the Regiment's task was to support the East India Company in its pursuit of trade with the various independent Indian states; their treaties and agreements had to be backed by military force, particularly against the French. The heat was relentless and, for that reason, the uniform was eventually adapted to make life cooler for the troops: white trousers and gaiters replaced kilts, linings were removed from jackets and feather bonnets were replaced with round hats.

The Regiment's first deployment in 1783 was against the French fort and seaport of Cuddaldore and the Palghautcherry fort occupied by Tippoo Sahib, Sultan of Mysore in the Carnatic.[4] The earlier Carnatic wars of 1740–1763 were a series of conflicts between the British, French, Marathas and Mysore for control of the coastal strip of eastern India from Nellore, north of Madras (now Chennai), southward into Tamil country. More often than not, the regiment's actions involved 'reducing fortresses perched high up on granite hills'.

In 1782, during the Second Anglo-Mysore War, the French retook Cuddaldore at the time of the American War of Independence and were besieged there in 1783 by the British.

During the siege French and British naval forces clashed off the Cuddalore coast.

> This army consisted of the 73rd and 78th [Seaforth] Highlanders, and the 101st regiment, with a considerable body of Native troops, and was subsequently reinforced by a detachment of Hanoverians under Colonel Wagenheim .... On the 13th of June a general attack was made on the enemy's position in front of the garrison. After a severe conflict, which lasted from four o'clock in the morning till near five in the evening, the enemy were driven from their principal defences, on their right; when a cessation of firing took place as if by mutual consent. It was the intention of General Stuart to renew the attack next morning, but the enemy retired within the garrison in the course of the night. In this affair, the 78th lost Captain George Mackenzie, and 23 rank and file, killed; and 3 sergeants, and 44 rank and file, wounded.

The siege failed, but the fort was returned to the British in 1795 in exchange for Pondicherry and Mahé, two French territories that British forces had captured earlier in the war. Fighting continued between the British and Mysoreans until the Treaty of Mangalore was signed in March 1784.

> There were five separate naval actions off the coast during and around 1782 contested by two of the greatest admirals [of the time]: France's Admiral comte Pierre André de Suffren de Saint Tropez, bailli de Suffren, and the British Sir Edward Hughes, all of which were indecisive. In one of the skirmishes, on 3 August 1782, 'the Regiment was represented by detachments who acted as marines. The battle raged all day and the French were defeated with loss of 1,088 killed and wounded. Our losses were 334 killed and wounded, which included 2 officers of the regiment'.

For fifteen years the regiment was instrumental in breaking the power of Tippoo Sahib, Sultan of Mysore, or, more popularly, the Tiger of Mysore. Tippoo was quite a character: when he wasn't pioneering rocket artillery he introduced a number of administrative innovations, including a new coinage system and calendar, and a new land revenue system, which initiated the growth of the Mysore silk industry. He expanded the iron-cased Mysorean rockets and commissioned the military manual *Fathul Mujahidin*. He deployed his rockets against advances of British forces and their allies during the Anglo-Mysore Wars, including the Battle of Pollilur and Siege of Srirangapatna.

On succeeding his father in 1782 he won critical victories against the British in the Second Anglo-Mysore War, negotiating the 1784 Treaty of Mangalore with them and ending the war.

In 1783 the three years for which the soldiers of the 78th had enlisted were up; they had agreed to 'enlist for three years or until the end of the Rebellion', the Rebellion being the American War of Independence which concluded with the 1783 Treaty of Versailles. They could be discharged or stay on, on payment of a ten-guinea bounty; 300 took the money while the rest went home. The regiment was reinforced with volunteers from regiments returning to Britain to be disbanded.

In 1786 cuts accompanied the period of peace reducing the number of regiments to seventy-seven; the 78th was renumbered the 72nd.

The 72nd in India

The years 1789 to 1792 saw the 72nd fighting in the Carnatic campaign as part of the European Brigade; a number of forts were taken as a prelude to the invasion of Mysore. As we will see, they excelled at the assault on Bangalore in 1791, successfully stormed the fortresses at Savendroog and Outra Durgam and captured Tippoo's capital, Seringapatam, which concluded the campaign. The East India Company rewarded the soldiers who took part in the campaign with a bounty that amounted to more than a year's pay.

The 72nd played a prominent part in the siege of Pondicherry in 1793 alongside the 73rd Regiment (or Lord Macleod's Highlanders or 71st Regiment, or Glasgow Light Infantry). In *Sketches of The Character, Manners, and Present State of the Highlanders of Scotland with details of The Military Service of The Highland Regiments* by Major General David Stewart we get a number of interesting glimpses of the experiences of the Scottish soldier fighting in India at this time; this in relation to PoW conditions in a religious setting:

> The steadiness of principle, and incorruptible fidelity, of these soldiers on this occasion, are recorded by Mrs Grant [*Superstitions of the Highlanders*]. 'A Highland regiment, commanded by Lord Macleod, was, during the war with Hyder Ali, engaged in an unfortunate encounter, where more than 100 men fell into the hands of that remorseless tyrant. They were treated with the most cruel indignity, and fed upon very sparing proportions of unwholesome rice, which operated as slow poison, assisted by the burning heat of the sun by day, and the unwholesome dews of night, to which they were purposely exposed to shake their constancy. Daily some of their companions dropped before their eyes, and daily they were offered

> liberty and riches in exchange for this lingering torture, on condition of relinquishing their religion and taking the turban. Yet not one could be prevailed upon to purchase life on these terms. These Highlanders were entirely illiterate; scarce one of them could have told the name of any particular sect of Christians, and all the idea they had of the Mahomedan religion was that it was adverse to their own, and to what they had been taught by their fathers; and that, adopting it, they would renounce Him who had died, that they might live, and who loved them, and could support them in all their sufferings. The great outlines of their religion, the peculiar tenets which distinguish it from any other, were early and deeply impressed on their minds, and proved sufficient in the hour of trial.[1]

Likewise, they acquitted themselves well at Coimbetore, for decades a town much coveted by Tippoo Sahib and the British during the Anglo-Mysore Wars. The city was taken by the forces of the British East India Company in 1768 but they were forced to abandon it due to treachery. Colonel Fullarton occupied the city in 1783 but later returned it to Tippoo Sultan through the terms of the Treaty of Mangalore. At the beginning of the Third Mysore War of 1790–1792 Coimbatore was once again taken by the British. Tippoo Sahib laid siege to the city twice and was repelled in the first, but successful in the second; Coimbatore surrendered in October 1791. The commanders of the garrison, Lieutenant Chalmers and Lieutenant Nash, were taken prisoner to Seringapatnam. Coimbatore fell to the British at the end of the Third Mysore War but was restored to Tippoo Sahib when the fighting stopped. Coimbatore was eventually annexed by the British on the defeat and death of Tippoo Sahib in 1799. Coimbatore was taken by the Polygars in 1800 and was an important stronghold in the Polygar Wars. It was made capital of Coimbatore district in 1865.

There were other clashes with Tippoo Sahib: at Bangalore in 1791 which Tippoo thought was impregnable; Outredroog, Savendroog, Outra Durgum (where the two companies engaged escaladed the five walls of the fortress in succession) and at Seringapatam, where they formed part of the left division in the battle before the town.

Outra Durgum

Short History of the Seaforth Highlanders, describes this action as follows:

> The fort at Outra Durgam was enclosed by five walls; this fort was taken by two companies of the 72nd without waiting for orders. Ladders were planted against the walls; a few men were over the walls in the twinkling

> of an eye; the first gate was unbolted, and the companies rushed through. They crashed down the second gate with their shoulders; inside, the passage was so narrow that only two could squeeze through abreast; the defenders hurled huge stones down on the attackers, but they passed the ladders forward overhead, and very soon the gallant Highlanders were crowding over the third gateway. The enemy fled on all hands, pursued by Highland bayonets and the last two walls were gained without opposition. Our two companies were soon in possession of every part of the fortress, and Lt MacInnes planted the colours on the highest pinnacle.[2]

The Siege of Bangalore 1791

A siege of the town and fortifications of Bangalore occurred during the Third Anglo-Mysore War by forces of the British East India Company, led by Charles, Earl Cornwallis against a Mysorean garrison while Tippoo Sahib harried the camps and positions of the besiegers. Arriving before the town on 5 February 1791, Cornwallis captured the town by assault on 7 February, and after six weeks of siege, stormed the fortress on 21 March.

The Siege of Seringapatam 1799

The siege of the well provisioned Seringapatam (5 April-4 May 1799) was the final conflict of the Fourth Anglo-Mysore War between the British East India Company and the Kingdom of Mysore. The British, with the allied Nizam Ali Khan, 2nd Nizam of Hyderabad and Marathas, achieved a decisive victory after breaching the walls of the fortress at Seringapatam and storming the citadel.

At 11.00 am on 4 May 1799 the British troops were briefed, and whisky and a biscuit issued to the European soldiers, before the signal to attack was given. The 'forlorn hopes', numbering seventy-six men, led the charge. The columns quickly formed, were ordered to fix bayonets, and began to advance …

Lieutenant-General Sir Alexander Campbell kept a diary and gives us some detail about the siege:

> When about 50 yards from the works, the sentinel challenged us, and instantly fired his piece, which was followed by a scattered fire from the rest of their party. We rushed among them, and those who did not save themselves by immediate flight were shot or bayoneted … by this time the general attack on the enemy's lines had commenced, and there was an almost connected sheet of fire from left to right: musketry, guns and rockets rending the air with their contending noise … we had now got into their camp, upon the right flank of their lines; they retreated steadily before us, and our fire and bayonets did great execution among them, the

> road being strewed with their bodies. We charged and dislodged them from the second choultry [a resting place, inn or caravansary for travellers] … we pursued the enemy to a large pagoda; they attempted to cross the river, but the place was so crowded with guns, tumbrils, bullocks, elephants, camels, followers, and heavens knows what that we were in the midst of them before they could escape, and for some minutes there was nothing but shooting and bayoneting … we pushed on through holes, over rocks and stones, falling and stumbling at every step, the enemy's shot reducing our numbers … .[3]

The battle comprised a series of encounters around Seringapatam during April and May 1799 between the combined forces of the British East India Company and their allies, numbering over 50,000 soldiers in total, and the soldiers of the Kingdom of Mysore numbering up to 30,000. The Fourth Anglo-Mysore War came to an end with the defeat and death of Tipu Sultan in the battle.

In the war with France and the Netherlands the Regiment was present at the capture of Pondicherry from the French, and for their services were permitted to carry 'Hindoostan' on their Colours.

In 1795 the regiment formed part of the force which landed at Trincomalee under their old commander Colonel, now Major General, James Stuart in the capture of Ceylon (Sri Lanka) from the Netherlands. This was the last service of the regiment in the East at that period. In 1797 they were moved from Ceylon to Pondicherry, when orders were received, in December, to draft the regiment, then 800 strong, into the corps on that station, and for the officers, non-commissioned officers, and invalids, unfit for service, to embark for England. The 'skeleton of the regiment' embarked at Madras in January 1798 after seventeen years of foreign service, and, after a short passage, landed at Gravesend. From there they were ordered to Perth, where they arrived in August, under the command of Lieutenant Colonel Hugh Fraser. The troops were issued with Highland dress after those seventeen uncomfortable years of tropical kit.

Recruitment at Perth was to be a problem over the next three years, not just for the 72nd but for all Scottish regiments. Whether it was the emaciated appearance of the few permitted to return home which discouraged the young local men, or the realisation that few of the many who had left Perth to join the regiment had come home or, more generally, the great drain of men from the Highlands at this period. Whatever, the corps failed to recruit even 200 men in three years. However, when removed to Ireland in 1800, the ranks were filled up to 900 with young men from the Scotch Fencible regiments.[4] Colonel Macfarlane, who succeeded to the command on the death of Lieutenant Colonel Fraser was now at the head of an efficient body of young men, which formed a 'fine regiment, possessing as pure and true a spirit as any corps'. It is worth repeating that one quarter of the men and officers were English and Irish, and three quarters Highlanders; and 'singular as it may seem, the former were as fond of the kilt and pipes as the latter, and many of them entered completely into the spirit of the national feeling. And, in all the solid essential qualities which form the character of the British soldier, they were perfect'.[5]

Cape Colony and the Kaffir Wars

In 1805 the 72nd then formed a part of the expedition, under Sir David Baird, against the Cape of Good Hope, stopping off at Madeira en route. And, to commemorate their gallantry at the Cape, they were able to display the words 'Cape of Good Hope, 1806', on their Colours. At the Cape they formed part of the Highland Brigade with the 71st and the 93rd advancing against the Dutch at Blaauberg, also known as the Battle of Cape Town, on 8 January 1806. Later they landed at Lospard's Bay under fire but chased the defenders into the Blue Mountains where they enjoyed a victory.

The Cape Colony had huge strategic importance. At this time it belonged to the Batavian Republic, a French vassal. The British decided to seize the colony in order to prevent it, and the sea route to India, from falling under French control. A British fleet was despatched to the Cape in July 1805 to forestall French troopships which Napoleon had sent to reinforce the Cape garrison.

The colony was governed by Lieutenant General Jan Willem Janssens, who doubled as commander-in-chief of its military forces. What forces he had, including foreign units in the pay of the Batavian government, were small and of poor quality. They demonstrated nicely the multi-nationalism of contemporary armies and included a regiment of foreign mercenaries from Waldeck, two regular Batavian battalions, a squadron of Batavian light dragoons, a troop of Batavian horse artillery and over 200 sailors and marines from two beached French warships, *Atlante* and *Napoleon*. The local troops Janssens mustered for the battle included 181 Hottentots, 224 Burghers out of Swellendam organised as dragoons and 54 Javanese artillerists with 104 Mozambiquan slaves serving as their auxiliaries, wagon drivers and carriers.

Baird began the battle with 5,399 men: his troops suffered 204 casualties, 189 wounded and fifteen killed. The Highland Brigade was in the thick of it. David Baird's despatches tell us that 'The Highland Brigade advanced steadily under a heavy fire of round shot, grape and musketry. Nothing could resist the determined bravery of the troops, and the number of the enemy served only to augment their ardour'.[1]

This was a small but significant military engagement during the Napoleonic Wars. After the British were victorious, peace was made under the Treaty Tree in Woodstock.[2] It established British rule over the Dutch Cape Colony, which was to resonate through the region during the nineteenth and twentieth centuries.

The 72nd spent the sixteen years after the Battle of Cape Town in the Cape stationed at Simon's Town, Cape Town and Stellenbosch. The posting was interrupted at the end of 1810 by a foray to the French owned island of Mauritius which capitulated without resistance.

Mauritius has an interesting history: a Dutch fleet, under Admiral Van Warwyck landed at what is now Grand Port and took control of the island in 1598, renaming the then uninhabited islands after Maurice, Prince of Orange, and establishing a succession of short lived Dutch settlements over the next 120 years, to exploit the local ebony forests and establish sugar production. France took control in 1715, renaming it Île de France. In 1810 the United Kingdom seized the island and, four years later, in the Treaty of Paris, France ceded Mauritius and its dependencies to the United Kingdom.

The 72nd remained for three years, returning to Cape Town in 1814, but not for long. In 1815 they made a lightning trip to India to fight against the Rajah of Nepal. By the time they reached Calcutta the trouble had blown over, so they returned to the Cape until 1821.

In 1804 the 72nd was permitted to raise a 2nd Battalion which was mostly stationed in Great Britain as a feeder battalion for the 1st/72nd, then, as we have seen, on active service in the Cape and Mauritius. Army cuts post-war with France led to the disbandment of the 2nd Battalion in 1816 at Londonderry.

In 1809 the 72nd was dealt a blow which would have had serious ramifications for morale and pride. George III had bizarrely agreed to order the Seaforth (and other Highland regiments: 73rd, 74th, 75th and 91st) 'to discontinue wearing the Highland costume'. Back came the tropical uniform with red jacket, white trousers and Glengarry bonnet. The regiment was also renamed the 72nd Regiment of Foot with the reference to 'Highland' erased. Effectively, the king was taking the Scotland out of those illustrious Scottish regiments which stood proudly among the best in the defence of the British empire around the world. *The Short History of the Seaforth Highlanders* describes it well: 'thus the nationality of the regiment was disowned.' The Mackenzie tartan and the jacket's yellow facing were ditched and the 72nd were compelled to don the white facings and pantaloons of a standard regiment of the Line. This they endured for fourteen long years although, unofficially, they managed to retain a number of Scottish traditions, including their pipers, and continued to use the drum beatings and fife tunes of the Scotch Duty.

The Kaffir War (1817–1821)[3]

Garrison duty in Scotland, Ireland and England kept the Regiment busy until 1817 when it embarked for the Cape and, in 1832, engaged in what is known as the sixth Kaffir War until its conclusion.[4] The Regiment was split into detachments charged with repelling cattle raids on the frontier and punishing transgressors in counter raids. They clashed endlessly with Bantu tribes intent on extending their territories and defended against Kaffir raids on Boer settlements. The Kaffirs were one of the main Bantu tribes.

After a short period back in Britain from December 1821 the regiment was garrisoned in the south of England and the Channel Islands. That period of home service was marked by the welcome news in 1823 that George IV had restored the 72nd to Highland Regiment status with the re-introduction of Highland dress; it was redesignated the 72nd or Duke of Albany's Own Highlanders. The main concession was that officers and men would wear trews instead of kilts; the trews were of the Royal Stuart tartan in the Prince Charles Edward Stuart sett. They returned to Edinburgh in September 1824 after twenty-four years away from Scotland and were stationed at Edinburgh Castle from where they could recruit in the Highlands and restore their quintessentially Scottish Highland character.[5]

His Majesty continued to say that he had also been pleased to approve of the regiment bearing the title of the '72nd or the Duke of Albany's Own Highlanders'. The excellent conduct of the Regiment, both in peace and war, resulted in the distinguished honour of being called after the Commander in Chief, the first Prince of the Blood Royal of Scotland, and in being restored to 'the proud position from which it had been so unaccountably removed fourteen years before'.

In 1825 the Regiment was back in Ireland on garrison duty until 1827 when it moved back over to London, quartered in the Tower and sharing duties with the Household regiments. The following year they marched to Canterbury and then to Gravesend whence they sailed to Cape Colony where the Kaffirs kept them busy again, this time for twelve years.

The Kaffir War 1834–1835

In 1834 the Kaffirs were resuming their truculent attitude in the eastern part of Cape Colony. A significant raid won them many a settler's cattle; the 72nd was involved in subduing the Kaffirs and restoring the cattle to their rightful owners.

By 1840 they were back in Great Britain.

Rioting in Lancashire 1840

Trouble at home occupied the regiment in 1842 when the Admiral Lord Rodney Pub in Waterside, Colne, was regarded by the authorities to be a hotbed of sedition and dissent on the introduction of power looms in Colne.

Cotton workers feared for their livelihoods: home and manual loom workers were being threatened by machinery. The workers had the support of the radical Manchester Socialist Group, the Chartists. Meanwhile, a government spy was embedded behind the bar at the pub to eavesdrop on the machinations of the rebels.

A march was organised to protest against these highly controversial power looms, from the pub up Waterside Road to Robert Shaw's premises in Colne Lane, Victoria Mills, and his Georgian residency next door. Shaw was the first and largest mill owner in Colne to introduce lower looms.[1]

The Lancashire Telegraph reported:

> This situation led to the Riot in Waterside. The Militia was then called from Burnley to Colne, where the Cloth (Piece) Hall was used as a Barracks. It was during this initial disturbance that the local constable, Joseph Halstead, aged 44 years, was isolated and killed in Clayton Street, which stretched up as far as Market Street in those days … . His gravestone in Colne Cemetery reads: 'Barbarously murdered while engaged in his duty as a Special Constable during the riot of 10th August 1840.[2]

Richard Boothman, a weaver, who always pleaded his innocence, was convicted as a Chartist murderer. With his original death sentence commuted to transportation for life, he was shipped to Tasmania; he arrived in Hobart on 13 January 1842.

The years 1843–44 were spent in Ireland on garrison duty again with 1844–1848 on further garrison duties in Gibraltar along with the 79th Cameron Highlanders, the first of many postings which saw both regiments serving together.

In February 1848 the 72nd left Gibraltar for the West Indies only to be stricken on landing by a yellow fever epidemic which claimed four officers and fifty-nine other ranks.[3] Garrisons included Trinidad and Barbados while detachments were also stationed at St Lucia, Demerara, Grenada and Tobago.

In 1851 the regiment moved north to Halifax, Nova Scotia, marching in September of that year to New Brunswick and then back to Halifax in 1853.

While the 72nd was kicking its heels in Canada, the world further east was increasingly tense with the expansionist Russians eyeing India and the Middle East, and the Crimean War about to erupt, with Sevastopol under siege as the regiment sailed for Ireland.

Since the depot companies in Ireland had followed orders to provide every last man in order to bring other Highland regiments up to strength, the 72nd found itself more than 300 men short of establishment. The service companies sailed for Malta in December 1854 while the depot companies remained in Ireland to recruit. The service companies arrived in Malta in January 1855 but were delayed there until May.

Crimea 1855–1856

The 72nd were to join the expedition to Kertch but did not land. Instead, they spent six days at anchor during which twenty-two NCOs and men perished from cholera.

The 72nd eventually disembarked at Balaclava in May 1855 joining the 42nd, 79th and 93rd Highlanders. For two months the Regiment toiled in the trenches during the siege at Sevastopol until the Russian base was captured. Finally, they moved with the Highland Brigade to support the Sardinian army against an anticipated Russian assault on Kamara, the day after their fighting in the Battle of Chernaya (from the Chyomaya River on the outskirts of Sevastopol) on 16 August. The battle was fought between Russian troops and a coalition of French, Piedmontese and Ottoman troops. The battle, involving 58,000 Russian troops against 28,000 French ended in a Russian retreat and a victory for the allies. At Sevastopol the 72nd was detailed to lead the storming party but the Russians evacuated their positions the night before. One year later the Regiment was still there, plagued by disease which took one officer and 101 other ranks. When the 71st and 92nd Highlanders arrived along with the 1st and 2nd Battalions of the Royal Scots the Brigade was redesignated as the Highland Division.

The expedition to Kertch

In the Crimean campaign it took part in the expedition to Kertch.[1] There were accusations of war crimes by the British. In the House of Commons Thomas Milner Gibson (Lib.) probed this allegation:

> I wish, Sir, to put a question to the noble Lord at the head of the Government in reference to the recent operations at Kertch and other places in the Sea of Azoff. Grave charges have been made against the character of Englishmen and English officers, which I do not believe, and which, if not true, ought to receive contradiction from the Ministers of the Crown. I have seen the same statement made in private letters and published in the public journals. It is stated in *The Times* newspaper, that—

> 'When the allies entered Kertch the following morning the population made their submission, and offered bread and salt to the conquerors, in accordance with the Russian custom, and they were assured that they would be protected, and that their lives and property should be spared.'

The correspondent goes on to say that destruction of property followed; and more than that—

> 'Towards evening Turkish stragglers from the camp, and others who had fallen out of the line of march, flocked into the town, and perpetrated the most atrocious crimes. To pillage and wanton devastation they added violation and murder.'[2]

The port of Kerch commanded access to the Sea of Azov, an important supply route for Sevastopol.[3]

Much to the disgust of the British, a previous Anglo-French expedition to capture Kerch had been abandoned in sight of its objective when the French force was suddenly recalled. However, on 22 May 1855 a second expedition was launched which was successful, opening up the way into the Sea of Azov and destroying the Russian naval squadron there.[4]

Around this time the regiment was increased to seventy-one officers and 2,256 other ranks of whom forty-seven were drummers and pipers.

Back to the UK, the 72nd disembarked at Portsmouth on 31 July 1856 and were ordered to parade at Aldershot the following day for inspection by Queen Victoria. They were then despatched to the Channel Islands until April 1857, before joining the 79th in garrison at Shorncliffe in Kent. In August and September that year they sailed for Bombay to help quell the Indian Rebellion. The 72nd was posted to central India where it successfully checked the spread of the mutiny and hunted down bands of rebels.

India 1857–8: The Indian Mutiny

The Indian Rebellion of 1857 was a critical uprising in India against the rule of the East India Company, which functioned as a sovereign power on behalf of the British Crown. The rebellion began on 10 May 1857 in the form of a mutiny of sepoys of the Company's army in the garrison town of Meerut, forty miles (64km) north-east of Delhi. Troops of the HEIC armies of the different presidencies (Bengal, Bombay and Madras) were called *sepoys*, in the case of infantrymen, and *sowars*, in the case of cavalrymen. It then erupted into other mutinies and civilian rebellions, chiefly in the upper Gangetic plain and Central

India, although incidents of revolt also occurred farther north and east. The rebellion posed a real military threat to British power in that region and ended only with the rebels' defeat in Gwalior on 20 June 1858.

During the Mutiny, the Regiment was engaged in mopping up fleeing rebels when they had been expelled from areas of insurrection such as Delhi and Lucknow. It then sailed to Kota-ki-Serai (Kotah), a sizeable walled city located in the south-east of the northern Indian state of Rajasthan, via Bombay, marching to Nasirabad to join up with a force of about two brigades. At Kotah the British Resident and his sons had been slain by mutineers, the Rajah was complacent and the locals rebellious and supported by mutineers. The attack took the form of three columns, the first of which comprised 260 men of the 72nd. The city duly fell, thanks largely to the efforts of the 72nd.[1] Over seventy guns and a large ammunition magazine were captured. It was there that Lieutenant Cameron was awarded the VC.

Colonel Aylmer Spicer Cameron VC CB

Colonel Aylmer Spicer Cameron VC CB, born in Perth, was commissioned as an ensign in the 72nd Highlanders on 9 July 1852 and promoted to lieutenant in August 1854. He served in the Crimean War and was present at the siege of Sevastopol in 1855 before going to India after the outbreak of the Mutiny.

Cameron was 24 years old when the following action took place on 30 March 1858 at Kotah for which he was awarded the VC:

> For conspicuous bravery on the 30th of March 1858, at Kotah, in having headed a small party of men, and attacked a body of armed fanatic rebels, strongly posted in a loop-holed house, with one narrow entrance. Lieutenant Cameron stormed the house, and killed three rebels in single combat. He was severely wounded, having lost half of one hand by a stroke from a tulwar [a type of curved sword or sabre].[2]

In addition to receiving the VC, for his services in India Cameron was twice Mentioned in Despatches and, in December 1859, promoted to captain.

The 72nd was in barracks at Neemuch when, on 6 August 1858, Risaldar Wali Shah and Kotha-Havaldar Mahavir declared a sepoy rebellion at Sehore cantonment near Bhopal. In October the Regiment was split among the columns pursuing the rebels and played a leading role in saving the State of Bhopal from falling into rebel hands; it had marched 110 miles in seventy-four hours to get there and fight. In the following May, Lieutenant Vesey led a detachment of 100 men on camelback and returned to quarters after spending seventeen months under canvas and marching an unbelievable 3,000 miles.

The 72nd remained in India until 1865, stationed at Mhow with detachments at Indore, later moving to Poona before embarking for home in late 1865. First stop was Edinburgh Castle and then, in May 1867, accompanied by their families, Aldershot. The soldiers moved up to Manchester in October before returning to Ireland in February 1868. Two years later they embarked again for foreign service in India leaving the depot companies in Ireland.

Disembarking at Bombay in 1871 the 72nd spent the next seven years in what is modern-day Pakistan at stations including Umballa (1871), Peshawar (1871), Nowshera and Cherat (1875) and Sialkot (1876–1878).

Meanwhile, in 1873, under the Localization Scheme the 72nd Depot companies were linked with 91st Argyllshire Highlanders at Stirling Castle until 1881.

The Second Anglo-Afghan War 1878–1881

The Second Anglo-Afghan War was fought between the British Raj and the Emirate of Afghanistan from 1878 to 1880, when the latter was ruled by Sher Ali Khan of the Barakzai dynasty. The war was part of what was known as the 'Great Game' between the British and Russian empires. The aim was to thwart Russia's expansion southwards and end its threat to India.

1878 saw the 72nd join with Sir Frederick Roberts leading the Kabul Field Force against the Amir of Afghanistan. The Regiment excelled at Peiwar Kotal, dislodging the entrenched enemy with the help of 5th Gurkhas and 2nd Battalion 8th (King's) Regiment. Lord Roberts later said, 'I cannot praise them too highly, the 72nd is a splendid regiment.'

The war comprised two campaigns: the first began in November 1878 with the British invasion of Afghanistan in which the Amir, Sher Ali Khan, was forced to flee. Ali's successor, Mohammad Yaqub Khan, immediately sued for peace and the Treaty of Gandamak was signed on 26 May 1879. The traditionally neutral Afghanistan, sandwiched between India and Russia, raised tension by welcoming a Russian embassy to Kabul. In response, the British sent an envoy and mission led by Sir Louis Cavagnari to Kabul but, on 3 September, the mission was massacred and the conflict was re-ignited by Ayub Khan which led to the abdication of his brother Yaqub. Britain was having none of this and despatched Major General Frederick Roberts VC with the Kurrum Valley Field Force to establish a mission in Kabul.

Charasiab 1879

The Battle of Charasiab was fought on 6 October 1879. On the evening before Roberts' force reached Charasiab, a small town 7.5 miles south of Kabul, where he camped overnight, awaiting the arrival of the baggage train. The next morning saw a large force of regular Afghan soldiers, equipped with artillery and reinforced by local tribesmen, in the hills ahead. It was led by Nek Mohammed Khan, Governor of Kabul and uncle of Yakub Khan, whose intention was to attack the British. The 72nd led the attack and, eventually, the Afghan army was repelled at the Peiwar Kotal pass; by 3.45pm Roberts had opened the route to Kabul. He resumed his advance and occupied Kabul on 13 October.

British casualties were eighteen killed and seventy wounded, while Afghan deaths exceeded 300. Twenty Afghan field guns with ammunition and food were captured, including an 8-inch brass howitzer previously presented to the Afghan government by the British. The British force was equipped with two Gatling guns, the first time those guns were used in action. The 72nd were accompanied by a squadron of 9th Lancers, F/A Brigade Royal Horse Artillery, G/3 Battery Royal Artillery, the 67th Foot and 92nd Highlanders and various units of the Indian Army. The battle was the last occasion on which the 72nd carried its Colours into action.

With the Treaty of Gandamak in May 1879, Yakub Khan, Amir of Afghanistan, agreed to accept the British Mission but, six weeks later, the embassy staff were murdered. Roberts was despatched again with orders to occupy Kabul.

Lance Corporal George Sellar VC

On 14 December the Highlanders scaled the Asmai Heights just outside Kabul, defeating the enemy with a bayonet attack and killing 600 Afghans. Lance Corporal George Sellar was awarded the Victoria Cross for his valour: Sellar was about 39 years old, when the following deed took place:

> For conspicuous gallantry displayed by him at the assault on the Asmai Heights, round Kabul, on the 14th December, 1879, in having in a marked manner led the attack, under a heavy fire, and, dashing on in front of the party up the slope, engaged in a desperate conflict with an Afghan who sprang out to meet him. In this encounter Lance-Corporal Sellar was severely wounded.[3]

The Battle of Maiwand and *the Retreat to Kandahar, July 1880*

The Afghans, however, were not taking this lying down. Elsewhere they were amassing a strong army, and a serious reverse for the British occurred at the hands of Ayub Khan with two brigades of British and Indian troops under Brigadier General George Burrows defeated. It was, however, a Pyrrhic victory given that between 2,050 and 2,750 Afghans were reportedly killed, and about 1,500 wounded. The 72nd was in barracks in Kabul when all this was going on.

When word of the disaster reached Kandahar the following day, a relief force was despatched which met the retreating force at Kokeran. The Regiment, 800 strong, was part of the 2nd Brigade; 322 miles were covered in twenty-two days, an average of fifteen miles a day. The British were routed but managed a withdrawal. Of the 2,476 British troops involved, the British and Indian force lost twenty-one officers and 948 soldiers killed, and eight officers and 169 men were wounded: the Grenadiers lost 64 per cent of their strength and the 66th lost 62 per cent, including twelve officers; cavalry losses were much smaller.

Ayub Khan succeeded in shutting the British up in Kandahar, prompting General Frederick Roberts' famous 314-mile relief march from Kabul to Kandahar in August in twenty-two days over unforgiving terrain and ever subject to attack. With only three days to prepare, Roberts was leading an army of 10,000 men, 11,000 animals and 8,000 camp followers. Temperatures ranged from a searing 110 degrees Fahrenheit to a bone-aching freezing point at night. There were no losses to enemy action. The resulting Battle of Kandahar on 1 September was a decisive victory for the British. The 72nd lost two officers and eleven men, including the CO Lieutenant Colonel Francis Brownlow CB.

The loss of the Queen's Colour and Regimental Colour of the 66th (Berkshire) Regiment of Foot at the Battle of Maiwand, following so soon after the loss of the Colours of the 2nd/24th (2nd Warwickshire) Regiment at the Battle of Isandlwana on 22 January 1879, during the Anglo-Zulu War, resulted in Colours no longer being taken on active service.

The second campaign ended in September 1880 when the British decisively defeated Ayub Khan outside Kandahar. The new Amir, Abdur Rahman Khan, hand-picked by the British, ratified and confirmed the Gandamak treaty once more. When the British and Indian soldiers had withdrawn, the Afghans agreed to let the British attain all objectives, as well as create a buffer between the British Raj and the Russian Empire.

Two weeks after the battle the 72nd marched out of Afghanistan and travelled by train to rejoin their families at Mean Meer; in November it moved on to Lucknow.

At this time the 72nd Seaforth was part of the Kurram Valley Field Force, 2nd Infantry Brigade under Brigadier General J.B. Thelwell, along with 21st Punjabis, 56th Rifles and 5th Gurkha Rifles.

In 1881 there was more substantive change for the Seaforth. Under the Army Reforms, the 72nd Duke of Albany's Own Highlanders joined with the 78th Highlanders (Ross-shire Buffs), with the former becoming the 1st Battalion Seaforth Highlanders and the latter the 2nd Battalion. The official designation of the amalgamated regiment was Seaforth Highlanders (Ross-shire Buffs, The Duke of Albany's).

To trace the progress and development of the old 78th we must retrace our steps to 1793 when the 78th Highlanders was first raised.

Chapter 2

The 78th Highlanders 1793–1881

Francis Mackenzie was a shrewd man; he was well aware in 1793 that war with France was in the offing and more infantry regiments would be required. Astutely, he offered to raise yet another Highland regiment from the Mackenzie clans. On the anticipated outbreak of war in 1793 the offer was accepted and he received authority in a Letter of Service to raise what became, by coincidence (and confusingly), the 78th Highlanders, the same number as the Earl of Seaforth's Highland Regiment before being re-numbered as the 72nd. Francis Mackenzie was Lieutenant Colonel Commandant.

Between August and October the 78th was posted to Guernsey to guard the coast against French invasion and assist French Royalists in Brittany after the Revolution. In January 1794 they moved to Newport, returning to Guernsey in March. On 8 February 1794 a new battalion was raised: the 2nd/78th.

The 1st/78th first saw action in the Netherlands during the Revolutionary War, fighting at the defence of Nijmegen in November 1794 as part of the British-Hanoverian expeditionary force under Prince Frederick, Duke of York and Albany, along with Dutch and Austrian allies, in a bid to halt the French revolutionary forces. It was not a success for the allies: for example, in a bayonet attack there the Regiment lost one officer and seven men; a further four officers and sixty men were wounded. In the freezing January of 1795 the 78th withdrew to Bremerhaven in Germany.

The Regiment moved back to England in April 1795 and then sailed to France, landing at l'Île Dieu, off the Brittany coast, in September 1795, after which the French Royalist force collapsed and the 1st/78th was posted back to Poole in England.

Later in 1795 the 2nd/78th deployed to South Africa, capturing Cape Town, Wynberg and Muysenberg from the Dutch. It took part in the successful attack by a British fleet under Sir George Elphinstone on the Dutch Cape Colony, then held by the Batavian Republic: the attack led to the capitulation by the Dutch Navy at Saldanha Bay and the capture of the colony by British forces in September 1796.[1] The 2nd/78th, ably assisted by marines, landed at, and captured, Simonstown with further successes at Wynberg. Cape Town surrendered and the colony soon capitulated.

In November 1795 the 1st and 2nd Battalions were amalgamated, forming the 78th Highlanders (Ross-shire Buffs).

They set sail for India on the 10th, arriving at Calcutta whence they marched to Fort William, a fort in Hastings, Calcutta (Kolkata).

The 2nd Maratha War and the Battle of Assaye 1803

In 1803 the 78th assisted the Marquess of Wellesley (Wellington's older brother) when they established an operational base by taking the Maratha fortress at Ahmednuggar. The Battle of Assaye followed: Wellesley's 7,000 strong force with twenty-two cannon against some 40,000 Marathas with 100 cannon. The 78th was on the left flank of one of three echelons and joined in the rout. It was also part of the successful attack at the Battle of Argaum and at the capture of the apparently impregnable Gawilghur, the final battle of the war. This major success left the East India Company in control of a significant part of central India. All troops were rewarded with prize money; a private soldier pocketed thirteen rupees.

The 78th remained around Bombay for the next three years and then garrisoned the Portuguese (a British ally) colony of Goa, which was also under threat from the French, from 1807 to 1811.

1804: Another 2nd Battalion

1804 was the year in which another 2nd Battalion of the 78th was raised, primarily as a feeder for the 1st Battalion. As before, the reason was fear of a French invasion while the British Army was decidedly thin on the ground. To that end, most new battalions were stationed in the south of England; the 2nd/78th were in barracks at Hythe in Kent for six months in 1805 being trained by the legendary Lieutenant General Sir John Moore who instilled the highest levels of discipline, morale and training for which he became famous.

The 2nd was on its way to Gibraltar in September 1805 when it passed a large fleet of French and Spanish ships en route to Trafalgar. The British transports took refuge in the mouth of the river Tagus at Lisbon. In May 1806 the Battalion sailed from Gibraltar to Sicily to support the Kingdom of the Two Sicilies whose king, Ferdinand, had been deposed by the invading French under Napoleon's brother Joseph. To deter a French invasion of Sicily itself the 2nd/78th, part of a force of 4,800, sailed for Italy, landing in Calabria and attacking the 6,400-strong French force under General Regnier. This was the Battle of Maida.

The Battle of Maida (or Santa Euphemia) 1806

The battle was fought on 4 July 1806. At dawn, General Sir John Stuart's force of 4,300 men with three field guns and eight mountain guns marched out to attack the French outside Maida. Sailing from Messina, Major General John Stuart led 5,236 Anglo-Sicilian troops to victory over about 5,400 Franco-Italian-Polish troops under the command of Général Jean Louis Ebénézer Reynier, inflicting significant losses while incurring relatively few in reply.

Of the landing, Ensign Joseph Anderson (later Lieutenant Colonel) of the 78th wrote:

> Our landing was but slightly opposed, because our convoy, the Endymion frigate took up her position as near the shore as possible, and by her fire soon cleared the beach and drove the enemy far beyond our first footing. He made a partial stand, however, on a rising ground inland; but as our troops advanced, and after a skirmish, we soon forced him to retreat on his supports and finally on his main body. We then halted for the day, and the enemy left advanced posts and videttes to watch our movements.[1]

The British force numbered 5,200 infantry, including the 78th and the 81st from Malta, with eleven guns. Hopton, in his *Battle of Maida 1806: Fifteen Minutes of Glory*, has the force as 8,000 with between 5,050 and 5,450 French opposing them.[2]

Hopton goes on to underline the inexperience of the 78th's troops, pointing out that, of the 650 men who fought at Maida, all but fifty were under-age: 'a corps of boys', although they fought valiantly despite sustaining the highest number of casualties. The local Sicilian men were impressed by their 'picturesque national dress' although the women, out of modesty, thought it 'ugly'.

The French force numbered 6,000, including some 1,500 cavalry and six guns. We know how, in the thick of the battle, the enemy De Watteville's Swiss Regiment was confused with another De Watteville's Swiss Regiment which, due to similar red coats, was allowed to approach the 78th and deliver a damaging volley. The 78th began to retreat but were brought back into the line by General David Stewart. After a frenzied fight between the 78th and the Swiss, the Swiss retired to the right and reformed on Digonet's Brigade.

General Stewart recounts how the fact that there were Swiss on both sides caused confusion.

> On the side of the French there was a Swiss Regiment, commanded by an officer of the family of Watteville, a family which had also a regiment in our

> service, and in the field that day. The Watteville Regiment in the French service was dressed in a kind of light claret-coloured uniform, something like scarlet when much worn, and with hats so much resembling those of the band of our Watteville's, that when this corps was seen advancing from their second line, the Highlanders, in their inexperience, believed they were our own, who had in some manner got to the front; and a word passed quickly to cease firing. The fire had accordingly slackened, before the voice of the mounted officers, whose elevated position enabled them to distinguish more clearly, could be heard, and the enemy, believing this relaxation to proceed from a different cause, advanced with additional boldness. This brought them so close that when the men were undeceived and recommenced firing, it was with such effect that, in ten minutes, the front was cleared, and the enemy driven back with great precipitation.[3]

It continues to relate how 'British discipline had held again and with two concentrated volleys at very close range and a counter charge from the 78th and 81st, reinforced by the 58th, brought up from the reserves had forced the enemy at the very last moment to retreat'.

Anderson again:

> We remained quiet and steady, but impatient, on our ground, and had a full view of our foes, as they boldly and confidently advanced, evidently expecting that they could, and would, walk over us; and so they ought to have done, for we afterwards ascertained they numbered upwards of nine thousand of their best troops, while our force did not much exceed six thousand men! Their cavalry was also more numerous, for we had only one squadron of the 23rd Light Dragoons [*this contradicts all other reports*] but ours was so admirably managed that it kept the others in check during the whole day.
>
> As soon as these formidable French columns came sufficiently near, and not till then, our lines were called to 'attention' and ordered to 'shoulder arms'. Then commenced in earnest the glorious Battle of Maida, first with a volley from our brigade into the enemy's columns and from our artillery at each flank without ceasing, followed by independent file firing as fast as our men could load; and well they did their work! Nor were the enemy idle; they returned our fire without ceasing, then in part commenced to deploy into line. The independent file firing was still continued with more vigour than ever for at least a quarter of an hour, when many brave men fell on both sides. Our brigade was then ordered to charge, supported by our second line, and this they did lustily and with endless hearty cheers, the

> French at the same moment following our example and advancing towards us at a steady charge of bayonets, the rolling of drums, and endless loud cheers. Both armies were equally determined to carry all before them; it was not till we got within five or six paces of each other that the enemy wavered, broke their ranks, and gave way, turning away to a man and scampering off, most of them throwing away their arms at the same time; but our men continued their cheers and got up with some of them, and numbers were either bayoneted, shot, or taken prisoners. The enemy was then fairly driven over the bridge by which they had advanced, or forced into the river, where numbers were captured or drowned.

By midday it was all over. The French 23rd and 42nd Regiments had remained largely intact and functioning. Concentrating his scattered troops round these two units, Reynier retreated into the hills protected by his cavalry. If the British had had cavalry the defeat of the French could have been even more comprehensive. However, there was no heavy cavalry and the soldiers were tired and ammunition low; the French were largely unmolested and able to retreat in good order.

The Proceedings of the Royal Artillery Institution report that 'all the French lay on their faces being stabbed in the back while all the British lay on their backs being shot in front'. In his *Sketches*, Major James Stewart of the 78th tempered the triumphalism when he wrote:

> The disadvantage so frequently experienced in the transmarine expeditions of England, occasioned by the want of ships for the conveyance of a sufficient number of troops, was now severely felt; for though the field was most favourable for the operations of cavalry, that arm was, on the present occasion, totally wanting. As soon as the ships had landed the infantry at St Euphemia, they were ordered back for the cavalry, who arrived the day after the battle.

Stewart suffered forty-five killed and 282 wounded. Out of a total of 6,440 soldiers, Reynier lost 490 killed and 870 wounded. In addition, the British captured 722 French soldiers and four cannon. The 1st Light Infantry lost half of its number either killed, wounded or captured.[4]

Maida showed that, with the earlier defeat of the French fleet at Trafalgar, England, no longer fearing invasion and having command of the seas, could land troops, and support them on any part of Europe accessible from the sea and defeat the French on land. Two weeks later, Gaeta fell to the French after a long siege, Stuart having missed an opportunity to assist the defenders of Gaeta.

Maida Hill and Maida Vale in London are named after the battle. A pub was built in Middlesex, north-west of London and named the 'Maida'. The pub sign showed a portrait of General Stuart, later Count of Maida.

The 78th formed part of the 2nd Brigade, as follows:

2nd Brigade:
Colonel Wroth Palmer Acland (69 officers, 1,272 men)
2nd Battalion, 78th (Highland) Regiment of Foot (Ross-shire Buffs) (eight companies, 36 officers, 702 men)
1st Battalion, 81st Regiment of Foot (Loyal Lincoln Volunteers) (eight companies, 33 officers, 570 men)

The Alexandria Expedition (Fraser Expedition) 1807

This was a failed British attempt to take Alexandria during the 1807–1809 Anglo-Turkish War and secure a Mediterranean base of operations against the Ottoman and French Empires. It was part of a larger strategy against the Ottoman-French alliance of Ottoman Sultan Selim III.

The expedition began in mid-February 1807 when a force of British troops stationed in Calabria and Sicily was ordered by General Fox, in Messina, to embark on transports with a destination rumoured to be Constantinople. Meanwhile, John Thomas Duckworth, second-in-command of the Mediterranean Fleet, sailed for Constantinople. After departure from Constantinople, as an Admiral of the White Squadron, he was to rendezvous with the transports in Aboukir Bay near Alexandria. However, by 17 March the fleet of transports with nearly 6,000 British troops approached Alexandria under command of General Alexander Mackenzie-Fraser.

Order of Battle: The British Army
Detachment, Royal Staff Corps
Detachment, Royal Artillery
Detachment, Royal Engineers (Sir John Burgoyne)]
3rd Squadron, 20th Light Dragoons
1st Battalion, 31st Regiment of Foot
1st Battalion, 35th Regiment of Foot
2nd Battalion, 35th Regiment of Foot
2nd Battalion, 78th Regiment of Foot
Regiment de Roll
Chasseurs Britanniques
Sicilian Regiment

- 6,000–8,000 British regulars under Mackenzie-Fraser, plus 1,500 British reinforcements under John Coape Sherbrooke, 5000-plus mercenary troops of Roll's Regiment, Chasseurs Britanniques, Sicilian, Greek and Balkan mercenaries
- Ottoman: 4,000–6,000 infantry (Tabuzoglu division), 1,500 cavalry (Hassan Pasha Division), 700 infantry (Rosetta's garrison) and an unknown, but large, number of Egyptian irregular troops and armed civilians (*fellahin*)

A hoped-for Egyptian Mameluke uprising against their Turkish rulers never materialised. The people of Alexandria, somewhat disaffected with Muhammad Ali, threw open the gates of the city to the British forces, making it one of the easiest conquests of a city by British forces during the Napoleonic Wars. Thus, Alexandria was captured briefly and occupied by the 5,000-strong expeditionary force, including the 2nd/78th, but attempts to advance inland were confounded. British forces were twice defeated by Turkish cavalry in battles at Rosetta in the Nile delta at the terrible cost of over 900 officers and men killed and many captured at the second siege of Rosetta alone.

Disaster followed disaster: at El Hamet the Turkish cavalry struck again and three companies of the 2nd/78th lost 163 soldiers, including their Commanding Officer, Lieutenant Colonel Patrick Macleod, who were slain.

The remnants of British forces in Egypt were forced to retreat to Alexandria, where they remained besieged without supplies. Using this caged army and the many prisoners as a bargaining tool, Viceroy Muhammad Ali compelled the British commanders to cease operations in Egypt, board their transports again and leave Alexandria empty-handed, having gained no significant influence in Egypt nor any influence over the Ottoman Empire's improving relations with France. On the contrary, the expedition united the populace behind Muhammad Ali, who seized power in Egypt. As Harrison[5] says, it also had the effect of convincing the British government that they should support Egypt as part of the Ottoman Empire.

Thanks to the Angus Macleod Archive we have the testimony of Angus Macleod, a soldier with the expedition, extracts from which follow. These illustrate the ruthless tactics used by the Regiment in recruitment campaigns, more like a press gang than anything else. Obviously, this was not unique to the Seaforth.

Kenneth McLeod

In the summer of 1804, the hated army recruiting agents of the Seaforth Mackenzie Landlord regime in Lewis were once again combing through the

Lewis villages pouncing on unsuspecting young men, and forcibly enlisting them into the 2nd Battalion of the 78th Seaforth Highlanders. The Seaforth Highlanders had volunteered to raise Battalions earlier in 1793 and 1794, and at first the Regiment was called the 78th Foot. In 1804 the Seaforth recruiting agents came to Calbost and according to tradition it was Norman 'Buidhe' Mackenzie who they first approached and he protested and pointed out that he should be exempt from military service because of his domestic circumstances. His mother was a widow and he was therefore the bread winner. The only other person in their family was his orphan cousin Kenneth Macleod who was fostered by his mother; accordingly, Kenneth was taken and that event is still remembered 200 years later by the Gaelic saying heard on the lips of older generations of Calbost people to this day:

> *Tormod Buidhe carach, chuir e mo, sheanar do'n airm.* Crafty Norman Buidhe sent my grandfather to the army.

Kenneth Macleod, *Coinneach Mor*, 'Big Kenneth' was born in 1776 and was therefore 28 years old when he enlisted in the army at Fort George on 4 June 1804; his height is given as 5ft 10ins, black hair, hazel eyes and swarthy. At the time that Kenneth Macleod and his Lewis compatriots were recruited for the British Army they would be speaking Gaelic only as there were no English or even Gaelic schools in the area where they could learn to read and write; therefore, it could hardly be said that they knew what they were called on to fight for in the distant overseas lands. We may be sure, however, they were told they were fighting for 'King and Country'. After a spell of training at Fort George, the 2nd Battalion Seaforth Highlanders, to which our Kenneth was attached, moved to Hythe Barracks and from there to Shorncliffe Barracks and then to Gibraltar, and on to Italy where they appear to have taken part in the glorious victory of the British at 'Maida' in Southern Italy.

After the battles of Rosetta and El Hamet, Kenneth Macleod tells us that, on 21 April, Lieutenant Colonel Patrick Macleod

> formed his men into a square, hoping assistance would come. They fought grimly until eventually Colonel Macleod, most of the officers and many of the men were killed, and there was no other course but to surrender. On surrendering on 21 April 1807 there was a mad scramble by the Turkish soldiers to take as many Prisoners-of-War as they could, because it was the Turkish custom that Prisoners-of-War became the private property of the soldier who took them, and a ransom was expected for each prisoner. In

> that way the British Prisoners-of-War were pulled and hauled and man-handled with little or no ceremony by the Turks … .

Kenneth Macleod, Calbost, was among those listed killed or taken prisoner at 'El Hammet', and his worldly effects and credits at the time were valued at only £1.22. Fortunately, it turned out that he was among the Prisoners-of-War, and he was therefore spared to spend his estate of £1.22.

Angus Macleod goes on to tell us how after the prisoners of war were sorted out by the victorious Turkish Army, they were made to march between two long avenues of poles topped with the heads of their slain comrades. The prisoners suffered 'barbarous treatment' at the hands of their enemies. The ground at 'El Hammet' was strewn with headless bodies as well as those who were severely wounded.

> Five hundred British Prisoners-of-War were taken to the slave market at Cairo and sold as slaves … . The conditions of imprisonment were terrible and it was at this time that many of the Prisoners-of-War became affected with ophthalmia [ophthalmitis], a disease of the eyes which caused inflammation and blindness. Ophthalmia first appeared among the soldiers at Gibraltar and it was attributed partly, at least, to the change of diet from their native Scottish food of fish, oatmeal and vegetables to a greater consumption of animal food than they were accustomed to. Our Kenneth was among those who were afflicted with ophthalmia and he therefore escaped being sold as a slave in Cairo.

After the debacles at El Hammet and Rosetta, the British Army retired to Alexandria and stayed for several months, waiting for help that never arrived from Britain. At length, General Fraser sent a flag of truce to the Pasha, offering to evacuate Egypt, providing all prisoners of war in the hands of the Turks were released. The terms were accepted readily. On 23 September 1807, the British troops re-embarked and set sail for Sicily. Kenneth Macleod of Calbost was discharged from prison hospital in Egypt in December 1807 where, as we have seen, he was suffering from ophthalmia. Subsequently, the blind and the wounded were sent home to Britain via Sicily and Malta in 1808. Eventually, Kenneth Macleod of Calbost's regiment arrived in the Isle of Wight where he spent some time in hospital. In 1809 he was back at Fort George from where he was discharged on 12 September 1809 as an invalided soldier with a disability of blindness, having served five and a half years in the army. He was granted a disability pension of £30 a year and £12 a year for a guide to lead him around.

Thomas Keith (c. 1793–1815) aka Ibrahim Aga

Thomas Keith was an apprentice gun-maker from Leith who became a soldier and the regimental armourer. Captured in Egypt, as a prisoner of war, he did something extraordinary for the times: he converted to Islam, changed his name to Ibrahim and joined the Ottoman military. As governor of Medina, he died in 1815 in a cavalry charge fighting the emerging power of the Saudi dynasty.

Keith enlisted in the 78th (Highlanders) Regiment on 4 August 1804 and went with the 2nd Battalion to join General John Stuart in the British campaign in Sicily in 1806. Keith then went to Egypt in the 1807 Alexandria expedition.

James Grant tells how he was captured at Al Hamed near Rosetta on 21 April 1807 where he and a drummer in his regiment, William Thompson, were bought as slaves by Ahmad Aga (nicknamed Ahmad Bonaparte).[6] It was there that the two Scots resolved to convert to Islam and change their names, Keith becoming Ibrahim Aga and Thompson Osman Effendi, later enjoying success as a doctor in Cairo. Keith had a quarrel with one of Ahmad's Mamluks, ironically a Sicilian. The Sicilian was killed in their duel and the Scot then sought the aid of the wife of Muhammad Ali Pasha, *wali* (protector) of Egypt. She sent Keith to the service of her son, Tusun Pasha. In 1811, Keith joined Tusun's expedition against the British-backed Wahhabis of Saudi Arabia who had invaded the Hijaz, a region in the west of Saudi Arabia. After a successful campaign, Keith was made acting governor of Medina in 1815 in Tusun's absence. He was killed in a Wahhabi ambush later that year. Thomas Keith is the subject of the 1987 novel *Blood and Sand* by Rosemary Sutcliff.

From 1809 to 1814 the 2nd Battalion was back in the south of England, supplying drafts to the 1st Battalion in Goa. In 1809 it moved to Fort George, leaving a 370-man draft under orders for India. From Fort George the main battalion moved to Aberdeen where it stayed until 1814.

The Walcheren Campaign 1809

The draft only got as far as Cowes on the Isle of Wight when it was diverted to join the Earl of Chatham's force in the disastrous Walcheren Campaign, aiming to take Antwerp with its docks and arsenal in autumn 1809. It suffered from an incompetent commander and substantial losses due to malaria, or Walcheren Fever. Starting on 30 July 1809, a British force of 39,000 men and 15,000 horses, together with field artillery and two siege trains, landed on Walcheren with a view to assisting the Austrians against Napoleon by opening another front, enabling navigation of the Scheldt and attacking the French fleet moored at Flushing (Vlissingen).

Although Flushing surrendered, the Austrians had already been defeated decisively at the Battle of Wagram in early July and, having effectively lost the war, were suing for peace. Meanwhile, the French fleet had moved to Antwerp and the British lost over 4,000 men to a disease dubbed 'Walcheren Fever', thought to be a deadly cocktail of malaria, typhoid, dysentery and typhus, as well as to enemy action, although only 106 died in combat. The survivors withdrew on 9 December.[7] The French suffered some 4,000 dead, wounded and captured.

Walcheren Fever

Things started to go wrong from the outset when the British seized the swamp of an island that was Walcheren at the mouth of the Scheldt, as well as South Beveland island, both in the Netherlands today. British troops soon began to contract Walcheren fever. Medical provisions for the expedition proved inadequate and reports that an occupying French force had lost 80 per cent of its numbers to the disease a few years earlier were ignored.[8]

The invasion of Java 1811

In 1811 the 78th had a change of scenery when the regiment departed Bombay for Java to evict the French who had occupied the Dutch-owned island and established the Batavian Republic in 1795. The Dutch considered Java their most valuable overseas possession.

The invasion was a successful British amphibious operation. Originally established as a colony of the Dutch Republic, Java remained in Dutch hands throughout the Revolutionary and Napoleonic Wars, during which time the French invaded the Republic and, as noted, established the Batavian Republic in 1795 and the Kingdom of Holland in 1806. The Kingdom of Holland was annexed to the First French Empire in 1810 and Java became a titular French colony; it continued to be administered and defended primarily by the Dutch.

The Dutch were at war with the British, and, from 1808, the Dutch governor in Java began fortifying the island to guard against British invasion, building fortifications such as Fort Cornelis. Anxiety was increasing because the British had recently captured the French islands of Réunion and Mauritius and the Dutch East Indian possessions of Ambon and the Molucca Islands, making an invasion of Java ever more likely.

Firstly, a flotilla of frigates patrolled off the island, raiding shipping and launching opportunistic amphibious assaults. On 23 May 1811 a party from HMS *Sir Francis Drake* attacked a flotilla of fourteen Dutch gun vessels off Surabaya, capturing nine of them. Merak, in north-western Java, was attacked and the fort defending the town largely demolished by a party from HMS

Minden and HMS *Leda* on 30 July. That same day HMS *Procris* attacked a squadron of six Dutch gunboats flying French colours, capturing five and destroying the sixth.

The Highlanders' Museum tells us that the 78th was part of a force 11,960 strong: 'the British landed twelve miles east of Batavia and defeated the first line of Franco-Dutch troops at the storming of Wettervreden and at Serondole. Batavia was left undefended, and part of the town had been razed to prevent the British from collecting booty. Troops were landed on 4 August and, by 8 August, the undefended city capitulated. The defenders withdrew to a previously prepared fortified position, Fort Cornelis, which the British besieged, capturing it early in the morning of 26 August.'

> Following a British attack on 10th of August (in which 100 British troops and 300 Franco-Dutch troops were lost), the Siege of Fort Cornelis took place. The fort was heavily defended by Dutch, French, and Indonesian troops. The invasion of the fort began on 25th of August at midnight and the Dutch officially surrendered on 18th of September 1811, resulting in Britain seizing control of Java [after the French stand at Samarand on September 16]. Total British casualties amounted to 960, with over 1,000 French, Dutch, and Indonesian deaths. [Stamford] Raffles was appointed Governor General of Java.

The Netherlands became independent of France in 1814 and the British subsequently returned the island to Dutch control. At the Siege of Cornelis, the commanding officer of the 78th was killed, along with over 160 other casualties. The same campaign saw the capture of Sumatra, Bali and Celebes.

The 78th Highlanders stayed in Java for five years after the invasion, suppressing Indonesian uprisings and undertaking minor expeditions.

The *Princess Charlotte* Tragedy 1816

Tragedy accompanied the troops and families of the 78th at the end of their Java tour. The families had been quartered in Goa, but eventually relocated to Java. When the Regiment received orders to depart the island the 400 troops and their families boarded the *Princess Charlotte* on 18 September. One day out to sea in the Bay of Bengal, the ship hit a rock and limped back to Batavia, but with no casualties.

Eleven days later, they re-embarked on the sister ship *Frances Charlotte*, destination Calcutta (Kolkata). On 5 November, the ship struck a sunken reef twelve miles off Preparis. The lifeboats had room only for 150 passengers, leaving

119 troops marooned on the uninhabited island of Preparis, north of the Andamans. The first ship sent to rescue the survivors was itself wrecked. Four days later, the merchant ship *Po*, en route from Madras to Penang, managed to rescue only twenty-seven more men while two rescuers and a boat were lost in the attempt. A number of the marooned died of drowning, starvation or exposure. All the regimental baggage and records were lost along with nearly £2,000 of regimental funds.

Finally, on 10 November, the merchant ship *Prince Blucher* approached the wreckage. Over the next three days, it rescued 316 passengers. The Government of Bengal sent two cruisers to rescue the remaining 110 of the 119 survivors who, by then, had been marooned for thirty-six days; the other nine had died. The survivors had run out of food and were too weak even to gather the meagre shellfish on the rocks at low tide. Others died of starvation shortly after rescue, and some from over-eating after having been starved for so long. Bad weather and damage to *Prince Blucher* prevented it from rescuing another ninety Europeans and forty Lascars who remained on the island. After nine days *Prince Blucher* arrived at Calcutta. In the end only eighteen people, including the two rescuers, died throughout the whole tragedy. On 1 March 1817 the 78th finally set sail for England on the *Prince Blucher*, docking at Portsmouth in June 1817 and then setting off again for Aberdeen where they arrived in July. The 78th had been overseas for twenty-one years.

Merxem, 1814

The 2nd Battalion was posted to Belgium in January 1814 as reinforcements for the 7,000-strong force which had landed in the Netherlands to ensure that the nation stayed in friendly hands. The force was almost immediately supplemented by the arrival of the 2nd King's German Legion Hussars on 27 December and, subsequently, by the reinforcements from Leith, the 2/21st and the 300-strong 2nd Battalion of the 78th ('composed mostly of boys', according to *A Short History of the Seaforth Highlanders*), which joined on 10 January 1814.

Andrew Bamford tells us that:

> Six British battalions, and elements of the King's German Legion (KGL), had been deployed to North Germany in 1813 to secure the Baltic ports; some of these troops, commanded by Major General Samuel Gibbs, could be drawn upon for the new army, but the remainder would have to come from units at home; all, including later reinforcements, were either single-battalion regiments or second, third, and fourth battalions. Most had seen no prior service, and none was at anything approaching full strength.[9]

He goes on to add that the initial objective of Graham's force, operating in conjunction with Bulow's Prussian corps, was Antwerp and, more specifically, the French squadron based there. During the advance, two combats were fought at Merxem, a village about three miles east of Antwerp, on 13 January and 2 February, the village being taken on the second occasion, and thereafter a bombardment of the French squadron began, lasting from 3 to 6 February. However, the withdrawal of Bulow's Prussians meant that Graham had also to fall back but, as an alternative, an ill-fated attack was launched against the fortress of Bergen op Zoom on 8 March. The repulse of this, and subsequent surrender of the greater part of those troops who had penetrated the French defences, brought an effective end to active operations. But with the ending of hostilities following the fall of Paris, Graham was ultimately able to negotiate the evacuation of both Bergen op Zoom and Antwerp by their French garrisons.

Casualty figures
French Forces Number engaged: 12,000; Casualties: 846 (7.05%)
Anglo-Prussian Forces Number engaged: 13,000; Casualties: 260 (2.00%)

With the abdication of Napoleon Bonaparte in March 1814, the 2nd Battalion remained in the Netherlands, independently assigned to garrison duties as part of the allied reserve at Nieuwport, so missing the Waterloo campaign. When the battalion returned home in February 1816 it was disbanded and merged with the 1st Battalion at Aberdeen to form a single-battalion regiment once again. The headquarters remained in Aberdeen with detachments in Perth, Fort George, Fort Augustus and Fort William.

More change followed in 1817 when the 1st and 2nd Battalions of the 78th were amalgamated at Aberdeen and, once again, became a single-battalion regiment.

The Calton Riots 1817 and the Scottish Radical Rising of 1820 (The Radical War)

A particularly ugly incident occurred in August 1817 when the 78th was ordered to send companies to keep the peace during riots in Calton in Glasgow. So fierce were the attacks on the troops escorting prisoners to jail that they had no option but to open fire on the rioters.

The Calton weavers' strike of 1787 has the dubious honour of being the first major industrial dispute in Scottish history, when troops fired on demonstrators, killing six of them, making the Calton weavers Scotland's first working-class martyrs.[1] They did not die in vain because in the end the strike helped establish a workers' movement which wrought fundamental changes in the relationship between workforce and employers.[2] The massacre is commemorated in a panel by Scottish artist Ken Currie in the People's Palace, Glasgow, commissioned on the 200th anniversary of the event.[3]

In 1787 Calton was a handweaving community where, at the peak of Calton's prosperity when the fly-shuttle was introduced, wages had risen to nearly £100 a year and weavers were elevated to the higher echelons in Glasgow society. However, mechanisation and an expansion of the labour force had then dramatically depressed wages.

In the summer of 1787, the journeymen weavers of Calton mobilised themselves and organised processions through the streets of Glasgow to protest at a 25 per cent wage cut and lockout. Angry strikers cut the webs from the looms of weavers who continued to work, emptied warehouses of stock and made bonfires in the streets. Christina O'Neill tells how 'mustering on September 3, attempts by the Magistrates and the Lord Provost to read the Riot Act were thwarted as strikers threw stones to drive them back'.[4] O'Neill continues:

> as the men marched to Glasgow Cathedral, the military [a detachment of the 39th Regiment under Lt Colonel Kellet] were sent to face them off at Drygate Bridge. Soldiers fired their muskets … . Three weavers were killed instantly and three were fatally wounded, with several more injured.

Only three of their names are known: James Page, Alexander Miller and James Ainsley.[5]

Disturbances later in the day were suppressed by the troops. On the following day more looms were wrecked, but the riots died out quickly.

In 1788 James Granger was tried in Edinburgh as the ringleader of the strike. Aged 38 he was married with six children. He was found guilty of 'forming illegal combinations'; his sentence was to be publicly whipped through the streets of the city at the hands of the common executioner, and then to be banished from Scotland for seven years. Granger later returned and took part in the 1811–1812 strike. He lived to the age of 75.

Calton was a prelude to, and a warning of, the subsequent 1820 Radical War, a week of strikes and unrest in Scotland, a culmination of Radical demands for reform which had become prominent in the early years of the French Revolution, but had then been repressed during the lengthy Napoleonic Wars.[6] Artisan workers generally, but particularly weavers in Scotland, wanted action to force the government to enact Luddite protective restrictions. The gentry, fearing a revolution in the shadow of the Peterloo Massacre in Manchester the year before, recruited militia while the government deployed a network of spies, informers and *agents provocateurs* to eradicate the movement.

As at Calton, the militia men who were deployed to drag the prisoners to Greenock jail were attacked by local people and the prisoners released. James Wilson of Strathaven was singled out as a leader of the march there and, at Glasgow, was executed by hanging before being decapitated. Of those seized by the army at Bonnymuir, John Baird and Andrew Hardie suffered a similar fate at Stirling after making short defiant speeches. Twenty other Radicals were sentenced to transportation to penal colonies.

On Monday 3 April work stopped, particularly in weaving communities, over a wide area of central Scotland with an estimated total of around 60,000 downing tools.

Rumours spread that men were carrying out military drill at points around Glasgow, foundries and forges had been raided, and iron files and dyers' poles taken to make pikes. In Kilbarchan soldiers found men making pikes; in Stewarton around sixteen strikers were dispersed; in Balfron around 200 men had assembled ready for action. Pikes, gunpowder and weapons called 'wasps' (a sort of javelin) and 'clegs' (a barbed shuttlecock to throw at horses) were on sale.

Troops were on standby in Glasgow, including the Rifle Brigade, the 83rd Foot, the 7th and 10th Hussars and Samuel Hunter's Glasgow Sharpshooters. That evening 300 radicals skirmished with a party 'of cavalry', but no harm was done that day. Sixteen hussars and sixteen yeomanry troops were shot at on 4 April. Next day, more regiments arrived in Glasgow, causing considerable excitement. Some signs of resistance being organised were reported and the army stood on alert well into the night, but no Radical attack materialised.

In the end ringleaders were executed and beheaded, including the UK's last beheading, while others were transported to Tasmania or New South Wales.

The effect of the crushing of this insurrection was to discourage serious Radical unrest in Scotland for many years. Lord Melville, the right-hand man of Lord Liverpool's government in Scotland, saw the suggested visit of King George IV to Scotland as an absolute political need, to engage the feelings of the common people and weaken the Radical movement. The event, largely organised by Sir Walter Scott, was a great success and, according to John Prebble brought a new-found Scottish national identity, creating widespread enthusiasm for the tartan 'plaided pageantry' that Sheriff Ranald MacDonald of Stirling was already enthusiastically engaged in as a Clan chieftain at Ulva and member of various 'Highland societies'.

At the suggestion of Walter Scott, unemployed weavers from the west of Scotland were employed on paving a track round Salisbury Crags in Holyrood Park next to Arthur's Seat. The path is still known as the Radical Road.

The cause of electoral reform continued and, with the Scottish Reform Act 1832, Glasgow got its first Member of Parliament. The event was largely overshadowed by English Radical events and was forgotten by school history and by history books, but the Scottish National Party historian and leader Jimmy Halliday (1927–2013) reintroduced the event into the curriculum. At an anniversary debate in the Scottish Parliament members of the various parties each found lessons for their different causes in the 'Radical War'.

After the unedifying law-and-order patrols of Calton, the 78th moved to Belfast in November 1817 for nine years. Then followed eleven years in Ceylon, now Sri Lanka, from 1826 to 1837 where cholera and other tropical diseases tore through the ranks, killing 299 officers and men. In 1837 they returned to Ireland, arriving in February 1838. Civil unrest in Canada required the regiment to supply volunteers, rendering it below strength. Accordingly, they returned to Scotland to recruit in Glasgow and Edinburgh. India in 1842 and Aden took the 78th to 1857 and the Persian War.

Ceylon 1826

In 1826 Ceylon was officially British Settlements and Territories in the Island of Ceylon with its Dependencies from 1802 to 1833; then it was the Island of Ceylon and its Territories and Dependencies from 1833 to 1931. Initially, the area it covered did not include the Kingdom of Kandy, which was a protectorate but, from 1817 to 1948, the British possessions included the whole island of Ceylon.

The regiment would have been dealing with the fall-out from the discontent of the Kandyans with life under the protectorate as determined by the Kandyan Convention of 1815 and the subsequent guerrilla war which escalated into the Uva Rebellion in 1817. The main cause of the rebellion was the British authorities' failure to protect and uphold the customary Buddhist traditions, which were viewed by the islanders as an integral part of their lives. A scorched earth policy was pursued, and all males between 15 and 60 were driven out, exiled or killed. The British Crown annexed the Kingdom of Kandy to British Ceylon in 1817.

India 1842 and Kabul

In 1842 the 78th was in India. Those were troubled times in British India. Edward Law, 1st Earl of Ellenborough (1790–1871) was Governor-General from 1842 and, according to Hugh Chisholm, 'his administration was from first to last a subject of hostile criticism. The events chiefly in dispute are his policy towards Afghanistan and the army and captives there, his conquest of Sind, and his campaign in Gwalior'.[1]

Chisholm continues, telling us that Ellenborough went to India to 'restore peace to Asia' but his whole term of office was occupied by war. On his arrival, the news that greeted him was of the horrendous massacre of Kabul and the sieges of Ghazni and Jalalabad, while the sepoys of Madras were on the verge of open rebellion.

William Dalrymple tells how the massacre took the lives of 4,500 British and Indian troops under Major General William Elphinstone along with 12,000 camp followers on the snowbound march back from Kabul to Jalalabad to avoid the uprising in the Afghan capital.[2] The civilians were the families of Indian and British soldiers, plus workmen, servants and other Indian camp followers. The final stand was made just outside a village called Gandamak on 13 January. Many also died from exposure, frostbite or starvation.[3]

Elphinstone's questionable leadership is an example of how the ineptitude and indecision of a senior officer can compromise the morale and effectiveness of a whole army. It is generally agreed that Elphinstone totally failed to lead his soldiers, but at the same time exerted enough authority to prevent any of his officers from exercising any semblance of command in his place. Sadly, Elphinstone was not the only one.

In his proclamation of 15 March 1842, Ellenborough stated with characteristic clarity and eloquence the duty of first inflicting some signal and decisive blow on the Afghans, and then leaving them to govern themselves under the sovereign of their own choice. Unhappily, when he left for upper India and learned of the failure of General Sir Richard England, he instructed George Pollock and William Nott, who were advancing triumphantly with their avenging columns to rescue the British captives, to fall back. The army proved true to the governor-general's earlier proclamation rather than to his later fears. The hostages were rescued and the scene of Sir Alexander Burnes's murder in the heart of Kabul was burned down.

A punitive expedition was arranged hastily, requiring the 78th to replace the troops on their way to Afghanistan. At this point, July 1842, the 78th could boast over 1,000 men who spent the next three years in Karachi and Poona.

As we have seen, Fairrie describes the years 1844–1845 as 'the most melancholy period in the history of the 78th, for cholera struck the regiment bringing losses on a scale which it never encountered in battle'. It happened in 1844 when the Seaforth Highlanders were relocating to Karachi and marching to Sukkur in Sind. Early the next year the 300 survivors returned to Bombay, having lost 535 officers and men, as well as 202 wives and children, in eight months. A monument in Edinburgh's St Giles' Cathedral commemorates this wretched episode.

The cholera pandemic 1817–1828[1]

> The Indian origins of cholera and its almost global dissemination from Bengal made the disease a convenient symbol for much that the west feared or despised about a society so different from its own. One of the strongest expressions of this antipathy arose from the epidemiological connection between cholera and Hindu pilgrimage.
>
> David Arnold, *Past & Present*

The disease first emerged in the 1800s from what was then Calcutta; since then, seven cholera pandemics have swept the world. Epidemics tended to occur after wars, civil unrest, or natural disasters, when water and food supplies become contaminated with *Vibrio cholerae*, and is encouraged by crowded living conditions, not least barracks and camps, and poor sanitation.

The 1817–1824 pandemic started at the Kumbh Mela, a major Hindu pilgrimage and festival. It probably would have gone largely unnoticed but what brought it startlingly to European attention were the 10,000 or so British soldiers serving in India who succumbed.

The British Army, marching overland to Nepal and Afghanistan, and the Royal Navy and merchant shipping must take some of the responsibility for such extensive transmission with their seemingly unchecked movements by land and sea throughout the region.

The pandemic brought out the worst (again) in British colonialism and supremacist dogma when the disease gave rise to an explosion of anti-Asian sentiment and xenophobia. Medical professionals of the time were also heard making moral judgements and racist generalisations of Indian people on pilgrimages. During the outbreak, British authorities launched inquiries into the conditions of South Asian people on pilgrimages and eventually classified pilgrims as a 'dangerous class' who were then placed under surveillance.

The good news, and there was precious little, for the 78th was that by 1845 the regiment was back up to strength, thanks to some energetic recruiting throughout Great Britain and Ireland, not least a draft of 100 men from the 2nd Foot, Queen's Royal Regiment. The 78th stayed within the Bombay Presidency at Poona, Kirkee and Belgaum.

The demographics at this time are interesting. Before the pandemic the 78th had been 91 per cent Scottish but the arrival of 732 new men changed all that. Post-pandemic, only 47 per cent were Scots, 30 per cent English and 23 per cent Irish.

Aden 1849–1853

This is the broad situation the Regiment's soldiers would have found themselves in when they disembarked in the port of Aden. In 1839 Britain had captured Aden from the Sultan of Lahej in what was a strategic rather than commercial undertaking, protecting the lines of communication with India. With British Somaliland on the 'horn of Africa', Aden provided control of the entrance to the Red Sea. Western Aden and Eastern Aden, from 1840 and 1882 respectively, were British Protectorates until 1967, although in 1840 nominally the Abdali sultan retained his status.

In the 1840s and 1850s Aden was marked by the suppression of the Abdali anti-British unrest and the treaty signed with the British by the Sultan of Lahej Shaykh Muhsin ibn Fad.[1] In 1850 Aden became a freeport and two years later a Catholic church was built.

From 1853 to 1857 the regiment was in Poona.

The Anglo-Persian War 1857

Persia, now Iran, was a key player in the 'Great Game', the Anglo-Russian struggle for hegemony in Central Asia. The British wished Afghanistan to remain independent on friendly relations as a buffer against Russian expansion towards India and naturally opposed the spread of Persian influence in Afghanistan because they believed that Persia was influenced by Russia. In response to Persia's attack on Herat, the British governor-general in India, acting on orders from London, declared war on 1 November. The Anglo-Persian War lasted from 1 November 1856 to 4 April 1857.

Although Herat had been part of Iran under the Qajar dynasty when the war broke out, it had declared itself independent under its own rebellious emir, placing itself under the protection of the British in India in alliance with the Emirate of Kabul, predecessor of the modern state of Afghanistan. The port of Bushire was taken and became the British base; reinforcements, including the 78th from Poona, were awaited.

The war resulted in the Persians withdrawing from Herat and signing a new treaty surrendering claims on the city; the British then withdrew from southern Iran.

January 1857 saw the Regiment join the Persian Expeditionary Force, disembarking at Bushire in the Persian Gulf, the country's most important commercial port. The second division was led by Brigadier General Havelock and Major General Sir James Outram KCB, who had arrived in India from England with instructions to take over command and direct British operations in Persia. The Bombay government granted Outram the 14th King's Light Dragoons, 78th Highlanders, 23rd Native Light Infantry, 26th Native Infantry, Jacob's Scinde Horse, one troop of horse artillery, two field batteries, and a light battalion composed of ten companies from different native infantry regiments. The 78th was embroiled in the battles of Khushab (or Koosh-ab) and Mahommerah. Khushab was the biggest single engagement of the war. The resulting battle honour, Koosh-ab was awarded to the North Staffords, then the 64th, the 68th Durham Light Infantry and the Seaforth.

The Battle of Khushab

Having taken Borazjan without a fight, the British expeditionary army was withdrawing to Bushire on 7 February after plundering the garrison's stores and taking the town's governor as prisoner. It was ambushed by a smaller Persian force under Sohrab Khan Qashqai, drawn up in battle order to its rear.

George Henry Hunt,[1] tells us that the Persian cavalry contingent surrounded the British force on all sides and galloped around them. The Persian cavalrymen aimed to instil fear and cause confusion among the British rank and file by sounding British bugle calls. Given that English officers were once employed by the Qajar military, the Persian army was well-versed in several standard British bugle calls. The buglers of the Qashqai cavalry sounded 'Cease Fire' and 'Incline to the Left' orders which had no effect on the Highlanders but the 20th Native Infantry reportedly stopped firing, thinking that it was their own force firing on them. The Persian light skirmishers fired a salvo and then stopped firing in that direction. The Persian cavalry engaged the 78th head on at various points during the skirmish. The British Army adopted an oblong formation as the five heavy guns of the Persian artillery opened fire with round-shot. Hunt adds that, while the Persian artillery had calculated the range very accurately, there were few casualties given the lengthy bombardment. However, one shot dealt considerable damage to the 64th (2nd Staffordshire) Regiment and blew off one of Lieutenant Greentree's feet, while severely wounding Captain Mackler. During this engagement, Outram's horse fell and rolled over him, rendering the general incapacitated for the duration of the ambush. His chief of staff, Colonel Lugard, took command of the British forces and quietly covered the mishap, ensuring few others knew of Outram's condition until the next morning.

The battle ended with a British victory. The troops returned to Bushehr.

On the morning of 8 February, the Persian army under Shoja ol-Molk drew up in line at the walled village of Khushab. With the clearing of the morning mist the two sides began exchanging cannon fire.

George Hunt[2] tells us that the British brigades began manoeuvring into different positions, forming two lines, with the first consisting of the 78th Highlanders and a contingent of Indian sappers to their right; the rest included the 26th Regiment Native Infantry, 2nd European Light Infantry, and 4th Rifle Regiment at the far left of the line. The second line included Her Majesty's 64th Regiment to the right, the 20th Regiment Native Infantry and the Belooch Battalion to the left. Outram placed the light infantry battalions to counter the Qajar centre, while a detachment of 3rd Cavalry covered the Qashqai Cavalry. The Governor of Borazjan was present at the British rear but was forced off his horse to his knees when attempting to signal the Persian army to his presence. As the British lines advanced, Hunt and Townsend cite few casualties among the Highlanders and 26th Native Infantry but note that the 1st Brigade, 1st Division fared worse against the Persian bombardment. The British records cited one officer and eighteen men killed, with four officers and sixty wounded. Other records, however, cite 220 killed and 64 wounded. The British claimed Persian casualties to be approximately 700 and considered the battle a British victory with only ten lost, and none of those in the 78th. The Persian government saw it differently and published an alternative version of Khushab, considering the battle to be a Persian victory in which the British casualties amounted to 1,000 killed and wounded.

The British were also victorious at Mahommerah. On 4 March a treaty was signed in Paris bringing an end to hostilities. Over the next few months, the force returned to India and, in October, withdrew from Bushire. Most of the forces were soon deployed in Central India to quell the Indian Mutiny.

When the 78th later attacked the Persian camp at Mohomrah near the Shat-el-Arab waterway the Persians fled, having been bombarded by Outram's navy.

The Indian Mutiny, or the 'First War of Independence', 1857–1859

As we have seen in our coverage of the 1st Battalion, the Indian Mutiny, or Rebellion, of 1857 was a critical insurrection against the rule of the British East India Company. The rebellion began on 10 May 1857 with a mutiny of sepoys of the Company's army in Meerut, forty miles north-east of Delhi. It then erupted into other mutinies and civilian rebellions, chiefly in the upper Gangetic plain and central India, though incidents of revolt also occurred farther north and east. The rebellion posed a threat to British hegemony in that region and was contained only with the rebels' defeat in Gwalior on 20 June 1858. On 1 November 1858, the British granted amnesty to all rebels not involved in murder, although they did not declare hostilities to have ended formally until 8 July 1859.

The Indian Rebellion was fuelled by deep resentments fostered by oppressive British-style social reforms, harsh land taxes, summary and disrespectful treatment of some rich landowners and princes, as well as scepticism about the so-called improvements brought about by British rule. Many Indians rose against the British; however, it should be said that a majority also fought for the British, seemingly content with British rule. Violence, which sometimes descended to terrible atrocities, was inflicted on both sides, on British officers, and civilians, including women and children, by the rebels, and on the rebels, and their supporters, including sometimes entire villages, by British reprisals; the cities of Delhi and Lucknow were laid waste in the fighting and the British retaliation.

The 78th landed at Calcutta, disarmed mutinous sepoys at Barrackpore and then hastened to Allahabad, forming part of General Havelock's force. From there the objective was to recapture Kanpur (Cawnpore) and on 12 July they engaged the rebels at Futtehpore, drove them out of town and captured twelve guns. More victories followed at Aong and Nuddi.

Havelock's Force:

HM 64th Foot (from Persia)	435 men	Maj Sterling
HM 78th Highlanders (from Persia)	284 men	Col Hamilton
HM 84th Foot (from Pegu)	190 men	Lieut Ayrton
1st Madras Fusiliers (from Madras)	376 men	Maj Renaud
Voluntary Cavalry (from Allahabad)	20 men	Capt Barrow
Royal Artillery (from Ceylon)	96 men	Capt Maude
	1,403 British	
Native Troops		
Regiment of Ferozpore (Sikhs)	448 men	Capt. Brasyer
13th Irregular Cavalry and 3rd Oude Cavalry	95 men	Lieut Palliser
Artillery	18 men	
	561 Native	

Havelock then advanced to Kanpur which had been besieged by 3,000 mutineers under Dandhu Path, better known as Nana Sahib who had earlier sent an army to check the advance of General Havelock to Kanpur. As we have seen, it was defeated at Fatehpur on 12 July. Nana Sahib then sent a follow-up force under his brother, Bala Rao.

Havelock was a popular general, his career damaged when his family's fortune evaporated and he could not afford to buy the necessary promotions. But he had his critics, one of whom described him as 'an old fossil, dug up and only fit to be turned into pipe clay'. His orders, however, were simple: relieve the garrisons at Cawnpore and Lucknow and 'take prompt measures for dispersing and utterly destroying all mutineers and insurgents'.

On 15 July, the British forces defeated Bala Rao's army in the Battle of Aong. During the battle, Havelock captured a number of rebel soldiers who provided some valuable intelligence when they informed the British that there was an army of 5,000 rebel soldiers with eight artillery pieces further up the road. This obviously had a bearing on Havelock's strategy.

The Siege of Cawnpore 1857[1]

Situated as it was on the Grand Trunk Road and Grand Trunk Canal beside the Ganges, Cawnpore became a vitally important garrison town, straddling key communication lines. The commander, General Hugh Wheeler, was confident, though, that the mutiny 'might pass them by'. By June 1857, the Indian Rebellion had spread to several areas near Cawnpore, including Meerut, Agra, Mathura and Lucknow. However, the sepoys at Cawnpore initially remained loyal. Unusually for a high-ranking British officer, Hugh Wheeler was conversant with the local language, had adopted local customs, and was married to an Indian woman. He was confident that the sepoys at Cawnpore would remain loyal to him. Indeed, he had 'a gross overconfidence in the loyalty of the sepoys under his command', and sent two British companies (one each of the 84th and 32nd Regiments) to besieged Lucknow.

In 1857 Cawnpore was garrisoned by four regiments of native infantry and a European battery of artillery. The 300 or so East India officers apart, the European contingent was a motley collection of 300 military families and 150 business owners, barbers, operators of toll roads, telegraphs and railway engineers. Unsurprisingly, the native servants wasted no time in leaving. According to Caleb Wright, the most suitable defensive location for the British was the magazine located in the north of the city. It had thick walls, ample ammunition and stores, and also hosted the local treasury. However, General Wheeler bizarrely decided to take refuge in the south of the city, in an entrenchment composed of two barracks surrounded by a mud wall with poor provisions.[2]

The local situation was complicated by Nana Sahib, the adopted heir of the last great Maratha king Baji Rao; after defeat by the British, he had settled in luxurious exile at Bithur. For thirty-three years the British paid the prince a lavish pension but, by some breathtaking diplomatic clumsiness, the East India Company decided that Baji Rao's pension and honours would die with him and would not be passed on to any successors. Nana Sahib lobbied hard, sending an envoy, Azimullah Khan, to London to petition Queen Victoria directly, but to no avail. This dispossessed and now disaffected Hindu aristocrat would surely come back to haunt Wheeler.

On 10 May in Meerut the small but mostly contained disturbances exploded into a full blown mutiny – again through British arrogance and diplomatic and religious insensitivity. New-style cartridges were the cause of this cataclysmic mutiny. On 9 May, eighty-five cavalry *sowars* (lancers) of the 3rd Bengal Cavalry refused to use their newly-issued cartridges, despite claims that no defiling fat had been used in their manufacture. The eighty-five were found guilty and sentenced to life imprisonment, clapped in irons and jailed. Next day a group of sowars descended on the town and released their comrades. When British officers tried to intervene, they were cut down or shot. Bungalows were torched with all Europeans considered fair game. By the end of that bloody Sunday about fifty European men, women and children lay dead. The mutiny spread from Meerut and Delhi to Agra, Muttra, Lucknow and Bhurtpore during May. However, Cawnpore appeared to remain loyal. British officers dutifully slept amongst their sepoys and sowars in order to show their confidence in their men. In fact, General Wheeler was so out of touch that, when a relieving force of two companies of the 84th arrived on 2 June, he sent one of those companies plus one of the already arrived 32nd (a total of two officers and fifty men) on to Henry Lawrence at besieged Lucknow, totally misjudging how useful they could have become to the defence of Cawnpore in the coming days.

According to P.C. Gupta, the rebellion broke out in Meerut on 10 May 1857.[3] Cawnpore was home to the 1st, 53rd and 56th Native Infantry and the 2nd Bengal Cavalry. These regiments, in common with the other regiments of the East India Company Army, consisted of British officers and Indian soldiers. The total number of native troops in Cawnpore in 1857 was about 3,000, compared to about 300 British soldiers (the officers of the Native Regiments, a small number of men of the 84th Regiment, some invalids from the 32nd Regiment, and a few artillerymen and Madras Fusiliers). Although the sepoys in Cawnpore had not rebelled, the European families began to drift into the entrenchment as the news of rebellion in the nearby areas reached them. The entrenchment was fortified, and the Indian sepoys were ordered to collect their pay one by one, so as to avoid an armed mob gathering.

Wheeler's entrenchment contained two large barrack buildings, one used as a hospital, and various outlying buildings. A trench had been hastily dug and the earth from it formed a wall about four-feet high. Several batteries of guns were set up. In all there were about 1,000 people in the entrenchment, but only about 300 were soldiers, the rest being civilians and, mainly, women and children. The entrenchment was ill-equipped for a long siege. Food was not plentiful, water was a particular problem as the only well was in an exposed position, guns were in short supply, and the hospital building burned down when hit by a missile.

The forces at Wheeler's disposal were pathetically small at around 250. He had forty-nine soldiers of the 84th, seventy-nine of the 32nd (mostly sick), fifty-nine artillery and forty-three Eurasian drummers and fifers to defend about 1,000 civilians. Tensions were growing. On the night of 2 June a drunken Lieutenant Cox fired on his own guard. He missed, was disarmed and thrown into jail for the night. The following day the sowars were less than impressed when a hastily convened court failed to convict him of firing on his own troops: one rule for the English and another for the Indians. Paranoia was setting in when rumours led some to believe that the Indian troops were to be summoned to a parade, where they were to be massacred. All those factors conspired to encourage them to rebel against East India Company rule.

On 5 June the sowars started torching buildings, looting and generally causing mayhem. The 56th panicked and fled. European artillery opened up on the fleeing sepoys, assuming they were mutineers too. If they hadn't been before, they were after. To make matters worse, the 53rd, Wheeler's old regiment, was caught in the crossfire. The confusion and panic had led the British defenders to fire upon what was probably the most loyal unit in the area.

The unforgiving pre-monsoon humidity and heat was certainly neither friend nor help and was the main catalyst for the unrest. As we have said, the single well was in the line of fire of enemy artillerymen and snipers who were able to take pot shots at the increasingly desperate and thirsty defenders. Water extraction would take place at night to stand any chance of replenishment. A second dried-up well served as a makeshift burial chamber: dead bodies were piled up outside the buildings awaiting nightfall when they would be dragged and unceremoniously dumped. Smallpox, dysentery and cholera broke out and ravaged the steadily weakening defenders. By 21 June, the defenders had lost a third of their number. General Wheeler suffered his own personal tragedy when his son, Lieutenant Gordon Wheeler, was decapitated by a round-shot in the final assault on the barracks.

The first major assault by Nana Sahib was on the evening of 12 June. However, the attacking soldiers were convinced that the British had laid out gunpowder-filled trenches and did not enter the area. As we noted, on 13 June the British lost their hospital building to a fire, which destroyed most of their medical supplies and caused the deaths of a number of wounded and sick artillerymen who burned alive in the inferno.

Nana Sahib and his advisers had come up with a plan to end the deadlock. They enlisted a female European prisoner, Rose Greenway, to approach the entrenchment to initiate negotiations. She carried a note to the defenders explaining that Nana Sahib was willing to offer safe passage to Allahabad from the Satichaura Ghat, a landing on the Ganges, for everyone who laid down their arms.

According to Mowbray Thomson, one of the few survivors, Wheeler was implacably opposed to surrender:[4]

> Sir Hugh Wheeler, still hopeful of relief from Calcutta, and suspicious of treachery on the part of the Nana, for a long time most strenuously opposed the idea of making terms; but upon the representation that there were only three days' rations in store, and after the often-reiterated claims of the women and children, and the most deplorable destitution in which we were placed, he at last succumbed to Captain Moore's expostulations, and consented to the preparation of a treaty of capitulation.

General Wheeler rejected it, ostensibly because it did not bear a signature and that therefore no personal guarantee had been offered. Next day, 25 June, a second note was brought, by a different female prisoner, the elderly Mrs Jacobi and signed by Nana Sahib himself. This caused a division between the survivors: those determined to hold out and those wishing to trust Nana Sahib. Wheeler was in favour of holding out, but some of his officers persuaded him of the sense in escorting the surviving women and children to safety. The general relented and offered to lay down his arms in return for safe passage. The bitter pill was sweetened somewhat when he won the concession allowing the British troops to take their sidearms and sixty rounds each.

The day designated to board the boats to take them down the Ganges to Allahabad was 27 June. Wheeler was at the head of the column destined for embarkation at Satichaura Ghat. Caleb Wright tells us that Nana Sahib had sent a number of carts, *dolis* (litters) and elephants to enable the women, the children and the sick to reach the river banks. The British military were escorted by a large contingent of the rebel army. The party reached the Satichaura Ghat by 8.00am where Nana Sahib had arranged around forty boats. Looters all the while were frantically grabbing the personal effects of those further down the column. More locals swarmed into the entrenchment, hoping to find things of value left behind by the defenders. Confusion reigned at the river when the Indian boatmen, instead of pushing off, jumped overboard on hearing bugles sounding and made for the banks. In doing so they knocked over the cooking fires on the boats, thus setting some of the boats ablaze. Tatya Tope, Nana Sahib's commander in chief of forces in the Cawnpore region, ordered the 2nd Bengal Cavalry and some artillery pieces to open fire on the hapless Europeans. One account graphically, and perhaps over-imaginatively, describes the mayhem as

> The British opened fire on them. Perhaps it was all a terrible mistake, but from prepared positions on the riverbanks the sepoys showered the boats with a storm of grapeshot and musketry. Women screamed, the boats caught fire, the river turned red and corpses floated downstream. Indian cavalry troopers rode into the shallows and slashed at the wounded with their sabres.

Another account describes it as follows:

> On 27 June what remained of the garrison marched out towards the landing stage. The sick and the women were carried out in palanquins, and the children who could not walk were carried by some of the sepoys who had been trying to kill them a few days before. By 9.00am all were embarked in large clumsy vessels with thatched roofs which looked, from a distance, 'rather like floating haystacks'. Suddenly, and without warning, a shot was heard. Fearful of treachery, and with nerves tattered by three weeks of siege, the British immediately opened fire. The Nana's men replied with grapeshot and ball, and the little fleet was soon ablaze. One boat succeeded in getting away, and four of its occupants finally reached safety.[5]

Christopher Hibbert points out that there is no evidence to show who fired the first shots or whether the massacre was pre-planned.[6] Some historians believe that the Satichaura Ghat massacre was the result of confusion, and not of any plan implemented by Nana Sahib and his associates.[7] Lieutenant Mowbray Thomson, one of the four male survivors of the massacre, believed that the rank-and-file sepoys who spoke to him did not know of the killing to come.[8] Wheeler, his wife and elder daughter were amongst those killed in the ensuing massacre.

> The massacre was merciless. Bullets flew from all directions as the Europeans desperately attempted to scramble into the burning boats. There was no return fire as the British had been disarmed as part of the surrender terms. The relative shallowness of the river caused further difficulties in getting the boats moving as they scraped along the bottom of the riverbed. Bodies were falling everywhere as grapeshot and musket fire raked the boats from both banks. Mutineer cavalry sowars moved into the water to try and finish off any remaining Europeans with swords and pistols. Women and children were inevitably caught up in the deadly fire. Two boats seemed to drift off – General Wheeler's boat, which had started the mutineers in their murderous fire in the first place and a second boat which was quickly

> holed beneath the waterline with round shot fired from the bank. There was a panicked exodus from this second boat to try and attempt to make it to General Wheeler's boat which was slowly drifting to safer waters. Meanwhile back at the boarding point, the carnage continued. It then stopped almost as suddenly as it started when the mutineers suddenly ceased fire. Any remaining women and children were taken prisoner and escorted to Savada House. Any remaining men were cut down where they stood. Approximately 120 women and children were thus taken away.[9]

There was worse to come for Wheeler's boat and the sixty or so fugitives on board. Mutineers pursued them relentlessly along the riverbanks with the boat frequently grounding on sandbanks. Trying to dislodge the boat under fire was particularly perilous and not everyone was able to rejoin the boat whenever it floated free; General Wheeler's own family members were probably killed in the water trying to free the boat. Lieutenant Thomson led a last gasp desperate charge out of the river into the mutineers which worked and allowed them to capture some vital ammunition. The next morning yet another grounding resulted in another charge by Thomson and eleven volunteers. Whilst Thomson had been fighting, an attack had been launched from the opposite bank leaving the remaining defenders exhausted. With most of the remaining men shot or wounded, the rest had no choice but to raise the white flag. They were ignominiously escorted off the boat and taken back to Savada House, Nana Sahib's headquarters. It was here that Nana Sahib ordered the execution of all the remaining men, including General Wheeler, whilst the women and children were taken to Savada House to be re-united with the earlier survivors from Bibighar. The surviving British men were forced to sit on the ground while Nana Sahib's soldiers prepared to fire on them. Their Sahib granted the British chaplain Moncrieff's request to read prayers before they died.[10] The British were initially wounded by the guns and then finished off with swords.[11]

Unbelievably, Thomson's small band of desperate men had yet more to contend with:

> The survivors ran barefoot for three miles to try and evade any pursuing mutineers. Mutineers pursued but were wary of getting too close as Thomson's party laid several ambushes and mini-counter-attacks. The party found some refuge in a small shrine. They blocked the doorway with the bodies of mutineers who had hastily charged the position. Appreciating the difficulties of a frontal assault, a group of mutineers went around the back and started digging from behind. Another group attempted to smoke the British out – but the wind took the smoke in the opposite direction.

> Gunpowder was added to the fire to thicken the fire later in the day. This prompted the British to try a last gasp charge through the thick black acrid smoke. Six of the British were cut down, but the rest managed to bayonet their way to the riverbank where they flung themselves into the river and tried to swim to safety. A group of villagers beckoned the five soldiers to their side of the bank only to start clubbing them as they reached that bank. One was killed leaving just the four – including Thomson – to swim to the centre of the river. They drifted downstream as best they could – although they now had to worry about crocodiles too. They came exhaustedly ashore a few hours later. Their fortunes finally turned for the better when they were discovered by Rajput matchlockmen who worked for the Raja Dirigibijah Singh who had remained loyal to the British. They were taken, or rather carried, to the Raja's palace.

These four British soldiers were the only male survivors from the British side, apart from Jonah Shepherd, who had been captured by Nana Sahib before the surrender. The four men included two privates named Murphey and Sullivan, Lieutenant Delafosse and Lieutenant (later Captain) Mowbray Thomson. The men spent several weeks recuperating, eventually making their way back to Cawnpore which was, by that time, back under British control. Murphey and Sullivan both died soon after from cholera; Delafosse went on to join the defending garrison during the Siege of Lucknow, and Thomson took part in rebuilding and defending the entrenchment a second time under General Windham, eventually writing an account of his experiences.[12]

One of the few positive and uplifting stories to come from all this concerned another survivor. Amy Horne, a 17-year-old Anglo-Indian girl had fallen from her boat and had been swept downstream during the riverside massacre. Soon after scrambling ashore, she encountered Wheeler's youngest daughter, Margaret. The two girls hid in the undergrowth for a number of hours until they were discovered by a group of rebels. Margaret was taken away on horseback, never to be seen again (it was later rumoured that she survived and was married to a Muslim soldier) and Amy was led to a nearby village where she was taken into the protection of a Muslim rebel leader in exchange for converting to Islam. Just over six months later, she was rescued by Highlanders from Sir Colin Campbell's column on their way to relieve Lucknow.

The surviving 120 British women and children were moved from the Savada House to Bibighar, 'The House of the Ladies', a villa in Cawnpore. As we know, they were later joined by other women and children, the survivors from General Wheeler's boat. Another group of British women and children from Fatehgarh and some other captive European women were also confined to Bibighar. In total, there were around 200 women and children in Bibighar.[13]

Unfortunately, Nana Sahib entrusted the care of these survivors to a sex worker called Hussaini Khanum, also known as Hussaini Begum. She put the captives to work grinding corn for *chapatis*. Poor sanitary conditions inevitably led to deaths from cholera and dysentery.[14]

Nana Sahib used the prisoners as a tool for bargaining with the East India Company. As we have seen, the Company forces, comprising around 1,000 British, 150 Sikh soldiers and thirty irregular cavalry, had set out from Allahabad, under Henry Havelock, to retake Cawnpore and Lucknow.[15] The first relief force assembled under Havelock included the 64th Regiment of Foot and 78th Highlanders, recalled from the Anglo-Persian War. Nana Sahib demanded that the East India Company forces under Havelock and Colonel Neill retreat to Allahabad. However, the Company forces carried on regardless towards Cawnpore. Nana Sahib sent an army to check their advance. The two armies clashed at Fatehpur on 12 July, where General Havelock's forces emerged victorious and captured the town.

The battle on 15 July resulted in heavy casualties on both sides but cleared the road to Cawnpore for the British.

Crucially, Nana Sahib was informed that the British troops led by Havelock and Neill were showing violence against the Indian villagers. Pramod Nayar believes that the ensuing Bibighar massacre was a violent reaction to the news of violence perpetrated by the advancing British troops. Other suggestions for the atrocity are that there was a fear of future identification of key ring leaders if the prisoners were allowed to go free.

Nana Sahib, and his associates, including Tatya Tope and Azimullah Khan, agonised over what to do with the captives at Bibighar. Some of Nana Sahib's advisors had already made up their minds to kill the captives as revenge for the executions of Indians by the advancing British forces. The women of Nana Sahib's household were outraged and went on a hunger strike, but their protests were in vain.

Finally, on 15 July, an order was given to murder the Bibighar women and children. The details of the incident, such as who ordered the massacre, are by no means clear.[16]

The rebel sepoys executed the four surviving male hostages from Fatehghar, one of them a 14-year-old boy. But they refused to obey the order to kill women and the other children while some of the sepoys agreed to remove the women and children from the courtyard. But Tatya Tope threatened to execute them for dereliction of duty. Nana Sahib left the building because he did not want to be a witness to the unfolding slaughter.

The British women and children were ordered to come out of the assembly rooms, but they refused to do so and instead clung to each other. They barricaded themselves in, tying the door handles with clothing. At first, around twenty rebel soldiers opened fire from the outside of the Bibighar, firing through holes in the boarded windows. The soldiers of the squad that was supposed to fire the next rounds were so disturbed by the scene that they discharged their shots into the air. Soon after, on hearing the screams and delirium inside, the rebel soldiers threw down their weapons and refused to kill any more.

A furious Begum Hussaini Khanum denounced the sepoys as cowards and had her aide finish the job of killing the captives. She hired some butchers from the bazaar who hacked the women and children to death with cleavers. When it seemed that all the captives had been slaughtered the butchers left.

However, a few women and children had managed to survive by hiding under dead bodies. It was agreed to dump the bodies of the victims down a dry well using a team of sweepers and when the rebels arrived next morning to dispose of the bodies they discovered that three women were still alive, as well as three children aged between four and seven. The surviving women were thrown into the well by the sweepers who then threw the three little boys into the well one at a time, the youngest first. The retribution and reprisals visited on the people of Cawnpore and the rebels was no less sickening than the original atrocities.

Havelock's force, including the 78th, reached Cawnpore on 16 July and captured the city unopposed. A detachment of British officers and soldiers set off for the Bibighar to rescue the captives under the assumption they would still be alive. However, when they reached the site, they found it deserted and blood-splattered. Piles of children's clothing and women's hair blew on the wind and lodged in tree branches around the compound; the tree in the courtyard nearest the well was smeared with the brains of numerous children and infants who had been dashed headfirst against the trunk and thrown down the well.[17]

The hideous discovery of the massacre is recorded by Major G.W.P. Bingham of the 64th (2nd Staffordshire) Regiment of Foot, one of the first soldiers to visit the scene after the capture of the city on 17 July:

> The place was literally running ankle deep in blood, ladies' hair torn from their heads was lying about the floor; poor little children's shoes lying here and there, gowns, frocks and bonnets belonging to these poor creatures scattered everywhere. But to crown all horrors, after they had been killed, and even some alive, all were thrown down a deep well in the compound. I looked down and saw them lying in heaps. I very much fear there are some of my friends included in this most atrocious fiendish of murders.[18]

The 2,000 troops, racked with dysentery, cholera and heatstroke, took ten days to advance the 100 miles from Allahabad to Cawnpore. When they entered the town, on the 17th, they still hoped to bring release to the women and children imprisoned there. Instead, they found a slaughter-house. 'I am not exaggerating,' wrote one officer, 'when I tell you that the soles of my boots were more than covered with the blood of these poor wretched creatures.' Bloodstained clothing was scattered about, as well as leaves ripped out of the Bible and out of another appropriately titled book, *Preparation for Death.*

The British troops were struck with horror and incandescent at one and the same time when they processed what had happened. They engaged in a retaliatory orgy of violence of their own against the local population of Cawnpore, including looting and burning of houses, their justification being that none of the local non-combatants had done anything to prevent or stop the massacre.

Brigadier General Neill, who took the command at Cawnpore, instigated a programme of swift and vicious drumhead military justice, culminating in summary execution for any sepoy rebel captured from the city who was unable to prove he was not implicated in the massacre. Rebels confessing to or believed to be involved in the massacre were forced to lick the floor of the Bibighar compound while being whipped, after it had been wetted with water by low-caste Indians. The sepoys were then religiously disgraced and humiliated by being forced to eat beef, if Hindu, or pork, if Muslim. The Muslim sepoys were sewn into pig skins before being hanged, and low-caste Hindu street sweepers were employed to execute the high-caste Brahmin rebels to add additional religious disgrace to their punishment. Some were also forced by the British to lick clean other buildings stained with the blood of the recently deceased, before being publicly hanged.

Most of the prisoners were hanged within direct view of the well at the Bibighar and buried in shallow ditches by the roadside. Others were shot or bayoneted, while some were also tied across cannon that were then fired, an execution method initially used by the rebels, and the earlier Indian powers, such as the Marathas and the Mughals. When the ordnance was available, it was not unusual to blow alleged rebels from guns. It was maintained that this hideous and atrocious behaviour embodied 'two valuable elements of capital punishment; it was painless to the criminal and terrible to the beholder'.

> With great ceremony the victim was escorted to the parade ground while the band played some lively air. The victim's back was ranged against the muzzle of one of the big guns and he was strapped into position. Then the band would fall silent and the only sound would be the faint crackle of the portfire, as it was lowered to the touch-hole. With a flash and a roar,

> an obscene shower of blood and entrails would cover both the gunners and observers.[19]

'Remember Cawnpore!' became a war-cry for the British soldiers for the rest of the conflict. Acts of summary violence against towns and cities believed to harbour or support the rebellion also increased. In one village, a detachment of Highlanders caught around 140 men, women and children. Ten men were hanged without any evidence or trial. Another sixty men were forced to build the gallows from wooden logs, while others were flogged and beaten. In another village, when around 2,000 villagers came out in protest brandishing *lathis*, long, heavy iron-bound bamboo sticks used as weapons, the Highlanders surrounded them and set the village on fire. Villagers trying to escape were summarily executed by the Highlanders.

Pratul Chandra Gupta[20] tells us that, on 19 July, General Havelock resumed operations at Bithoor. Major Stevenson led a group of Madras Fusiliers and Sikh soldiers to Bithoor and occupied Nana Sahib's palace without any resistance. The British troops seized guns, elephants and camels, and set the palace on fire.

In the end, the British left the room at Bibighur untouched, and filled in the well only partially. Why? So that they could stand as terrible reminders to new troops from the UK that their duty must be sustained by a desire for revenge. One soldier, his head full of tales of atrocities, reported: 'I seed two Moors [Indians] talking in a cart. Presently I heard one of 'em say "Cawnpore". I knowed what that meant; so I fetched Tom Walker, and he heard 'em say "Cawnpore", and he knowed what that meant. So we polished 'em both off.'

Revenge was not confined to uneducated soldiers. At Cawnpore, Brigadier General James Neill issued an order on 25 July that every captured rebel, whether proved guilty or not, 'will be taken down to the house and will be forced to clean up a small portion of the bloodstains. The task will be made as revolting to his feelings as possible .... After properly cleaning up his portion, the culprit will be immediately hanged.' The guilty men, of course, had fled long before Neill arrived. Neill proudly reported that 'a Mohammedan officer of our civil court, a great rascal' had objected. He was flogged, and 'made to lick up part of the blood with his tongue'. Then, in Old Testament terms expressing the fanatical desire for vengeance which infected many British, Neill concluded: 'No doubt this is a strange law, but it suits the occasion well, and I hope I shall not be interfered with until the room is thoroughly cleansed in this way .... I will hold my own, with the help and the blessing of God. I cannot help seeing that His finger is in all this – we have been false to ourselves so often.'

Neill was not alone in what was now a mindless reign of terror which perhaps started to become an excuse for inhumane atrocities, atrocities that were a repellent form of public entertainment put on by incorrigible sadists. By the middle of June 1857, they had begun what one nineteenth-century historian of the Mutiny, I.W. Kaye, called a 'Bloody Assize'. Indiscriminate lynchings were commonplace. 'Volunteer hanging parties,' wrote Kaye, 'went out into the districts, and amateur executioners were not wanting to the occasion. One gentleman boasted of the numbers he had finished off quite "in an artistic manner", with mango trees for gibbets and elephants for drops, the victims of this wild justice being strung up, as though for pastime, in the form of figures of eight.'

With Cawnpore taken, Havelock addressed the 78th in what reads like a clumsy attempt to rewrite recent history:

> In the whole of my career I have never seen a Regiment behave better, nay more I have never seen anyone behave as well as the 78th Highlanders this day. I am not a Highlander but I wish I was one.

The Havelock Force then proceeded to Lucknow. Havelock was, however, dogged not only by large bodies of mutineers, but also by heatstroke and disease. Though he was victorious in a number of engagements, his troops were too weak to follow up their successes, and twice he was forced to fall back on Cawnpore. There he was able to regain sufficient strength to defeat, on 16 August, a large force of mutineers who attempted to retake the city. But reinforcements arrived, and on 19 September Havelock was at last able to set out once again to relieve the long-besieged people in the Lucknow Residency.

Cartridges: their religious and cultural significance

The difficulties experienced with cartridges at this time are both legion and infamous. They involved a potentially explosive mix of religious sensibilities and technological change. For years the East India Company had relied on a simple smoothbore musket until it was decided to introduce a more accurate muzzle-loading Enfield rifled musket. One way of speeding up the loading process was to use a paper cartridge with the bullet sitting on the exact quantity of powder needed. The loader had to bite this paper cartridge to expose the powder. The original cartridges, made in Britain, were coated in tallow to help protect them from the elements.

Unfortunately, and significantly, the tallow was made from beef and pork fat. To the average British user of the cartridges, that was not a problem. Hindu and Muslim users, however, were horrified at the prospect of biting fat which would have defiled them. Although the EIC realised its blunder quickly and replaced the animal fat with vegetable fat, the damage had been done. To

Hindus and Muslims, their worst fears of being ritually humiliated had become a reality. Many assumed that this had been a deliberate policy by evangelising Europeans looking to impose their own religion on the sub-continent. Indian battalion after battalion refused to use the new cartridges. Some even refused to handle them when officers allowed them the option of tearing open, instead of biting the cartridges.

As far as most of those officers were concerned, an order was an order and refusing to obey an order was mutiny. Different commanders handled the situation in different ways, some with more sensitivity than others. The first shots were, literally, fired by (an inebriated) Mungal Pandy on 29 March at Barrackpore. Protesting against the disbanding of a unit that had disobeyed orders to use the cartridges, he shot at a British sergeant-major and a lieutenant and engaged them in a sword fight. He saw both of them off but then shot himself in the chest when a General Hearsey arrived in the parade ground. The authorities at Barrackpore were fortunate to have the European 84th Regiment to hand so that disarming the Indian battalions could be done with the threat of force to any sepoys thinking of refusing to hand over their guns. Not all stations would be so fortunate.

The Siege of Lucknow 1857

The state of Oudh/Awadh had been annexed by the East India Company and the Nawab Wajid Ali Shah was exiled to Calcutta the year before the rebellion broke out. This characteristically high-handed action by the East India Company was greatly resented within the state and throughout India.

On 30 May, the day of the Muslim festival of Eid ul-Fitr, most of the Oudh and Bengal troops at Lucknow erupted into open rebellion. In addition to his locally recruited pensioners, Sir Henry Lawrence, an experienced administrator who took up the Residency only six weeks before the rebellion began, also had the bulk of the British 32nd Foot at his disposal; they were able to drive the rebels away from the city.

On 4 June there was a rebellion at Sitapur, a large and important station fifty-one miles from Lucknow, followed by another at Faizabad, one of the most important cities in the province, and by outbreaks at Daryabad, Sultanpur and Salon. Thus, in the course of ten days, British authority in Oudh practically evaporated.

A reinforced Havelock Force arrived at and established itself at the Alam Bagh – a walled enclosure two miles from Lucknow from which the enemy had recently been dislodged. After an ill-fated and poorly organised reconnaissance mission, in which sepoys loyal to the British were hacked to death and many others died of heatstroke within sight of the Residency, Lawrence retreated within. The sixty-acre Residency had been besieged by mutineers since July; it was garrisoned by about 855 British officers and men, 153 armed civilian volunteers and 712 native troops. Then there were the 1,280 non-combatants including hundreds of women and children. The defenders were up against a force of well over 20,000 Indian mutineers.

The truth was that the Residency was little more than a bungalow surrounded by the native town. 'The whole place from a military point of view, was utterly untenable', according to *A Short History of the Seaforth Highlanders*. Indeed, 'the defence of the Residency was a nightmare' since the Residency lay in the midst of several palaces, mosques and administrative buildings, as Lucknow had long been the royal capital of Oudh. Lawrence initially refused permission for these buildings to be demolished, urging his engineers to 'spare the holy places'. Unfortunately, during the siege they were to provide good vantage points and cover for rebel snipers and artillery. One military commander, Colonel Sir John Eardley Inglis of the 32nd Regiment, described this poor decision as 'our very tenderness to the religious prejudices and respect to the rights of our rebellious citizens and soldiery'.

Casualties were obviously high. Deadly sniper fire was soon supplemented by heavy artillery. On 1 July a shell burst in the room occupied by Lawrence. On being urged to move to a safer place he misguidedly replied that he 'did not believe that the enemy had an artilleryman good enough to put another shell into that small room.' He was wrong. They did. About 8.00am next day, while he lay exhausted on his bed, there was 'a sheet of flames and a terrific report'. To the cry from one of his aides, 'Sir Henry, are you hurt?' he replied, 'I am killed.' His pain dulled by chloroform, Lawrence survived for two days despite 'a fearful wound in his hip'. In his lucid periods he dictated orders and requested that on his tomb should be placed the simple inscription 'Here lies Henry Lawrence who tried to do his duty. May God have mercy on him'. In the night of 4 July, he was, without ceremony, buried with other dead in a large pit.

The women and children were confined to the cellars, and lived a terrible, subterranean existence punctuated only by alarm and death. Food was rationed, each person receiving 'attar or flour, which we made into chapatis; rice, dhal or peas; salt and meat'. There were no proper cooking facilities so everything was cooked together, with ships' biscuits and some water, into a stew. 'But as the saucepan was of copper and could not be relined during the siege, the food when it was turned out was often perfectly green – hunger alone could make it enjoyable.' As ever in war the women and children suffered most. The heat was stifling – there were no coolies to pull the punkah fans. When the besiegers attacked the Residency, all the lights were extinguished and the children lay trembling in the darkness until the defenders had routed the Indians.

The defenders, their number constantly depleted by military action as well as disease, were able to repel all attempts to overwhelm them. Several sorties were mounted, attempting to reduce the effectiveness of the most dangerous rebel positions and to silence some of their guns.

The rebels in Oudh were a mediocre lot, but pre-eminent among the civilians there was a woman of strong character and a real sense of purpose. Begum Hazrat Mahal, who began her career as a dancing-girl, had caught the eye of the King of Oudh and bore him a son. After the rising in Oudh, the sepoys approached a number of the ex-king's concubines to persuade them to put up one of their sons as king. All refused until it was the turn of Hazrat Mahal. She immediately agreed that her ten-year-old son, Birjis Qadr, should be proclaimed king and that she should be regent during his minority. She raised funds, issued orders, and gave speeches to encourage the fight and as a result her men forced the British forces to retreat to the Lucknow Residency and that is where we find them under siege for almost five months.

William Howard Russell, correspondent with the *London Times*, noted in his diary: 'This Begum exhibits great energy and ability. She has excited all Oudh to take up the interests of her son, and the chiefs have sworn to be faithful to him.'

A 'government' of sorts was formed under Hazrat Mahal. Unbeknown to the Residency, Begum toured through Oudh connecting with other rebel leaders. Military intelligence did come to aid the British, however, through a native spy who several times was able to make his way through the rebel forces to Havelock's camp; and on 23 September a letter came from Sir James Outram, who had been sent to supersede Havelock but instead volunteered to serve under him until Lucknow was relieved. In his letter Outram informed the commander of the garrison that the relieving force would be there in a few days.

Outram arrived at Cawnpore with reinforcements on 15 September. The force numbered 3,179 and was composed of six British and one Sikh infantry battalions, with three artillery batteries, but only 168 volunteer cavalry. They were divided into two brigades, under the disputatious Brigadier General James Neill and Colonel Hamilton of the 78th Highlanders.

The force encountered heavy resistance at the Charbagh Canal, with half the officers and one third of the men of the 78th either killed or injured, but succeeded eventually after nine out of ten men of a forlorn hope were killed storming a bridge. They then turned to their right, following the west bank of the canal. The 78th Highlanders took a wrong turning, but were able to capture a rebel battery near the Qaisarbagh palace, before finding their way back to the main force. After further heavy fighting, by nightfall the force had reached the Machchhi Bhawan. Outram proposed to halt and contact the defenders of the Residency by tunnelling and mining through the intervening buildings, but Havelock insisted on an immediate advance. He feared that the defenders of the Residency were so weakened that they might still be overwhelmed by a last-minute rebel attack. The advance was made through heavily-defended narrow lanes. Neill was one of those killed by rebel musket fire. In all, the relief force lost 535 men out of 2,000, incurred mainly in this last rush. By the time of the relief, the defenders had endured a siege of eighty-seven days and were reduced to 982 fighting personnel.

On 25 September, after intense fighting, Havelock smashed his way through to the Residency. 'The half-famished garrison,' wrote Havelock, 'contrived to regale me, not only with beef cutlets, but with mock turtle soup and champagne.' But Havelock and Outram could do nothing in return. The force they had brought to Lucknow was not strong enough to break out again.

Although Outram and Havelock both recommended storming the Kaisarbagh palace to secure the British position, Campbell knew that other rebel forces were threatening Cawnpore and other cities held by the British, and he ordered Lucknow to be abandoned. The evacuation began on 19 November. While Campbell's artillery bombarded the Kaisarbagh, to deceive the rebels that an assault on it was imminent, canvas screens were erected to shield the open space from the rebels' view. The women, children and sick and wounded made their way to the Dilkusha Park under cover of the screens, some in a variety of carriages or on litters, others on foot. Over the next two days, Outram spiked his guns and withdrew after them.

At the Dilkusha Park, Havelock died of a sudden attack of dysentery on 24 November. The entire army and convoy now moved to the Alambagh. Campbell left Outram with 4,000 men to defend the Alambagh, while he himself moved with 3,000 men and most of the civilians to Cawnpore on 27 November.

The first siege had lasted eighty-seven days, the second a further sixty-one. The siege was raised on 17 November, the 78th having remained there throughout. Campbell returned to retake Lucknow, with the attack starting on 6 March. By 21 March 1858 all fighting had ceased.

Despite it all, there is one uplifting story to come out of the siege, as given in Richard Holmes's *Sahib*.

> The garrison's morale ebbed and flowed as hopes of relief were dashed and raised...there were Scots amongst the relieving force. On 25 September the women and children were assembled 'in trembling expectation ... how the rough and bearded soldiers of the 78th rushed amongst them, wringing their hands with loud and repeated gratulations' wrote Surgeon

Home. 'How the rough-looking men took the children up in their arms, caressed them and passed them back to others.[1]

Mrs Germon tells us how the joy and excitement continued:

> The most exciting scene I ever witnessed – the Piper sprang on a chair and he and Mrs Anderson claimed acquaintance – he asked where she came from and – she said 'Edinburgh' and he answered 'so do I and from the Castle Hill' and then they shook hands and he sent round word that there was a lady from Edinburgh and then gave another tune on his bagpipes... the confusion and excitement was beyond all description – they lost a great number of men coming through the city.[2]

One outcome of the siege was that the 78th earned no fewer than six Victoria Crosses. They were:

- **Lieutenant Herbert T. Macpherson, 25 September**

He was thirty years old, and a lieutenant in the 78th Highlanders (later The Seaforth Highlanders) during the Indian Mutiny when the following deed took place at the siege of Lucknow for which he was awarded the VC:

For distinguished conduct at Lucknow, on the 25th September, 1857, in setting an example of heroic gallantry to the men of the regiment, at the period of the action, in which they captured two brass nine-pounders at the point of the bayonet.[3]

- **Surgeon Joseph Lee, 25/26 September**

- **Assistant Surgeon Valentine M. McMaster, 25 September**

McMaster was a twenty-three-year-old assistant surgeon when the following action took place at the first relief of Lucknow for which he was awarded the VC:

For the intrepidity with which he exposed himself to the fire of the enemy, in bringing in, and attending to, the wounded, on the 25th of September, at Lucknow.[4]

- **Colour Sergeant Stewart McPherson, September 26**

McPherson saw action in Persia and India before Bengal. He was approximately thirty-eight years old, and a colour sergeant. His actions during the Siege of Lucknow earned him the Victoria Cross. His citation reads:

For daring gallantry in the Lucknow Residency on the 26th September, 1857, in having rescued, at great personal risk, a wounded Private of his Company, who was lying in a most exposed situation, under a very heavy fire. Colour-Serjeant McPherson was also distinguished on many occasions by his coolness and gallantry in action.[5]

- **Private Henry Ward, 25/26 September**

Ward was about thirty-four years old, and a private in the 78th Regiment of Foot during the Indian Mutiny when the following deed took place on 25 and 26 September 1857 in Lucknow, for which he was awarded the VC:

For his gallant and devoted conduct in having on the night of the 25th, and morning of the 26th of September, 1857, remained by the dooly (a litter to transport people) of Captain H.M. Havelock, 10th Regiment, Deputy Assistant-Adjutant-General, Field Force, who was severely wounded, and on the morning of the 26th of September, escorted that Officer and Private Thomas Pilkington, 78th Highlanders, who was also wounded, and had taken refuge in the same dooly, through a very heavy cross fire of ordnance and musketry. This soldier remained by the side of the dooly, and by his example and exertions kept the dooly bearers from dropping their double load, throughout the heavy fire, with the same steadiness as if on parade, thus saving the lives of both, and bringing them in safety to the Baillie Guard.[6]

Ward later became the personal servant of Sir Henry Havelock whose life was saved by Ward in his VC action. He later attained the rank of quartermaster-sergeant.

- **Private James Hollowell, 26 September**

Hollowell was about thirty-four years old, and a private in the 78th Regiment of Foot during the Indian Mutiny when the following deed took place on 26 September 1857 at the Siege of Lucknow for which he was awarded the VC:

> A party, on the 26th of September 1857, was shut up and besieged in a house in the city of Lucknow, by the rebel sepoys. Private James Hollowell, one of the party, behaved, throughout the day, in the most admirable manner; he directed, encouraged, and led the others, exposing himself fearlessly, and by his talent in persuading and cheering, prevailed on nine dispirited men to make a successful defence, in a burning house, with the enemy firing through four windows.[7]

The experience of women in the Indian Mutiny

We learn from Barbara J. Starmans:

> For the wives of the British officers who were stationed in India, the initial reports from Meerut inspired absolute terror. It was reported that few were spared in the savage attack and that the victims of the rebels included Mrs Chambers, a pregnant woman whose unborn baby was ripped from her womb and Mrs Dawson, who was burnt to death.[1]

Sadly, this bestial treatment of women is not unusual in the history of warfare and has been a hallmark of conflict the world over since early man fought with early man.[2]

Mrs Maria Vincent Germon, wife of one of the commanders of an outpost at Lucknow, first heard of the horrible news from Meerut when she dined at the home of the Brigade Major of Lucknow. On Friday, 15 May 1857, she wrote in her diary:

> it was rather alarming for one living alone as I was, my husband being on city duty. Mr B— walked home with me about half-past 8, at 9 I went to bed, taking good care to have a shawl and dressing gown close to the bed. Charlie's orderly slept in the verandah with the servants, as he had done all the week; the B—-s had kindly offered me a bed, but I had declined it. I had one door, as usual, open close to the bedroom at which the punkah-wallah pulled the punkah the other two were sleeping by him; the watchman, bearer, orderly, and two doggies, forming quite a guard around the door; the Ayah and her child slept in a room adjoining; and, notwithstanding the alarm, I think I never slept sounder in my life.[3]

Starmans continues:

> The following morning, Maria Germon dispatched [Charlie's] her husband's meals for the day as usual, the fare consisting of bread and butter, quail, mango-fool and some vegetables and sat in the garden to enjoy her coffee, despite the news of the prior day. That morning, she went into the city, visiting with other families and found that everyone was much distressed at the recent news and that the Residency in the city was being transformed into a sanctuary for ladies and the sick. Becoming increasingly nervous, Maria visited her husband and asked if she could remain with him but he sent her home after calming her. That night when she retired, she armed

> herself with a dagger which she called an *Affghan knife* but eventually drifted to sleep.
>
> The next morning, she arose as usual and set off for church after dispatching her husband's provisions and observed seven companies of the 32nd Queens entering the military camp. There was much activity that day with troops coming and going and rumours flew back and forth amongst the families. Maria was invited to spend the night with friends but eventually declined. Her husband's Subadar [a rank in the Indian Army equivalent to a British lieutenant] had sent his salaam and two Sepoys to guard her house and the idea of having Sepoys as guards unnerved her a little but after checking with the Adjutant, she acquiesced to the guards and rested well that night.

The lull continued until Monday 25 May 1857 when Charlie was summoned at 3.00am by Sir Henry Lawrence, the commander, who ordered that all ladies should leave the cantonments and go to the Residency for protection. Maria gathered her belongings, taking her valuables and coffee and provisions, and clambered aboard the carriage of friends. They passed many other carriages filled with ladies and children all heading for the Residence. When they arrived, the Residency was crowded with ladies and children and they went to see if they could lodge with Doctor Frayrer, whose house was in the grounds of the Residency. Maria, along with another lady shared their hostess's room; three beds under one punkah. The heat was intense and they could not sleep well. During the days, they met at breakfast, then amused themselves with work, reading or music, lunched at 2.00pm and dined at 7.30. The Padre gave a reading in the evening, they prayed and then retired for the night. Although they shared a room at the Frayrers', it was much better than at the Residency where each room was filled with six or eight ladies and their children, their servants crowded onto the verandas. On Wednesday they heard that the Commander-in-Chief had died of cholera at Umballah and that Dr Frayrer's brother had been killed by insurgents. Two husbands of the women had also been killed. One left a widow and seven children, another a new bride. Reports continued to come in of other Sepoy regiments who had joined the mutiny and it was reported that Colonel Birch, the commandant of the 41st had been shot by his men, his daughter captured by the fugitives.

Mrs Germon's diary continues:

> We passed the night without an accident, though the roof was hit by round shots. Mrs F—'s little boy Bobby very ill. he looks a perfect skeleton: as for

> Mrs D——'s youngest boy, you can count his bones; they are only just covered with skin. it is a terrible time for poor children; they pine for fresh air.

On Wednesday, 19 August, one of the children died.

> After breakfast Mrs D—-'s poor baby was sewed up by Mrs—— in a clean table cloth, she having first dressed it in a clean night-dress and lace cap, and crossed its little arms on its breast; the little thing was carried to the hospital to await its burial, at night.

Things got increasingly worse when we hear that

> At Jhansi the brutes had burnt the children before their poor mothers' eyes, and then killed the wives, and then the husbands. At Cawnpore they found only two living beings and a heap of dead women and children, being those who escaped the massacre at the boats. They say the place where the murders were committed was a most heart-rending sight; not a soldier left it with a dry eye. We heard also of the B—-s of our regiment having been murdered at Hissar. Ever one was trying to get news of his friends; scarcely one but heard bad news.

The following year in 1858 the 78th joined the Rohilkhand Expeditionary Force and fought at the successful battle of Bareilly and against the rebels who had occupied the treasury and burnt public records.

The 78th were one of five Highland regiments in the infantry force: Highland Brigade, under Lieutenant Colonel Leith Hay CB, 93rd Highlanders

- HM 42nd Highlanders – Lt Col Cameron
- HM 79th Highlanders – Lt Col Taylor CB
- HM 93rd Highlanders – Lt Col Ross
- 4th Punjaub Rifles – Lt McQueen
- Belooch Battalion – Capt. Beville
- HM 78th Foot – Brig. Stisted
- 7 Coys HM 64th Foot – Lt Col Brigham CB
- HM 78th Highlanders – Col Hamilton
- 4 Coys HM 82nd Foot – Col The Hon P. Herbert CB
- 2nd Punjaub Infantry – Lt Col Greene
- 22nd Punjaub Infantry – Capt. Stafford
- Detachment Bengal Sappers and Miners – Lt Col Harness RE

May 1859 saw the regiment, 532 strong, set sail for home. Fairrie tells us that 'of the regiment which had arrived in India 17 years earlier, only 59 were still serving with it'.[4] Arriving at Fort George on 15 September, in Nairn and Inverness they were fêted by the locals as 'The Saviours of India'. A runic cross celebrates the campaign, erected on Edinburgh Castle esplanade.

Four years were spent in Aldershot and Shorncliffe in 1862, then a year in Dublin before a tour in Gibraltar until 1867, followed by a four-year posting to Canada, where they were initially in Montreal and then Halifax, Nova Scotia and New Brunswick.

In 1871 the 78th was back in Ireland and took part in security operations in Ulster until 1873. Based in Belfast, four companies deployed to Londonderry. The sectarian violence was particularly bad in Belfast and Lisburn and then, in early 1873, in Monaghan, Downpatrick and Ballymena.

In May that year they were back at Fort George sharing the depot with the 71st but overcrowding meant that two companies had to be accommodated in Aberdeen. 1874 saw them in Aldershot, brigaded with the 42nd, 79th and 93rd Highlanders in a Highland Brigade which was inspected by the Czar of Russia. Then there was Edinburgh and Ireland in 1878 before returning to India in 1879 travelling by train to Poona, the fifth time they had been there.

The Regiment left for Afghanistan in February 1879 during the Second Anglo-Afghan War; the posting was prompted by a raid on a British column at Maiwand. At the Battle of Maiwand in July 1880 between 2,050 and 2,750 Afghans were killed, and probably about 1,500 wounded. British and Indian forces lost 969 soldiers killed and 177 wounded. After a freezing winter under canvas at Kandahar the 78th returned to Sitapur in India in May 1881.

1881 was an important year for the 78th for it was then that, under the Territorial Scheme, they became the 2nd Battalion Seaforth Highlanders while the existing 72nd was redesignated the 1st Battalion Seaforth Highlanders. The full name was now Seaforth Highlanders (Ross-shire Buffs, The Duke of Albany's).

It was only in 1920 that the definite article, 'The', officially became part of the regimental title. The depot was moved from Stirling to Fort George and the territorial area reverted to Ross-shire and Lewis. 1882 was a good year too when the Mackenzie tartan kilt was restored to the uniform for the first time since 1809.

Chapter 3

Seaforth Highlanders 1st and 2nd Battalions: 1881–1899

1882 also saw much exchanging of troops between what had become the 1st and 2nd Battalions. The 1st (formerly the 72nd) left India for Aden, arriving there in February, albeit somewhat depleted by having left behind a number of men to keep the 2nd Battalion (the 78th) up to something approaching strength while serving in India. However, in August, the 1st was reinforced by two companies of the 2nd Seaforth from Lucknow.

The Battle of Tel El-Kebir 1882

The Egyptian army, led by the Minister of War, Colonel Arabi Pasha, rose up in 1882 against the Khedive, the Turkish Viceroy, impatient with government corruption and foreign interference in their affairs. The 1st Battalion landed at Ismailia to help put down the mutiny of the Egyptian army. The Highland Brigade had begun their night march at 2.00am, fixed bayonets at 5.00 and wiped out the mutineers at Tel El-Kebir (70 miles north of Cairo) within an hour. Official British figures gave a total of fifty-seven British troops killed while approximately two thousand Egyptians died. The British Army had more casualties due to heatstroke than enemy action. They then joined other units on the march to Zig-a-Zag, impressively covering the thirty-three miles by 7.00pm in intense heat. Later that year, in October, they returned to England where they remained until late 1896.

Later that year the 1st Seaforth returned to Britain to their new base at Parkhurst on the Isle of Wight, while those Lucknow reinforcements returned to Lucknow. In 1885 the Dervish Revolt in Sudan and the killing of General Charles Gordon demanded a new expeditionary force to go to Egypt. The 1st Seaforth took the place of the Foot Guards at Windsor Castle; when they returned the 1st moved on to Aldershot. In the new year they sailed from Portsmouth to Edinburgh for two years in the castle with recruiting forays as far afield as the Orkney Islands, Caithness and Sutherland, Skye and Lewis. Not only did this replenish the ranks of the 1st but it also provided 1,000 men for the 2nd in India between 1882 and 1888. This, of course, chimed with the Childers Reforms of the army, as detailed above.

In March 1888 the 1st moved west to Glasgow's Maryhill Barracks and then, in the next year, back to Ireland until 1895 with deployments in Dublin, Fermoy and Tipperary. Despite the recruitment drives in the Highlands the regiment was not helped by the sparse populations in these areas. And so it was that the Seaforth Highlanders were opened to general enlistment, which accounts for the large number of Englishmen and Irishmen in the ranks prior to the First World War. 1895–1897 saw the 1st in Aldershot for two years. In 1897 it changed roles with the 2nd and headed out to Malta for a year where they inherited 500 men who had not completed their overseas service from the 2nd.

In 1893, Mortimer Durand, the British Anglo-Indian diplomat and member of the Indian Civil Service was despatched to Kabul to sign an agreement with Rahman for fixing the limits of spheres of influence, as well as improving diplomatic relations and trade. On 12 November 1893, the Durand Line Agreement was reached, leading to the creation of a new North West Frontier Province.

The International Occupation of Crete 1897

The article by Jonathan Dewhirst honouring Second Lieutenant Percy John Finch, 1st Battalion Seaforth Highlanders on the International Occupation of Crete begins with a question: 'Does this sound familiar? Sectarian fighting and ethnic cleansing. Christians fighting Muslims, with atrocities on both sides. Massacres, and refugees fleeing the countryside for cities. Polarisation of communities along religious grounds. Entry of peacekeeping forces.' And then an answer: 'Just to prove there is nothing new under the sun, that is not Kosovo or Ireland or Cyprus, it is Crete, in 1897. An island that was part of the Ottoman Empire but which, in early 1897, witnessed a declaration of autonomy by its majority Greek Christian population, followed by a Greek invasion of the island in their support. Cue the fighting alluded to above, with allegations of atrocities emanating from both sides.[1]

What was it all about? In 1896, the six Great Powers – Austria-Hungary, France, the German Empire, Kingdom of Italy, Russian Empire and the United Kingdom – persuaded the Ottoman Empire to agree to institute reforms in their administration of Crete, controlled by the Ottomans since 1669, to protect the interests of the island's Christian population, with whom many Greeks sympathised. When the Ottomans did nothing other than torch parts of Chania and massacre Christian inhabitants on 23/24 January 1897 a revolt broke out the following day among the Cretan Christians to force the union of Crete with Greece. One hundred or so revolutionaries gathered at Akrotiri, hell-bent on bringing about the Union of Crete with Greece. With the support of Greek Army troops and Greek Navy warships operating along its coast, the insurgents overran much of the countryside while Ottoman troops generally retained control of Crete's large towns and outposts scattered around the island.

Keen to force the Ottomans to implement the reforms promised in 1896 and to avoid a war erupting between Greece and the Ottoman Empire, which conceivably might lead to a Greek defeat and could spread to become a general war in Europe, the six Great Powers intervened to enforce the Ottoman reforms. They applied pressure on the Ottomans not to reinforce their garrisons on Crete, in effect imposing a blockade on Crete, and, following Ottoman approval, established control of the island. In exchange, they assumed responsibility for the general safety of the Ottoman garrisons on the island. Troops from the armies of five of the powers (Germany declined to send any) arrived to occupy key Cretan cities in late March and April 1897.

In May 1896 the British battleship HMS *Hood* and a French gunboat had arrived in Cretan waters to protect their countries' interests and citizens in the face of unrest on Crete. When major rioting broke out in Candia (now Heraklion) on 6 February 1897, men from the British warship on station, the battleship HMS *Barfleur*, intervened to bring the situation under control and protect British subjects by bringing them aboard *Barfleur*. With the situation rapidly deteriorating on the island, ships of the Austro-Hungarian Navy, French Navy, Italian Royal Navy (*Regia Marina*), Imperial Russian Navy and Royal Navy all arrived in Crete's waters in early February 1897 as a show of naval might intended to demonstrate the Great Powers' commitment to end the fighting and come to an arrangement that would protect Christians on the island without separating it from the Ottoman Empire. This became known as the International Squadron.

But Greece acted to support the Cretan Christian insurgents. The Greek Navy ironclad *Hydra* arrived off Crete in early February 1897, nominally to protect Greek interests and citizens on Crete and, on 12 February, a Greek Navy squadron consisting of the steam sloop-of-war *Sphacteria* and four torpedo boats under the command of Prince George of Greece and Denmark arrived at Canea with orders to support the Cretan insurrection and harass Ottoman shipping. But the admirals of the International Squadron let Prince George know that they would use force if necessary to prevent any aggressive Greek actions in and around Crete, so Prince George's squadron departed Cretan waters on 13 February and steamed back to Greece.

However, the situation continued to escalate on 14 February when a Greek Army expeditionary force commanded by Colonel Timoleon Vassos, consisting of two battalions of Greek infantry, about 1,500 men, and two batteries of artillery landed at Platanias, west of Canea. Vassos proclaimed that his troops had come to occupy Crete on behalf of the King of Greece and unilaterally proclaimed Greece's annexation of Crete. This prompted the island's Ottoman *vali* (governor), George Berovich (also known as Berovich Pasha), to flee to Trieste on 14 February aboard the Russian battleship *Imperator Nikolai I*. Vassos's declaration was a direct challenge to both the Ottoman Empire and the Great Powers and Berovich's departure left Crete with no functioning civil authority. To address both matters, the International Squadron took its first direct action on 15 February 1897 by landing 450 sailors and marines, 100 each from France, Italy, Russia and the United Kingdom and fifty from Austria-Hungary, from the warships anchored at Canea and raising the flags of all six Great Powers over Canea. This was the start of both the international occupation of Crete and the role of the International Squadron's admirals in managing the island's affairs through the Admirals' Council.

Troops of the Austro-Hungarian, British, French, Italian and Imperial Russian Armies, something not dissimilar from a modern United Nations' peacekeeping force, began landing in Crete to take up occupation duties in late March and early April 1897. By early April, about 2,500 troops of the five armies were ashore.[2] The troops ashore came under the overall command of the Admirals' Council, which instructed the British Major General Herbert Chermside, overall commander of the occupation forces ashore, that he should not base any of his troops beyond the range of the International Squadron's guns.

After the International Squadron's bombardments in late March, organised insurgent operations against Ottoman and European forces ended with hostilities thereafter limited to sporadic sniping. However, as late as 21 April 1897, the British battleship HMS *Camperdown* anchored off Canea where Ottoman troops, Muslim civilians and a force of British and Italian soldiers were besieged by an estimated 60,000 insurgents. Its aim was to deter insurgents who had begun a demonstration with two artillery pieces that threatened the town.

Meanwhile, the Greco-Turkish War of 1897, also known as the Thirty Days' War, had erupted on the mainland of Europe with Greek forces crossing the border into Ottoman Macedonia on 24 March 1897 followed by an official declaration of war on 20 April. As the Great Powers had expected, the war ended quickly in a disastrous Greek defeat and a ceasefire went into effect on 20 May 1897.

As we know, on 18 March 1897 the 1st Battalion Seaforth Highlanders was in Malta; the British government announced that it was sending the Battalion to Crete. It comprised eighteen officers, 582 other ranks and five horses, a field hospital staffed by two officers and eighteen other ranks; one officer and five other ranks of the Army Service Corps and seventy-five mules with seventy-five Maltese mule drivers.[3] The kit left much to be desired, so, after deficiencies, particularly in helmets and gaiters, were made good and a number of additional personnel taken onboard, including a farrier, staff officer and military clerk, to assist Colonel Chermside, the British Military Commissioner, the Seaforth set sail, arriving in Crete on 24 March.

One company disembarked at Canea but most of the battalion, the remaining 650 men of 1st Seaforth, plus auxiliary personnel, went on to Candia, landing there on the 26th.[4] In Canea the Seaforth initially shared accommodation with the French 8th Marine Infantry in Nazimen Barracks but eventually moved out to tented accommodation in Halepa. In Candia, the intention was for the battalion to be accommodated in barracks but, due to the unscheduled arrival of Italian troops and 'objections to the various sanitary features in the proposed quarters', they moved to tents and then huts on the town walls.[5]

The British troops stationed in Canea at this time consisted of D and G Companies 1st Seaforth Highlanders commanded by Major S.B. Jameson and 184 men of No. 4 Battery Mountain Artillery, Royal Artillery, the latter recently arrived from Malta and about to be transferred to Candia [Iraklion].[6] The bulk of the British troops, 390 men of 2nd Royal Welsh Fusiliers and the remaining 650 men of 1st Seaforth, plus auxiliary personnel, were stationed in Candia.[7]

Unhappy camping
From: Army Medical Department, Report for 1897:

> At Canea the detachment of British troops was at first quartered with the other international Forces and with the Turks in the flag redoubt. As, however, the place was filthy and overcrowded, our troops were soon removed to a camp in the Municipal Gardens, where they occupied a new building intended as a theatre, which afforded room for about 100 men, the remainder being encamped in an adjoining field .... Our troops remained in this camp until August, when in consequence of the prevalence of fever and the ground having become much fouled, it was, on the recommendation of the Principal Medical Officer, Malta, who visited the island at this time, moved to the residential suburb of Halepa, about two miles from Canea, where an excellent site overlooking the sea was found, and where water was obtained from a spring where contamination seemed impossible.

Unfortunately for the Seaforth, and the other troops in Crete, the existence of goats in both Malta and Crete had serious health implications. Mediterranean

Fever (Brucellosis), transmitted from infected goats, was to prove, along with dysentery and malaria, a major cause of casualties amongst the British.[8]

In Candia meanwhile:

> With the exception of the men occupying the Greek Hospital, all the troops have been accommodated in Indian-pattern European privates' tents, which were pitched on the western ramparts which encloses the town from sea to sea. The space was scanty and some digging was necessary before the tents could be properly pitched .... Clay being plentiful, the men were able to make well-raised puddled floors which were easily kept clean, even in bad weather. When it became known that the huts would not arrive before winter set in, wooden linings were supplied for the walls of the tents, and added greatly to the comfort of the men. A proportion of marquees was supplied for hospital purposes; but they are not well suited for standing camps, and compare very unfavourably in comfort with the European privates' tents, for which they were discarded.[9]

The Soldiers' Pocket-Book tells us that there were three types of issue tent in India (and elsewhere) in the 1880s: the Staff-Sergeant's tent, (S-S tent) the European (or English) Privates' tent (EP tent) and the circular tent (bell tent). Native soldiers had a Lascar 'pal'.

In 1897 the British Army adopted khaki for the uniforms of its troops serving overseas; home-based troops had to wait until 1902. However, records do not reveal whether the first two battalions to arrive on Crete in 1897, the 1st Seaforth Highlanders and 2nd Royal Welsh Fusiliers, were issued with khaki before reaching the island. Whatever, the Scots still had to wear their kilts, both at home and abroad, as contemporary photographs show.

The *Illustrated London News* of 24 April 1897 reported:

> Captain Granville Egerton, of the Seaforth Highlanders, who is in command of one of the detachments of British troops now in Crete, has seen some years of active service. He received his commission in 1879, and proceeded at once to Afghanistan, where he was seriously wounded before the year was out in the operations around Cabul. He subsequently took part in the advance on Candahar and distinguished himself in the battle there fought. In the Egyptian Campaign of 1882, he was Adjutant to the 1st Battalion of the Seaforth Highlanders and took part in the Battle of Tel El-Kebir.

On 19 April 1897, under command of Captain Egerton, seventy-five men of 1st Seaforth Highlanders were sent to join the existing international detachment of seventy-five Austrians, seventy-five French, ninety Italians and two Italian guns, guarding the neck of Akrotiri peninsula, outside Canea. The force was placed there to prevent Christian insurgents from attacking the town from the north-east and remained there until June.

This extract gives us an interesting glimpse into Egerton's opinion of his allies:

> I did not trust the Italians a yard, and had no great confidence in the French, but my Austrian detachment officers and men, were reliable to the last degree. The Italians were very fond of the English and were ready to black our boots, and they have never forgotten how much we assisted towards a united Italy. The Austrians were on very friendly terms always, their officers were nearly all gentlemen, which was not certainly the case with most of the other foreign officers.
>
> The Russians we saw little of, they were mainly kept outside of Canea, on account of their rowdy habits. Their Colonel was an ex-Guardsman exiled from St Petersburg for his numerous crimes. He was often seen drunk.[10]

The Seaforth Highlanders stayed in Crete until November 1897 when they returned to Malta.

The Germans and Austro-Hungarians left Crete in April 1898 due to their interest in maintaining relationships with the Ottoman Empire, leaving the four remaining powers to negotiate a settlement. The Ottomans were evicted in late 1898. The Cretan State, created by the decisions of the International Squadron's admirals as they negotiated the status of Crete on behalf of their governments, existed until 1913. Foreign troops continued to garrison the island until 1909 and Royal Navy ships remained on station there until 1913. In 1913, after the Greek victory in the Second Balkan War, Greece formally annexed Crete in the Treaty of Athens.

Having left Crete, the Seaforth Highlanders, including Egerton, went on, via Malta, to take part in the campaign in the Sudan. There, Egerton was twice Mentioned in Despatches and eventually went on to command 52nd (Lowland) Division at Gallipoli, surviving the war and retiring from the army with the rank of major general in 1919.

Sudan 1898

In 1898 the 1st Battalion was called up to assist in the reconquest of Sudan, a reconquest of territory lost by the Khedives of Egypt in 1884 and 1885 during the Mahdist War (1881–1899).[1] The British had failed to organise an orderly withdrawal of Egyptian forces from Sudan and the defeat at Khartoum left only Suakin and Equatoria under Egyptian control after 1885. The conquest of 1896–99 eliminated the Mahdist state and re-established Anglo-Egyptian rule, which remained until Sudan became independent in 1956.

When that British force was sent to re-conquer Sudan in 1896 it was seen by many as retribution for the death of General Gordon, which had caused 'a wave of patriotic outrage amongst the British'.

Lord Kitchener needed to be sure that he had sufficient strength to defeat the Mahdist forces in their backyard, so he summoned reinforcements: a brigade under Major General William F. Gatacre arrived in Sudan at the end of January 1898. According to Dominic Green, the Warwicks, Lincolns, Seaforth and Cameron Highlanders had to march and ride on camelback the last thirty miles as the railway had not yet reached the front line.[2]

Atbara

Mahdist forces initiated skirmishes and tried to outflank Kitchener by crossing the Atbara, but they were outmanoeuvred and removed from their zareba.[3] The Egyptians steamed upstream and raided Shendi. Eventually, at dawn on 8 April, the Anglo-Egyptians mounted a full frontal assault on the forces of Osman Digna with three infantry brigades, holding one in reserve. Fighting lasted less than an hour and concluded with eighty-one Anglo-Egyptian soldiers killed and 478 wounded to over 3,000 Mahdist troops dead.

The Khalifa's forces then withdrew to Omdurman, abandoning Metemma and the Sixth Cataract so that the Egyptian army could pass unmolested. The Sudan Military Railway was extended southwards and additional reinforcements arrived. By mid-August 1898 Kitchener had at his command 25,800 troops, composed of the British division with two British infantry brigades and the Egyptian Division with four Egyptian brigades under Major General Hunter. Unfortunately, the gunboat *Zafir*, moving upriver, foundered and sank at Metemma on 28 August. Meanwhile, the Khalifa attempted to lay a mine in the river to prevent the Egyptian boats from bombarding Omdurman, but this resulted in the mine-laying ship *Ismailia* being blown up with its own mine.[4]

Omdurman

The Battle of Omdurman was fought between a British-Egyptian expeditionary force, commanded by Horatio Herbert Kitchener, and a Sudanese army of the Mahdist Islamic State, led by Abdullah al-Taashi, the successor to the self-proclaimed Mahdi, Muhammad Ahmad. Kitchener commanded a force of 8,000 British regulars and a mixed force of 17,000 Sudanese and Egyptian troops. Among those present was 23-year-old soldier and reporter Winston Churchill as well as a young Captain Douglas Haig. Churchill rode with the

21st Lancers. He published his account of the battle in 1899 as *The River War: An Account of the Reconquest of the Soudan*. Also present as a war correspondent for *The Times* was Colonel Frank Rhodes, brother of Cecil, who was shot and severely wounded in the right arm.

Abdullah's followers, calling themselves the *anṣār* and known to the British as Dervish warriors, numbered around 50,000, including some 3,000 cavalry.

The final advance on Omdurman began on 28 August.[5] The defeat of the Khalifa's forces at Omdurman was effectively the end of the Mahdist state. Over 11,000 Mahdist fighters died at Omdurman, and another 13,000 were seriously wounded with 5,000 taken prisoner. An eyewitness describes the carnage, with particular reference to the effective use of state-of-the-art Maxim machine guns:

> They could never get near and they refused to hold back. ... It was not a battle but an execution. ... The bodies were not in heaps – bodies hardly ever are; but they spread evenly over acres and acres. Some lay very composedly with their slippers placed under their heads for a last pillow; some knelt, cut short in the middle of a last prayer. Others were torn to pieces ... .[6]

Machine guns apart, the battle was also ballistically significant because it was the first time that the Mark IV hollow-point bullet, made in the arsenal in Dum Dum, a city in West Bengal, was used in a major battle. It was a highly effective expanding bullet.[7]

The charge of the 21st Lancers was to be one of the last cavalry charges in British military history. There were later cavalry charges in the First World War and at least one in the Second World War, although the last wasn't a full regimental attack.

On the British, Egyptian and Sudanese side Kitchener's force lost forty-seven men killed and 382 wounded. The Khalifa retreated into Omdurman but could not rally his followers to defend it. Kitchener entered the city, which formally surrendered without further fighting while the Khalifa escaped.

The battle had opened with a flotilla of twelve British gunboats bombarding Omdurman, damaging part of the city walls and, in an act of iconoclasm, the tomb of the Mahdi, wrecked by naval gunfire on Lord Kitchener's orders:[8] the dome of the *qubba* was destroyed by gunboat fire from Kitchener's Nile fleet.[9] Michelle Gordon tells how the Mahdi's body was dug up and decapitated. This decapitation was highly symbolic, recalling as it did General Gordon's death at the hands of the Mahdist forces in 1885.[10] The headless body of the Mahdi was dumped unceremoniously into the Nile.[11] Lord Kitchener kept the Mahdī's skull and it was rumoured that he intended to use it as a drinking cup or ink well.[12]

According to Winston Churchill, Kitchener 'carried off the Mahdi's head in a kerosene can as a trophy'.[13] Michelle Gordon's 2019 paper, *Viewing Violence,*

> addresses the photographs [of the atrocities] in the wider context of violence throughout the British Empire and in the context of other images of British violence. That such photographs are not commonly viewed and discussed speaks to wider issues regarding popular perceptions of the 'benevolent' British Empire, particularly in comparison to its European counterparts.

Simon Harrison demonstrates that Kitchener was not alone in this ghoulish fetish, where senior British military collected enemy skulls as trophies. Allegedly the Mahdi's skull was later buried at Wadi Halfa.[14] There is still considerable controversy raging over the conduct of Kitchener and his troops during and immediately following the battle. Later, in February 1899, Kitchener unsurprisingly, flatly denied that he had ordered or permitted the Mahdist wounded and those trying to surrender to be massacred by his troops; that Omdurman had been looted; and that civilian fugitives in the city had been deliberately fired on.[15] There is no evidence for the last accusation, but some foundation for the others.[16] M.W. Daly records that in *The River War* Winston Churchill was scathing of Kitchener's conduct, and in private correspondence he said that 'the victory at Omdurman was disgraced by the inhuman slaughter of the wounded and that Kitchener was responsible for this'. The Mahdi's tomb, the largest building in Omdurman, had already been looted when Kitchener gave the order for it to be blown up. Kitchener commanded that the Mahdi's remains be dumped in the Nile. He considered and discussed keeping his skull, either as some kind of trophy or as a medical exhibit at the Royal College of Surgeons. Eventually, however, the head was buried, although those anecdotes about its having been turned into an inkpot or a drinking vessel continue to circulate.

When news of the desecration of the Mahdi's tomb reached Britain it caused considerable shock and revulsion. Some argued that the actions were justified due to the perceived 'savage' nature of the Mahdist forces. However, there was also widespread respect for the Mahdist forces as fighters, particularly among the British military. The success by the *anṣār* in breaking the British military square was famously remembered in Rudyard Kipling's poem 'Fuzzy-Wuzzy', a pejorative term for the Hadendoa Beja tribesmen, many of whom fought in the Mahdist army.[17]

Daly tells us that eventually Kitchener was required to write a letter of apology to Queen Victoria for the actions of his troops after the battle, particularly in relation to the desecration of the Mahdi's tomb and the treatment of his body.[18]

The tomb was reconstructed in 1947 under the direction of the Mahdī's son, Abd-al-Raḥman al-Mahdī. It is next to the Khalifa House Museum. The tomb has been listed as a site of 'outstanding cultural value' by UNESCO.[19]

Fragments of the tomb were taken back to Britain as triumphalist trophies; many of these fragments are now held in cultural institutions in the UK. At least three of the large brass finials from the domes of the tomb survive. One is held at the Royal Engineers' Museum in Kent, another at Blair Castle in Scotland and one at the Khalifa House Museum in Omdurman.[20]

The cultural and media response

By the early twentieth century the media was beginning to feature heavily in conflict, not least through press coverage and photo-journalism. The Battle of Omdurman appeared in several oil paintings which were exhibited in Britain. The charge of the 21st Lancers was especially popular and a number of artists portrayed the scene, including Stanley Berkeley, Robert Alexander Hillingford, Richard Caton Woodville, William Barnes Wollen, Gilbert S. Wright, Edward Mathew Hale, Captain Adrian Jones, Major John C. Mathews, and Allan Stewart.[21]

According to Stephen Bottomore, although the press corps had film cameras, no footage was shot of the actual fighting. What masqueraded as films of the battle, or preparations for it, were in fact spliced footage of training or troop movements far from the front. Such films maintained their popularity for months in Britain and were succeeded by short features such as the fictional *How Tommy Won the Victoria Cross: an Incident of the Soudan War* (1899) in which English soldiers survive a 'dervish' ambush.

The victory, and especially the charge of the 21st Lancers, was soon celebrated by songs on the popular stage, including 'What Will They Say in England? A Story of the Gallant 21st' by Orlando Powell[22] and Léonard Gautier's 'The Heroic Charge of the 21st Lancers at the Battle of Omdurman', published complete with piano score. William McGonagall was also among those inspired to doggerel patriotism in a hastily produced broadside, 'The Battle of Omdurman: a new poem: composed September 1898', soon to be joined by the equally spontaneous verse of Henry Surtees, one of the uniformed participants, in his 'The March to Khartoum and Fall of Omdurman' of 1899. In the following year there appeared a more polished performance in Annie Moore's poetry collection, *Omdurman and other verses*.[23]

In Sudan itself, the Khalifa had poets among his entourage; sadly, much of their work was either destroyed by the British after the battle, or by the poets themselves in fear of reprisal. Nevertheless, a lamentation by Wad Sa'd, who was an eyewitness of the defeat survived as part of the oral tradition.[24]

A fictional account of the battle soon appeared in G.A. Henty's series of adventure stories for boys, entitled *With Kitchener in the Soudan* (1903) and included a description of the battle.[25] The battle also featured in the 1972 film *Young Winston* and included the charge of the 21st Lancers in which Churchill took part.[26] Lance Corporal Jones frequently mentions his own participation in the battle during the comedy series *Dad's Army*.[27]

The 1st Seaforth were still in Cairo in 1903. The Boer War had come and gone but the role of the 1st was limited to supplying the 2nd Battalion with reinforcement drafts and two companies of mounted infantry. To mitigate the strain on the regular army the 3rd (Militia) Battalion Seaforth Highlanders joined the 1st in Cairo and served together for nearly eighteen months.

In 1882 the 2nd Battalion relocated from Sitapur to Lucknow where they were reinforced by 1st Battalion troops who did not make the trip to Aden with the rest of the battalion. The 2nd returned the compliment with two companies when the 1st moved on to Egypt, eventually returning to the 2nd in Lucknow. The 2nd moved from Lucknow to Bareilly until 1889.

The Hazara Expedition 1888–1891

Following the Indian Mutiny, India became a Crown Colony. The ratio of British to Indian troops was increased from 1:10 to 1:3 simply by posting more British regiments to India. Brigade formations were a blend of British and Indian regiments. The artillery was put under the control of the Royal Artillery.

The Indian Army comprised the three armies of the Presidencies of Bombay, Madras and Bengal. The Bengal Army, the largest, supplied many of the units for service on the North West Frontier. The senior regimental officers were British. Soldiers were recruited from across the Indian sub-continent, with regiments recruiting Sikhs, Punjabi Muslims, Pathans and Gurkhas. After the Mutiny the British authorities viewed the populations of the East and South of India as unreliable for military service.

The Punjab Frontier Force were known as 'Piffers', regiments formed specifically for service on the North West Frontier and controlled by the Punjab State Government. Imperial Service Troops of the various Indian states were nominally independent but under the protection and *de facto* control of the Government of India. The most important of those states for operations on the North West Frontier was Kashmir.

A British infantry battalion at this time comprised ten companies, with around 700 men and some thirty officers. A battalion had a Maxim machine-gun detachment of two guns and some twenty men. Indian infantry battalions were much the same, but without the Maxim-gun detachment. Senior officers were British; junior officers were Indian.

British regiments were issued with the single shot, drop-action Martini-Henry breech-loading rifle. This rifle was issued to Indian regiments in 1888 so that a number of the regiments in the Hazara Field Force had the Martini-Henry. The remaining Indian regiments were still using the Snyder rifle, a 'clumsy adaptation to a breech loader of the muzzle-loading Enfield rifle. Both rifles took a bayonet'.

The conquest of the Punjab by the British, following the Sikh Wars from 1845 to 1849, extended the frontiers of British India to the western boundary of the old Sikh State, along the Indus. On the northern side of the border, beyond British authority on the east bank of the Indus, lay the Black Mountain, home to the Hassanzai and Akazai tribes of Pathans.

> A British garrison was maintained at Oghi Fort, some ten miles east of the Upper Indus and some five miles south of the border line. Persistent and troublesome cross border fighting and raiding followed the establishment of the British border. The final incident, which caused the Indian Government to act, took place on 18 June 1888, when a patrol of sixty soldiers from 5th Gurkhas and nineteen police, commanded by Major Battye of the 5th Gurkhas and Captain Urmston of the Punjab Infantry, left Oghi Fort and patrolled up to the border at Chitabat. The patrol was fired on by tribesmen from across the border and began a withdrawal to Oghi Fort. Extracting troops from action with tribesmen on the North West Frontier was always tricky, as it was the tactic of the tribesmen to press a retreating force very closely. During this withdrawal both British officers were killed and their bodies stripped.[1]

In response, the Hazara Field Force was assembled and began its march on 4 October 1888, after an ultimatum to the tribes expired on the 2nd. The force comprised 10,000 troops in thirteen infantry battalions with three batteries of mountain guns and a company of Sappers and Miners. The force was formed into four columns and a headquarters. Three columns and the HQ assembled at Oghi Fort in the Agror valley, with the fourth assembled at Darband on the Indus river, all by 1 October 1888.

Regiments in the Black Mountain Expedition 1888:

- Royal Artillery; 2nd Northumberland Fusiliers; 1st Suffolk Regiment; 2nd Royal Irish Regiment
- 2nd Royal Sussex Regiment; 2nd Seaforth Highlanders; 15th Bengal Lancers, 34th Pioneers

- 40th Bengal Infantry; 2nd Sikhs; 3rd Sikhs; 14th Sikhs; 4th Punjab Infantry; 29th Punjab Infantry
- 1st/5th Gurkhas; No. 4 Hazara Mountain Battery; 3rd Company, Sappers and Miners
- Kashmir Contingent; Khyber Rifles

The Reserve Column, which was not brigaded, comprised 2nd Seaforth Highlanders, 15th Bengal Lancers, 2nd Sikhs and the Kashmir Contingent.

The first phase of the campaign ended with the Hassanzai and Akazai tribes requesting an armistice on 19 October. The second phase targeted the tribes that lived north of the Black Mountain such as the Allaiwals. The campaign ended when the Allaiwal village of Pokal was occupied and destroyed by the British on 2 and 3 November 1888.

This is how the then Commander-in-Chief in India, General Sir Frederick Roberts remembered the Black Mountain Expedition:

> A success from a military point of view, but … the determination of the Punjab Government to limit the sphere of action of the troops, and to hurry out of the country, prevented our reaping any political advantage. We lost a grand opportunity for gaining control over this lawless and troublesome district; no survey was made, no roads opened out, the tribesmen were not made to feel our power, and, consequently, very soon another costly expedition had to be undertaken.[2]

He goes on to tell how:

> A Fifth Column was formed from the Reserve Brigade, commanded by Colonel A. Murray of the Seaforth Highlanders and comprising a wing of 2nd Seaforth Highlanders (the old 78th), the 40th Bengal Infantry, the force from the Khyber Rifles, two guns from the Royal Artillery and two Gatling Guns. Brigadier General Channer accompanied the Fifth Column.
>
> The Fifth Column moved to Dilbori and, on 21st October 1888, to Trand on the border. The Fifth Column crossed the border and camped some three miles on the route north towards Thakot, which lies on the Indus and was the immediate target for this phase of the operations against the Pariari Sayids.

On 28 October 1888, a force left camp for the march to Thakot, with minimum baggage. This force was commanded by Brigadier General Channer and comprised troops from the 2nd Seaforth Highlanders, 3rd Sikhs, 34th Pioneers,

Khyber Rifles, two RA guns and two Gatling guns. The soldiers carried their weapons and ammunition, a blanket and one day's rations. Much of the route was down a steep mountainside. On reaching Thakot, the brigadier marched his force through the village, the pipers of the Seaforth Highlanders playing the pipe tune 'Oh but ye've been a lang time a coming'.

On 3 November 1888, a force comprising companies from the Northumberland Fusiliers, the Seaforth Highlanders, the 5th Gurkhas and the Khyber Rifles and the marksmen from the Suffolk and Sussex Regiments and the 24th Punjab Infantry with two guns, moved forward to destroy Pokal. Apart from the mosque Pokal was razed and the force began to retire, the Seaforth Highlanders and the Khyber Rifles providing the rear-guard.

The failure of the tribes to honour the agreements that ended the 1888 campaign led to a further two-month expedition by a Hazara Field Force in 1891. General Roberts commented that:

> the Black Mountain tribes, [having been] quite unsubdued by the fruitless expedition of 1888, had given trouble almost immediately afterwards. [The second expedition] was completely successful in political results as in its military conduct. The columns were not withdrawn until the tribesmen had become convinced that they were powerless to sustain a hostile attitude towards us, and that it was in their interest, as it was our wish, that they should henceforth be on amicable terms with us.[3]

In 1889 the 2nd left for Rawalpindi and was engaged in the second Black Mountain expedition of 1891. In 1893 they moved on to Ferozepore and then back to Britain. Two years later they were back in India forming part of the Chitral Expedition.

The Chitral Expedition 1895

The Chitral Expedition was sent to relieve the fort at Chitral, which was under siege after a local coup following the death of the former ruler. A British force of about 400 men was besieged in the fort until it was relieved by two expeditions, a small one from Gilgit and a larger one from Peshawar.

The background reveals a complex story replete with internecine murder and intrigue. From 1857 to 1892 the ruler of Chitral was Aman ul-Mulk of the Katoor dynasty. When he died in 1892 one of his sons, Afzal ul-Mulk, seized the throne, consolidating his rule by murdering as many of his half-brothers as he could.[4] The old ruler's brother, Sher Afzal Khan, who had been in exile at Kabul, covertly entered Chitral with a few supporters and murdered Afzal ul-Mulk. Another of the old ruler's sons, Nizam ul-Mulk, who had fled to the British at Gilgit, advanced westward from Gilgit, enlisting troops as he went, including 1,200 men Sher had sent against him. Seeing what was a hopeless situation, Sher fled back to Afghanistan while Nizam assumed the throne with British blessing; a British political resident called Lieutenant B.E.M Gurdon was installed.

Within a year Nizam ul-Mulk was murdered at the behest of his brother, Amir ul-Mulk,[5] while the two were out hunting. Umra Khan, a tribal leader from Bajour to the south marched north with 3,000 Pathans either to assist Amir ul-Mulk or replace him. Surgeon Major George Scott Robertson, the senior British officer at Gilgit, gathered 400 troops and marched west to Chitral and threatened Umra Khan with an invasion from Peshawar if he did not turn back. Amir ul-Mulk began negotiating with Umra Khan, so Robertson replaced him with his twelve-year-old brother, Shuja ul-Mulk. At this point Sher Afzul Khan re-entered the contest, presumably on the basis that Sher would take the throne and Umra Khan would get part of the Chitral territory. Robertson moved into the fortress for protection which increased local hostility. Since Umra Khan and Sher Afzul continued their march, secret messengers were despatched requesting help.

The fort held 543 people of whom 343 were combatants, including five British officers. The units were the 14th Sikhs and a larger detachment of Kashmiri Infantry. Artillery support was two RML 7-pounder mountain guns without sights and eighty rounds of ammunition. There were only 300 cartridges per man and enough food for a month. On the night of 18 April someone shouted over the wall that the besiegers had fled. The next morning a heavily-armed party found this to be true. Kelly's relief force entered Chitral on 20 April and found the besieged 'walking skeletons'. The siege had lasted six weeks and cost the defenders forty-one lives.

There was, though a significant problem with the stocks of grain in the fort in that the only grinding facility available to the garrison was a grinder manufactured by a Sikh soldier. This used soft stone with the result that fragments of grit got mixed with the flour, causing stomach problems for the soldiers. There was some rum and tea. The officers had some tobacco. There seemed to be enough *ghi* with which to cook the soldiers' food. The British officers ate ponies.[6]

Beynon in his *With Kelly to Chitral* gives this description of the Kashmir Rifles after the siege:

> The next day the Kashmir troops of the garrison came out and camped with us, and revelled in the fresh air after the poisonous atmosphere of the fort. Poor chaps! they were walking skeletons, bloodless, and as quiet as

the ghosts they resembled, most of them reduced to jerseys and garments of any description, but still plucky and of good heart. They cheered up wonderfully in a few days with good fresh air and sleep, and marched from Chitral quite briskly when they left.

The key elements of the Siege and Relief of Chitral were:

- The fighting on 3 March 1895, immediately before the siege, in which Captains Campbell and Baird were wounded.
- The Siege of Chitral Fort itself, involving Robertson and his officers.
- The loss of Captain Ross's party in the Goragh Defile, in its attempt to march from Mastuj to Chitral.
- The capture of Lieutenants Edwardes and Fowler at Reshun, on the route between Mastuj and Chitral and the loss of their party.
- Colonel Kelly's march from Gilgit in the east to the relief of the Fort.
- General Low's march from the south to relieve the Fort.

Meanwhile, the British had assembled 15,000 men at Peshawar under Major General Sir Robert Low, with Brigadier General Bindon Blood serving as his chief of staff. The Chitral Relief Force comprised some 15,000 British and Indian troops, 9,000 or so civilian followers and 30,000 transport animals, mules and camels. They set off about a week after Kelly left Gilgit.

The Division comprised:

First Infantry Brigade: Brigadier General Kinloch: 1st Bedfordshire Regiment, 1st King's Royal Rifle Corps, 15th Sikhs, 37th Dogras and two field hospitals.

Second Infantry Brigade: Brigadier General Waterfield: 2nd King's Own Scottish Borderers, 1st Gordon Highlanders, 4th Sikhs, the Guides Infantry and two field hospitals.

Third Infantry Brigade: Brigadier General Gatacre: 1st Royal East Kent Regiment (The Buffs), 2nd Seaforth Highlanders, 25th Punjab Infantry, 2nd/4th Gurkha Rifles and two field hospitals.

Divisional Troops: 11th Bengal Lancers, Guides Cavalry, 13th Bengal Infantry, 23rd Punjab Pioneers, 15 Battery, Royal Artillery, No. 3 Mountain Battery, Royal Artillery, No. 8 Mountain Battery, Royal Artillery, No. 2

(Derajat) Mountain Battery, three companies, Bengal Sappers and Miners, an engineer park, three field hospitals and a veterinary field hospital.

34th Punjab Pioneers joined the division at the end of March 1895.

Accompanying Low was Francis Younghusband who was officially on leave and serving as a special correspondent for *The Times.*[7] On 3 April they stormed the Malakand Pass which was defended by 12,000 local warriors.[8] There were significant engagements two and ten days later. On 17 April Umra Khan's men prepared to defend his palace at Munda but, finding themselves greatly outnumbered, they slipped away.

Inside the fortress the British found a letter from a Scottish firm offering Maxim guns at 3,700 rupees and revolvers at thirty-four rupees each. The firm was ordered to leave India. Low was still crossing the Lowari Pass on the day Kelly entered Chitral. Although Kelly reached Chitral first, it was the massive size of Low's force that forced the enemy to withdraw. The first man from Low's force to reach Chitral was Younghusband who, without permission, rode out ahead of the troops. That night Younghusband, Robertson, and Kelly shared the garrison's last bottle of brandy.

Umra Khan fled with eleven mule-loads of treasure and reached safety in Afghanistan. Sher Afzul was sent into exile in India. Robertson was made a Knight Commander of the Order of the Star of India. Eleven Distinguished Service Orders (DSOs) were awarded, along with Whitchurch's VC, and all ranks who took part in the siege were given six months' extra pay and three months' leave.

There was a small monkey living at the Chitral Fort. During the siege, the monkey wandered around the fort, along the parapets and up the outside of the walls. Neither side shot at it. The monkey caused havoc inside the fort by ransacking the soldiers' and officers' possessions. It was repeatedly confined inside a box to restrict its disruptive antics and just as repeatedly released by its sympathisers. Finally, the monkey was committed to military custody in the care of the ammunition guard.

There were also several dogs that wandered around the fort and its surroundings. The soldiers tied cans to their tails and drove them towards the besiegers' sangars and into the bazaar in the middle of the night to the alarm and astonishment of the Chitralis.

The Chitral Expedition is remembered in British history as a celebrated chapter in gallantry and valour, which has drawn extensive praise.

> The valour and endurance displayed by all the ranks in the defence of the fort at Chitral have added greatly to the prestige of the British arms, and will elicit the admiration of all those who read this account of the gallant defence made by a small party of Her Majesty's forces, and combined with the troops of His Highness the Maharaja of Kashmir, against heavy odds when shut up in a fort in the heart of an enemy's country, many miles from succour and support.

Commander-in-Chief, India, Sir George White:

> The military skill displayed in the conducting of the defence, the cheerful endurance of all the hardship of the siege, the gallant demeanour of the troops and the conspicuous example of heroism and intrepidity recorded, will ever be remembered as forming a glorious episode in the history of the Indian Empire and its army.

Viceroy of India, Lord Curzon:

The siege and relief of Chitral caused a sensation in late Victorian Britain. Alice F. Jackson wrote a book in 1897 entitled *Heroes of the Chitral Siege*, published by The Society for the Propagation of Christian Knowledge (SPCK).

Chapter 4

The 2nd Seaforth Highlanders in the Second Boer War 1899–1902 and After

In the two years leading up to the Second Boer War (1897–1899) the 2nd Battalion was at Dover and, then, Fort George.

The Second Boer War was an unforgiving and controversial conflict fought between the British Empire and the two Boer Republics (the South African Republic and the Orange Free State) over the Empire's influence in Southern Africa from 1899 to 1902.

Unsurprisingly, money was an element of the *casus belli*. Following the discovery of gold deposits in the Boer republics, there was a large influx of 'foreigners', mostly British from the Cape Colony. They were denied the vote, and were regarded as 'unwelcome visitors', in a word, invaders. So they protested to the British authorities in the Cape.

British Battles gives us some background:[1]

> In the months before hostilities the Boer commandant general, General Joubert, bought 30,000 Mauser magazine rifles and a number of modern field guns and automatic weapons from the German armaments manufacturer Krupp and the French firm Creuset. The commandoes, without formal discipline, welded into a fighting force through a strong sense of community and dislike for the British. Field Cornets led burghers by personal influence not through any military code. The Boers did not adopt military formation in battle, instinctively fighting from whatever cover there might be. The preponderance were countrymen, running their farms from the back of a pony with a rifle in one hand. These rural Boers brought a life time of marksmanship to the war, an important edge, further exploited by Joubert's consignment of magazine rifles. Viljoen is said to have coined the aphorism 'Through God and the Mauser'. With strong fieldcraft skills and high mobility the Boers were natural mounted infantry. The urban burghers and foreign volunteers readily adopted the fighting methods of the rest of the army.

The 2nd Battalion sailed on the SS *Mongolian* about 21 October 1899 and arrived at the Cape around 16 November. Along with 2nd Black Watch, 1st Highland

Light Infantry and 1st Argyll and Sutherland Highlanders, they formed the 3rd, or Highland, Brigade, at first under Major General Wauchope and, after his death, under Brigadier General Hector Macdonald.

The Battle of Magersfontein 1899

It was at Magersfontein that the Seaforth saw their first fighting in the campaign on 11 December 1899. The British troops failed to deploy from a compact formation during their advance and the defenders inflicted heavy casualties. The Highland Brigade suffered the worst casualties while, on the Boer side, the Scandinavian Corps was destroyed.

On its formation in 1899, the Highland Brigade consisted of the 2nd Battalion Black Watch, 1st Battalion Highland Light Infantry, 2nd Battalion Seaforth Highlanders and 1st Battalion Argyll and Sutherland Highlanders.

After the war 2nd Seaforth was posted to Dublin (1903–1904), Aldershot and Edinburgh (1904–1909), followed by Fort George from 1909 to 1912 and Shorncliffe until the outbreak of war in 1914.

The Bazar Valley Expedition 1908

From Egypt the battalion moved back to India in 1903 and was initially stationed at Nasirabad, then Nowshera in 1905 and Gora Dhaka in the Muree Hills in 1907. The first real action did not come until 1908 in the Bazar Valley campaign, a punitive expedition against the Zakka Khel clan of the Afridi, a Pashtun tribe inhabiting the mountains on the Peshawar border of the North West Frontier province about 3,000 feet above sea level.[2]

It was undertaken by the Bazar Valley Field Force, under command of General Sir James Willcocks.[3] The campaign began on 12 February 1908 and was concluded by a *jirga* and peace in March.[4] The main British elements were 1st Seaforth Highlanders and 37th Lancers. Regiments of the British Indian Army included sections of the 45th and 53rd Sikhs, the Madras Sappers and 5th Gurkha Rifles. Archibald Percival, later 1st Earl Wavell, participated as a junior officer.

The Mohmand Expedition 1908

Another punitive expedition, this time against Mohmand rebels whose fighting strength was estimated in 1907 at 21,500 armed with about 1,850 breech-loading rifles. Of the above, about 11,000 men and 750 rifles belonged to the Afghan tribes. Mohmand is in the south-western corner of Peshawar district.

1st Seaforth Highlanders formed part of 2nd Brigade along with Guides Infantry, 2nd Punjabis, 55th Rifles F.F., Sections C and D of No. 1 British Field Hospital and No. 102 Native Field Hospital.

General Wilcocks ordered a dawn attack in two columns on 24 April. The force withdrew around 11.00am, during which Lieutenant Gray and one private, both of the Seaforth Highlanders, were severely wounded. On 2 May a number of troops and artillery were moved to Jamrud. They were:

- The Reserve Brigade, with four guns, 80 Battery RFA, 28 Mountain Battery, and 1 Squadron of 19th Lancers, under Brigadier General Ramsay CB, from Peshawar to Jamrud.
- Two guns, 18 Battery RFA, from Shabkadar, and 23 Mountain Battery, Seaforth Highlanders and Guides Infantry from Jangli Burj, under Major General Barrett CB, to Peshawar, en route for the Khaibar.
- The 54th Sikhs by rail from Nowshera to Peshawar.

Further movements involving the Seaforth Highlanders were ordered on 10 May:

Major General Barrett, with 23 Mountain Battery and Seaforth Highlanders, marched from Peshawar to Naguman, halfway between Peshawar and Shabkadar, where they were joined at 11.00pm by 54th Sikhs from Jamrud, who took the place of the Guides Infantry, quarantined for cholera at Daudzai.

Brigadier General Ramsay's Brigade to Naguman, where they encamped alongside 2nd Brigade; 21st Punjabis rejoined this brigade at 7.00am.

The Highland Division 1908

The 51st (Highland) Division was raised in 1908, when the Territorial Force (TF) was established.[5] It was initially known as the Highland Division and, from 1915, 51st (Highland) Division.

The division did not get off to an auspicious start, earning the uncomplimentary nickname of 'Harper's Duds' after its commander, Major General George Harper.[6]

The Territorial Force was a part-time volunteer element of the British Army, created in 1908 to reinforce British land forces; it combined the nineteenth-century Volunteer Force and Yeomanry, was commanded by the War Office and administered by local county territorial associations. The Territorial Force was designed to reinforce the regular army in expeditionary operations abroad but, because of political opposition, it was assigned to home defence.

The doubts surrounding the Division's aptitude arose from the merciless way in which the manpower of the division was plundered in late 1914 and early 1915 to shore up the Regular Army troops of the original British Expeditionary

Force (BEF) on the Western Front. In August 1914 the division's infantry element had comprised twelve battalions in three brigades: the Seaforth and Cameron Brigade, the Gordon Highlanders Brigade and the Argyll and Sutherland Highlanders Brigade. A crisis on the Western Front in late 1914 in terms of troop numbers saw increasing numbers of individual TF battalions being seconded to Regular Army formations on the Western Front.

Chapter 5

The Seaforth Highlanders in the First World War

1st Seaforth Highlanders

War against Germany and its allies was declared by the UK on 4 August 1914. The 1st Battalion was then stationed at Agra as part of the Dehra Dun Brigade of 7th (Meerut) Division. When it left for France it became 19 Indian Brigade of 7th (Meerut) Division as part of the Indian Expeditionary Force A, sent to reinforce the British in France. It was part of the Indian Infantry Corps, while the Meerut Cavalry Brigade was detached to join 2nd Indian Cavalry Division in the Indian Cavalry Corps. The voyage from India was delayed by the lethal activities of the German cruisers *Emden* and *Königsberg* operating in the Indian Ocean, and by the slow speed of the transport vessels.[1]

The division landed at Marseilles on 12–14 October 1914 but there were further delays while the troops were re-armed with the latest pattern rifles and while the supply train could be improvised, using tradesmen's vans procured locally. The division finally got to see action at the battles of la Bassée, Aubers Ridge, First Messines and Armentières in October and November 1914, followed by the battles of Givenchy and Loos in 1915.

The Dehra Dun Brigade under Brigadier General C.E. Johnson comprised:

- 1st Bn Seaforth Highlanders
- 6th Bn Jat Light Infantry
- 2nd/2nd Bn King Edward's Own Gurkha Rifles (The Sirmoor Regiment)
- 1st/9th Bn Gurkha Rifles

The winter of 1914–1915 saw the 1st Battalion entrenched in the system opposite the German trenches in the area of Richebourg-St Vaast and Neuve Chapelle. They had to endure poorly-made trenches and faced an enemy whose supply of shells was markedly better than theirs. Front-line duty lasted, on two occasions, thirty-three and thirty consecutive days. The German attack at Givenchy inflicted severe losses on the battalion; the 4th (Territorial) Battalion joined at this point.

1915

Active in the Second Battle of Ypres, 9 March saw the Indian Corps take two lines of German trenches at Neuve Chapelle where the attack was preceded by a 480-gun bombardment.

The attempt to take Aubers Ridge on 9 May ended in disaster with the 1st and 4th Battalions taking between 450 and 500 casualties. On 25 September the Indian Corps was tasked with creating a diversion at the Battle of Loos, suffering over 100 casualties.

In November 1915 1st Seaforth transferred to Mesopotamia, arriving at Basra on Christmas Day despite the close attention of German submarines. From there the Division journeyed up the River Tigris to El Gharbi, disembarked and marched further upstream to relieve the beleaguered garrison at Kut-el-Amara. Still part of 7th Meerut Division, the battalion participated in a number of battles ending with the capture of Baghdad in March 1917. Sym tells how they attacked the Turks at Sheik Saad on 16 January 1916, losing twenty officers and 60 per cent of other ranks killed or injured.[2] Engagements at Wadi on 13 January and Umm el Hannah on 21/22 January followed. Casualties were horrendous as the troops had to cross open land to reach the enemy trenches. So reduced was the battalion that it had to await reinforcements before moving on. It could barely muster 100 rifles.

In February 1916 1st Seaforth linked with 2nd Black Watch until July 1916 due to heavy casualties sustained earlier by both units at Shaikh Sa'ad; together they formed the Highland Battalion. On 6 April the battalion passed through the Turkish positions at Umm el Hannah while the next day saw an aborted attempt on the Ottoman stronghold at Sanniyat. Successive attempts saw the Highland Battalion succeed in taking the Turkish positions but the trenches were too waterlogged to hold. The battalion remained in the front line despite losing forty-one officers and 880 men. Corporal Ware earned the VC during the operations.

In February 1917 the Seaforth and Black Watch battalions reverted to their original regiments while 19 Brigade, with the Seaforth at its centre, took three lines of Turkish trenches at Sanniyat. Another VC was awarded, this time to Sergeant Steele.

Baghdad, reached after a fourteen-day march, was the next objective; the city was entered on 11 March. With a brief to secure the remainder of the railway system in the region, actions were fought at Moushahdieh, Beled and Istabulat on 21 April. The battalion summered near Samarra and in November clashed with the Turks at Tekrit, after which it moved south to Basra whence it sailed to Egypt on 1 January 1918.

Two months of R&R (rest and refitting) were spent in Ismailia.[3] On 1 April the battalion relieved elements of 52nd (Lowland) Division, which was bound for the Western Front. The EEF undertook few operations during the hot weather of summer 1918, but the Meerut Division captured 'North Sister' and 'South Sister' Hills on 8 June and raided 'Piffer Ridge' on 27 June.

It subsequently took part in Allenby's advance through Palestine, including the Battle of Megiddo as part of Lieutenant General Bulfin's XXI British Corps operating on the right flank. On 21 September the battalion was involved in taking Beit Lid, having marched, with precious little water, thirty-four miles in forty-eight hours through arid territory. Prisoners were taken but it all came at a heavy cost in terms of casualties. Beit Lid was the battalion's last action in the war.

That autumn they moved north to Beirut and in October sailed to Tripoli in modern Lebanon, and a month later went back to Beirut. The Armistice was signed but the Seaforth remained in Beirut until March 1919 when they moved to Alexandria.

The battalion ended the war in Palestine and Khan Abdi north-east of Tripoli in the Levant.

In June 1919 they finally returned to Fort George where, with the 2nd Battalion, a re-organisation took place.

2nd Seaforth Highlanders

The 2nd Battalion was stationed at Shorncliffe Camp near Cheriton in Kent on 8 August 1914 as part of 10 Brigade of 4th Division. On mobilisation it moved to Strensall, near York, an important mustering point for troops prior to mobilisation. The reason was a last-minute decision to defend against an anticipated German landing on the north-east coast of Britain. As nothing transpired, apart from the German fleet's lethal bombardment of Hartlepool, West Hartlepool, Whitby and Scarborough, the battalion moved to Harrow for final preparations for France on 18 and 19 August and, entraining at Harrow on the 21st, crossed to France on the 22nd. The battalion landed at Boulogne as part of the Expeditionary Force, providing infantry support (the cavalry, artillery, engineers and field ambulances were still en route at this time) on the left flank of the French Army.

Their various actions on the Western Front included:

1914

The Battle of le Cateau, which occurred on 26 August, followed by the battles of the Marne and Aisne and the First Battle of Messines. The battalion sustained heavy casualties at the Aisne but, in October, assisted in the capture of the German-occupied village of Meteren.

Le Cateau was part of the Retreat from Mons. The Expeditionary Force and the French Fifth Army had retreated after being defeated at the Battle of Charleroi (21–23 August) with the British II Corps fighting a delaying action at le Cateau to hinder the German pursuit so that most of the British force could continue its retreat to Saint Quentin.

What happened next is as good an example as there is of the ineptitude which sometimes attends military decision making during war and the self-serving attitude of many generals. Le Cateau and Mons are twenty-five miles apart, but the British II Corps under General Sir Horace Smith-Dorrien was worn out. Max Hastings[4] tells how II Corps had found itself separated from the rest of the force because Sir Douglas Haig, commander of I Corps, who had fought his own independent rearguard action at Landrecies on 25 August, decided to retreat. Following that engagement, Hastings adds, Haig had rallied his troops, revolver in hand, but panicked, writing to the French High Command about the imminent debacle. He had greatly overestimated German numbers and was '[mentally] completely destroyed', as described by James Edmonds, Chief of Staff of 4th Division. Instead of reinforcing Sir Horace at le Cateau, he chose to retreat farther inland, marching for five days.

According to Wilkinson Bird, Colonel of the Royal Irish, oblivious to I Corps' retreat, Smith-Dorrien planned to continue the march but, early on 26 August, Smith-Dorrien had second thoughts after observing the exhaustion of his troops and the probable mayhem that could occur should the marching continue. Hastings[5] adds that Allenby, commander of II Corps' cavalry, joined the high-level squabble when he claimed that both his men and horses were 'almost finished' and that battle at le Cateau was inevitable since the enemy were so close. Sir Horace agreed. At 07.00 Henry Wilson at Expeditionary Force HQ ordered him to continue the retreat; he refused the order, confirming that the men were already fighting.

Major E. Campion described the 2nd Battalion's retreat from Mons:

> We left Beaumont at 2 am on 25th August and knew we were to cover a retirement of some sort, probably we thought of some trenches we had seen the Camerons digging near le Cateau. At 6.am, just short of a place called St Python , we halted and had our breakfast (bully beef, bread and jam), and here we heard the first sound of War; at first Artillery fire, but shortly afterwards the rattle of musketry away on our left … it was a beautiful morning; the landscape large, open and rolling … and away out

> there, out of sight, came the sounds of nations in anger, the deep mutter of guns, and the sharp rattle of rifles.

The Germans exulted in their victory. The historian of Infantry Regiment 93 wrote, in what has been called 'a neat piece of delusional writing':

> The Battle of Beaumont-Inchy [le Cateau] will always be one of the most glorious days in the history of the regiment, which demonstrated that in a frontal attack against an enemy that was heretofore considered unbeatable, the crack troops of the British Army, the 93rd was not merely their equal, it was superior. 75th Field Artillery Regiment said that the battle 'strengthened the self-confidence of the German troops' … all the more so because the British Army was made up almost exclusively of long-service active army troops, who were superbly trained and equipped.[6]

The battalion took part in the Christmas Truce of 1914, that unofficial ceasefire in the trenches of the front line where some British and German soldiers exchanged gifts and played football in no man's land.

1915

In April and May 1915 they were involved heavily in defending the Ypres salient while the counter-attack at St Julien proved to be the battalion's most costly attack thus far in the war with 348 officers and men lost.

May and Ypres brought poison gas from the Germans, for which protection was rudimentary. Sym describes it as 'no better protection against gas was available than the tying of a handkerchief over the nose and mouth.[7] As a result, twenty-four men were killed while a further 324 suffered from the effects of the gas to some degree or other. Fairrie[8] and Sym[9] tell us that those two dreadful months 'cost the battalion over 1,000 casualties'. These were replaced in July and the Battalion was transferred 'to the comparative quiet of the Third Army front between Albert and Arras'[10] where it remained for nearly a year.

This was the first deployment of gas by the enemy in the war. The National World War I Museum and Memorial in Kansas City MO describes this horrific new chapter in the history of chemical warfare as follows:

> On April 22, 1915 at 5 p.m. a wave of asphyxiating gas released from cylinders embedded in the ground by German specialist troops smothered the Allied line on the northern end of the Ypres salient, causing panic and a struggle to survive a new form of weapon.

The attack forced two colonial French divisions north of Ypres from their positions, creating a 5-mile gap in the Allied line defending the city. This was the first effective use of poison gas on the Western Front and the debut of Germany's newest weapon in its chemical arsenal, chlorine gas, which irritated the lung tissue causing a choking effect that could cause death.

A British officer describes the horrendous effect of the gas on the French colonial soldiers:

> A panic-stricken rabble of Turcos and Zouaves with grey faces and protruding eyeballs, clutching their throats and choking as they ran, many of them dropping in their tracks and lying on the sodden earth with limbs convulsed and features distorted in death.
>
> There was no technology to protect the soldiers from this new weapon; an operational gas mask was not available, so the Allied soldiers improvised with linen masks soaked in water and 'respirators' made from lint and tape.
>
> Stunned by their overwhelming outcome of the attack, the Germans tentatively advanced, losing an opportunity to exploit their success.[11]

A fascinating archival collection (viewable through the National World War I Museum's online collections database) recently acquired by the Museum examines this new warfare from the experience of a German officer and gas-school instructor. Kurt Eduard 'Fritz' Sabersky was the commanding officer of Sanitary Company 3 of the Prussian Guard Reserve Corps from 1915–16 and then an instructor at the Royal Prussian Army Gas School in Berlin from March 1917 to the end of the war.

The collection includes:

- Sabersky's identity card for his instructor position
- Draft of an instructional sheet 'Gas Defense in the Trenches' listing instructions to prepare for an attack including 'The sentry must also look out for suspicious odors' and 'protect the telephone device'.
- Week-long class schedules with subjects including:
    - artillery gas shooting
    - mortar gas shooting
    - gas defence weapons
    - first aid for gas illnesses
    - exercises for handling of gas masks and oxygen-protection devices
    - weather forecasting on the front (the air pressure and wind direction were very important measurements to determine the effectiveness of a gas attack)

- o animal protection
- o conduct during an enemy gas attack
- o gas drill in the field

In one weekly schedule there is a class on 'Warfare agents' that discusses gas mixture formulations such as percentage of chlorine to percentage of phosgene and 'Tactic for gas emission', with measurements for the optimum length of gas cloud and amount of gas in tons.

By the end of the war the Germans had produced the most poison gas with 68,000 tons, the French second with approximately 36,000 tons and the British approximately 25,000 tons. About three per cent of gas casualties were fatal, but hundreds of thousands suffered temporary or permanent injuries.[12]

Who, once having read it, can forget this excerpt from Wilfred Owen, *Dulce et decorum est*, published posthumously in 1920:

> Drunk with fatigue; deaf even to the hoots of gas-shells dropping softly behind. Gas! GAS! Quick, boys! – An ecstasy of fumbling Fitting the clumsy helmets just in time, But someone still was yelling out and stumbling And flound'ring like a man in fire or lime. – Dim through the misty panes and thick green light, As under a green sea, I saw him drowning. In all my dreams before my helpless sight, He plunges at me, guttering, choking, drowning.

1916

The Somme, the Battle of Albert, the Battle of le Transloy.

At the Somme, the 2nd was detailed to take the village of Beaumont Hamel. All in all, at the end of the first day, the British had suffered 57,470 casualties, 19,240 of which were killed. The Seaforth alone lost over 500 casualties. After four months of battling the 2nd Battalion helped to gain three to four miles of enemy-held territory.

Martin Middlebrook, in his *The First Day of the Somme*, recounts an eyewitness account from Private W.E. Aust, Hull Commercials, the 10th (Service) Battalion of the East Yorkshire Regiment, who witnessed a highly disciplined, but ultimately fatal, 2nd Seaforth withdrawal:[13]

> Another eyewitness, this time in the British front line, watched a less successful withdrawal. 'We saw the survivors of a kilted battalion returning down an enemy communication trench. Then they spread out in what is called Extended Order as though they were on a barrack square. The officer

> or NCO in charge rose and held up his arm. On his signal they all set off at a trot in perfect line towards our trenches. Within seconds a German machine gun was traversing them until the last man fell. I remember standing on the fire-step and screaming 'Bastards! Bastards! Bastards!' That was a word I never used.

Middlebrook[14] tells of another incident later that morning concerning the Quadrilateral Redoubt (*Heidenkopf*) which projected into no man's land, and an attack on it involving Sergeant Major Percy Chappell and a sergeant: having dodged intense German fire and leaping from shell hole to shell hole, Chappell reached the British soldiers in the Quadrilateral after springing over a German-held trench. Chappell

> found himself near a lieutenant colonel of the Seaforth who was organising the defence of the redoubt. The Germans in the trench he had just leapt were able to fire right into the British positions and the Seaforth colonel decided that they would have to be driven out.

Orders were given but

> Even while this message was being circulated, a Seaforth corporal collected an armful of grenades and walked steadily towards the Germans shouting and swearing in broad Scots, throwing grenades as he went. He caused confusion and loss amongst the Germans, but as he reached their trench he fell dead, hit by several bullets. Inspired by this brave action, the whole British line rose and charged the enemy, shooting and bayoneting, until the trench was clear of Germans and the redoubt secure again.

Sadly, it seems that the corporal was never decorated for his bravery.

1917

This was the year of the Battle of Arras, the First and Third Battles of the Scarpe, the Battle of Polygon Wood, the Battle of Broodseinde, the Battle of Poelcapelle and the First Battle of Passchendaele. At Arras, during the attack on the factory at Fampoux, the 2nd Seaforth lost 93 per cent of the battalion strength with 526 casualties.

Stuart and Buchan relate how 51st (Highland) Division made a concerted attack on the western outskirts of Roeux Wood and the chemical works.[15] To their left, 37th Division assailed the buildings west of Roeux Station and gained the line of their objectives on the western slopes of Greenland Hill, north of the railway. They add that on the left of the main British attack, the 63rd (Royal Naval) Division made rapid progress against Gavrelle and took the village. To the south of the Scarpe and east of Monchy-le-Preux, 29th Division gained the western slopes of the rising ground (Infantry Hill). The River Cojeul marked a divisional boundary within VI Corps. Guémappe to the north was the objective of 15th (Scottish) Division, attacking east from Wancourt towards Vis-en-Artois. Stewart adds that the objective was commanded by the higher ground on the south bank and it was not until 50th (Northumbrian) Division captured the rise on the south side of the Cojeul that the village was taken.

The final battle of 1917 in which the Seaforth engaged came in October at the Third Battle of Ypres, where the objective was to drive the Germans off the Passchendaele Ridge above Ypres. The cost to the Regiment was high: 457 casualties in the month.

The stories behind the two 2nd Seaforth Victoria Crosses earned there help convey the ferocity of the fighting.

Walter Ritchie VC

Ritchie's story is fascinating: 'Amid the terror and confusion of the first day of the Somme, a wounded drummer made it to the German parapet and, using a German bugle, he rallied his fellow Highlanders to charge.' Ritchie's VC was in fact 'a change of fortune which only the confusion of war could have created, because he had potentially faced a court martial'. The website continues:

> On 1 July, 1916, the Seaforth were advancing against German positions at Beaumont Hamel, but by midday shortages of ammunitions had forced a disorganised retreat. Ritchie had been wounded in the knee, but as an interviewer later put it: 'He raced through the Germans' deadly fusillade and, mounting the enemy parapet, sounded the charge.'

The citation for the Victoria Cross reads:

> For most conspicuous bravery and resource, when on his own initiative he stood on the parapet of an enemy trench and under heavy machine-gun fire and bomb attacks, repeatedly sounded the 'charge', thereby rallying many men of various units who, having lost their leaders, were wavering and beginning to retire.

Press reports at the time read: 'Like a bombshell, Mrs Helen Ritchie made the chance remark that Walter had been court-martialled for dropping and losing his drum in action and picking up a rifle.' Mrs Ritchie assured the press that 'the reprimand was a formality. He had in fact disregarded regulations about taking instruments into the trenches and he himself later commented that had things gone the other way, he would have been court-martialled, not decorated.' The bugle is now in the Highlanders' Museum at Fort George.

From http://www.victoriacross.org.uk/bbritchw.htm we learn that 'The exceptional and important "First Day of the Battle of the Somme" Victoria Cross awarded to Drum Major Walter Ritchie, 2nd Bn Seaforth Highlanders, has been sold at a Spink auction on 21 July 2022 in London. The estimated sale price was between £240,000 and £280,000. The sale hammer price realised £360,000.

Lieutenant Donald Mackintosh VC

One year later, in April 1917, Lieutenant Donald Mackintosh was also awarded the VC and, like Walter Ritchie, leaves us with another amazing story of courage and resilience.

https://www.universitystory.gla.ac.uk/ww1-biography/?id=4507 tells us how Lieutenant Donald Mackintosh enlisted in 1914 in the Royal Army Medical Corps (RAMC), and was posted to 3rd Scottish General Hospital, where he became an acting sergeant. He obtained his commission six months later on 12 February 1915 and joined the Seaforth Highlanders. After a year he was promoted to full lieutenant.[16]

On 21 March 1916 he was severely wounded and was transferred to le Touquet Hospital before returning to Britain. By July he had recovered and so returned to the 3rd Battalion.

At the first Battle of the Scarpe, part of the Arras Offensive of April 1917, Lieutenant Mackintosh served with the 2nd Bn Seaforth Highlanders.

> On 11 April 1917 north of Fampoux, France, during the initial advance, Lieutenant Mackintosh was shot through the right leg, but although crippled, continued to lead his men, and captured the trench. He then collected men of another company who had lost their leader and drove back a counter-attack, when he was again wounded and although unable to stand, nevertheless continued to control the situation.

With only fifteen men left he ordered them to be ready to advance to the final objective and with great difficulty got out of the trench, encouraging them to advance. He was wounded yet again and fell. He is listed as being killed in action on 11 April 1917, aged 21. Lieutenant Donald Mackintosh was posthumously awarded the Victoria Cross for his bravery.

His medal is now held by the Highlanders' Museum at Fort George. Donald is commemorated on the University of Glasgow War Memorial while two windows commemorating him were unveiled in December 1925 in the Elder Chapel of the Western Infirmary.

Extreme valour notwithstanding, reckless displays of bravery were, of course, discouraged, as related in Max Hastings's chapter on 'Mudlife' in *Catastrophe*:[17]

Colwyn Phillips of the Royal Horse Guards wrote ruefully from Ypres.

> The first thing we learn here is forget about 'Glory' ... rigorous discipline became necessary to avoid exposing even an inch of flesh. Lionel Tennyson of the Rifle Brigade deplored the carelessness of his battalion's neighbours, the Seaforth Highlanders: 'a most extraordinary lot of men; if a shell had not come over for twenty minutes or so, they get out of their trenches and start exposing themselves as if no battle was on. The consequence is that many get killed unnecessarily.

1918

1918 saw the battalion in a number of battles as the end of the war approached. They included the Somme, the First Battle of Arras 1918, the battles of Hazebrouck (Hinges Ridge), Béthune, advance into Flanders, the Scarpe, Second Arras, Drocourt-Queant, Canal du Nord, the Selle, Valenciennes, Lys, Hindenberg Line, and the final advance in Picardy.

At Arras the battalion faced the full onslaught of the final German offensive in March where they contributed to bringing it to a halt. This offensive, Operation MICHAEL, or the Kaiserschlacht, began on 21 March 1918. They then moved to la Bassée. Valenciennes was where the battalion ended its war.

It is interesting to look briefly at the role of the Territorials in the war and to appreciate the contribution they made to victory.

Chapter 6

The Territorials in the First World War

The Territorial Army

A Territorial's obligation was to attend at least one drill night, a weekend camp or two where he got to fire his rifle; summer camp allowed more firing practice. In the early days attendance at all of these earned a bounty of £5.00.

Naturally, many professionals looked down on these 'weekend soldiers' as amateurs. It should be said that many a Territorial regiment or battalion served with great courage and efficiency during the course of the war, rising to the occasion and saving the day on numerous occasions. In the event it didn't take long in either world war for the reservists to become competent professionals.

What was the shape of the British Army at the end of the nineteenth century and the early twentieth century, and what role did the reservist or territorial play in that army? According to Mitchinson,[1] it 'was a small, professional organisation designed to garrison the empire and maintain order at home, with no capacity to provide an expeditionary force in a major war. It was augmented in its home duties by three part-time volunteer institutions, the militia, the Volunteer Force and the yeomanry'. Beckett[2] and Hay[3] point out how the Second Boer War exposed weaknesses in the ability of the regular army to counter guerrilla warfare which required additional manpower to overcome. The only reinforcements available were the auxiliaries – nearly 46,000 militiamen served in South Africa and another 74,000 were enlisted into the regular army; some 20,000 men of the Volunteer Force volunteered for active service in South Africa; and the yeomanry provided the nucleus of the separate Imperial Yeomanry, for which over 34,000 volunteered.

It is important to distinguish between the two forms of reservists in the British Army. 'The Army Reserve may be called upon to fill vacancies in regular units as individuals or to provide additional formed units/sub-units for operations.' Most of the Army Medical Services today are reservists while regular battalions have been augmented by reservists.

The Army Reserve was known as the Territorial Force from 1908 to 1921, the Territorial Army (TA) from 1921 to 1967, the Territorial and Army Volunteer

Reserve (TAVR) from 1967 to 1979 and again the Territorial Army (TA) from 1979 to 2014.

The Army Reserve supports the Regular Army at home and abroad; throughout its history almost every major operation and theatre of war has seen reservists operate capably alongside their Regular counterparts.

How did it all begin? An Army Reserve was created by Childers with his enlistment terms which provided for a return to the Colours for those who left before the 12-year engagement had been completed. However, it was the Secretary of State for War, Richard Haldane, who created the Territorial Force (TF) in 1908 when the Territorial and Reserve Forces Act merged the previously civilian-administered Volunteer Force with the mounted Yeomanry.[4] It was commanded by the War Office and administered by local county territorial associations. The Act created a number of county associations which were responsible for funding, housing and equipping the units created for the Territorial Force. Before 1914 the Force faced considerable political opposition, particularly a strong movement that preferred to introduce compulsory national service, conscription, not least Lord Roberts, fierce critic of the Territorial Force and strong advocate of conscription as a better alternative. And there were working-class fears that the TF would be used against any instances of industrial action. *The Long, Long Trail* tells how 'the War Office proved to be miserly in funding the TF, with the effect being that when war came in August 1914 it was greatly under-manned and under-trained, struggled to find sufficient horses, transport and other equipment to effectively mobilise, and was generally regarded as being barely fit for purpose.'[5] At the same time, the Militia was renamed the Special Reserve of the Regular Army.

The Volunteer Force was a citizen army of part-time rifle, artillery and engineer corps, created throughout the British Empire in 1859. In the beginning it was independent but, after the Childers Reforms of 1881, the units of volunteers became increasingly integrated with the British Army before forming part of the Territorial Force in 1908. Originally the corps were to consist of approximately 100 all ranks under a captain, with some localities having sub-divisions of thirty men under a lieutenant. The purpose of the rifle corps was to harass the invading enemy's flanks, while artillery corps were to man coast guns and forts. Engineer corps were also set up, mainly to plant underwater mines for port defence. Stretcher-bearers attached to the rifle corps subsequently formed volunteer medical detachments affiliated to the Army Medical Corps. In a few counties, units of light horse or mounted rifles were formed. The need for volunteers to buy their own rifles and uniforms inevitably served to exclude the lower classes.

A royal commission in 1862 revealed that the Volunteer Force had a strength of 162,681 comprising:[6]

- 662 light horse
- 24,363 artillery
- 2,904 cngineers
- 656 mounted rifles
- 134,096 rifle volunteers, of whom 48,796 were in 86 consolidated battalions and 75,535 in 134 administrative battalions

In 1872, under the Regulation of the Forces Act 1871, jurisdiction over the volunteers passed from the county lord lieutenants to the Secretary of State for War and Volunteer units became increasingly integrated with the Regular Army, culminating in the Childers Reforms of 1881.

It was in the Second Boer War that the volunteers first tasted active combat, due to the prolonged campaign. Volunteer battalions formed Volunteer active service companies that joined the regular battalions of their county regiments.

By 1907 the Volunteer Force was indispensable to British defence planning. Consequently, the Territorial and Reserve Forces Act 1907 merged the Volunteer Force with the Yeomanry to form the Territorial Force in 1908 while the Militia was re-organised as the Special Reserve, to provide a body of trained men available for drafting to regular battalions as required during time of war.[7] The total cost of the Territorial Force was from then on to be met by central government.

Haldane's plan was to create a volunteer 'Territorial Force' to provide a second line for the six divisions of the Expeditionary Force which he was establishing as the jewel in the crown of the Regular Army. The Territorial Force, nicknamed 'Saturday Night Soldiers', would comprise fourteen divisions of infantry and fourteen brigades of cavalry, augmented with the full range of supporting arms and services, including artillery, engineers and medical support. The new Special Reserve was to take over the depots of the militia, as an expanded reserve for the Regular Army. Under much political pressure, Haldane changed the raison d'être of the Territorial Force in his Territorial and Reserve Forces Act to home defence at the last moment but did not alter the planned structure. By the end of April 1915, six full Territorial divisions had been deployed on active service.[8]

Thus, the TF was to take care of home defence while most of the regular army deployed to Europe as an Expeditionary Force. On mobilisation when war was declared the units would form a central mobile striking force and coast defence formations. In the event, the TF was mobilised, or embodied, for full-time war service as soon as war was declared. Men enlisting into the TF were not obliged to serve overseas, although they could sign up for it if they wished under the 'Imperial Service Obligation'.

Unsurprisingly, the TF was not thought to be an effective and viable military force by the regular army and was denigrated by those who preferred conscription, not least Lord Kitchener, who considered territorials to be 'led by middle-aged professional men who were allowed to put on uniform and play at soldiers'. Kitchener was all for the Territorial Force focusing on home defence and elected to raise the New Armies to reinforce the Expeditionary Force in France, thus sidelining the Territorials. However, the need to replace heavy losses suffered by the BEF before the New Armies were up to strength forced a reluctant Kitchener to deploy territorial units overseas; the consequence of this was that it compromised the force's ability to defend the homeland.[9] To replace the depleted foreign-service units, the Territorial Force was doubled in strength by creating a second line which mirrored the original first-line units. Second-line units assumed responsibility for home defence and provided replacement drafts to the first line. The second line competed with the New Armies for limited resources and, like them, was poorly equipped and armed. The military merry-go-round continued apace and gathered speed when, inevitably, the provision of reinforcements to the first line weakened the second line's home defence capabilities until, that is, a third line was raised to take over responsibility for territorial recruitment and training. The second line's duties were further diluted by the expectation that it, too, would be deployed overseas.

The New Armies in the early days formed an all-volunteer element of the British Army which was intended to raise 500,000 volunteers. Kitchener's original intention was that these men would be formed into units that would be ready to be put into action in mid-1916, but events dictated how they were actually deployed.[10] Kitchener Army units first saw action at the Battle of Loos in September-October 1915.

In the event, after the first two months of the war, TF territorials were volunteering for foreign service in droves, thus permitting territorial units to be deployed abroad. They were in the thick of it from early on, the force filling the gap left by the virtual destruction of the regular army that year and the arrival of the New Armies in 1915. Territorial units deployed to Gallipoli in 1915 and, following the disaster there, provided most of the British contribution to allied forces in the Sinai and Palestine Campaign. By the end of the war, the Territorial Force had fielded twenty-three infantry divisions and two mounted divisions overseas. It was demobilised after the war and reconstituted in 1921 as the Territorial Army.

For the terms of engagement of a TF soldier *The Long, Long Trail* gives us the details:

> Until the introduction of the Military Service Act (MSA) in 1916, most TF recruits were engaged for four years. This could be extended in blocks of four years. Thus, a man enlisting in 1908 would 'time expire' in 1912. This had an interesting effect on men during wartime: for example, a man enlisting in 1911 would time expire in 1915. His service was considered finished and he could go home. Unfortunately, as long as he met the MSA criteria, he could be re-enlisted by being conscripted. This applied from 2 March 1916 for single men and 25 May 1916 for married men. Any man time expiring after those dates could also be re-enlisted and usually was. The MSA terms required the man for the duration of the war.

1/4th (Ross-Highland) Battalion Seaforth Highlanders

On the outbreak of war, 1/4th Seaforth mobilised at Dingwall, to set up defences at Nigg for the defence of the naval base in the Cromarty Firth. In August they went south to Bedford and were brought up to strength. The 1/4th landed at le Havre as part of 152 Brigade in the 51st (Highland) Division in November 1914. A scarlet fever epidemic kept it in the rear areas until December when it joined the 1st Seaforth in 19 Indian (Dehra Dun) Brigade of 7th Indian (Meerut) Division.

March 1915 saw 1/4th Seaforth join the attack on Neuve Chapelle, taking 168 casualties. In May the 1/4th with the 1st Seaforth lost over 200 more casualties at the unsuccessful attack on Aubers Ridge. The Battle of Loos began on 25 September and it was there that they made an early contribution to the prosecution of chemical warfare when 100 men were detailed to protect cylinders of poison gas. The much reduced battalion did not take part in the battle.

In the following year they fought in the Battle of the Somme from 22 to 26 July, enduring ferocious fighting attempting to take High Wood. They returned in the fourth phase of the Somme offensive on 3 October, the Battle of the Ancre. The following month saw them joining 51st (Highland) Division at Beaumont Hamel. In 1917 they were at Arras, suffering over 200 casualties but succeeding in their objective and taking 167 prisoners. The German positions at the chemical works at Roeux on the River Scarpe canal fell to them next. At the end of July they joined in the attack at Ypres, encountering German gas attacks. They suffered 200 casualties but gained 1,000 yards nevertheless.

In November they participated in the first major tank offensive at Cambrai; 324 tanks deployed. The breakthrough cost them 300 casualties, though. More heavy casualties followed during their stand against the German offensive in March 1918 on the Beaumetz-Morchies line. That July the 1/4th moved south to Eparnay with 51st (Highland) Division to support the French Army and encountered some of the most savage fighting of the war. The war ended for the battalion in October 1918 in the advance towards Valenciennes where they lost over 300 casualties, gaining ground nevertheless.

One of the 168 casualties in the fighting around Neuve Chapelle in March 1915 was Second Lieutenant Charles Grant Tennant. There is a memorial to him, a window in the parish church, Fairlie, Cunninghame, Strathclyde.

The Imperial War Museum:[11]

> Two Light Stained Glass Window with the subject of Courage and Endurance, the dedication is across the two lights.
>
> To The Glory of God And In Loving Memory of Charles Grant Tennant 2nd Lieut. 4th Seaforth Highlanders Only Son of James and Henrietta Grant Tenant of Fairlie Ayrshire Who Gave His Life For His Country Near Neuve Chapelle France on 9th May 1915 Aged 33 Years

Charles is also remembered on the le Touret Memorial, Richebourg (panel 38–39). He features prominently in Lynn MacDonald's *1915: The End of Innocence*. Here are some extracts from his correspondence:[12]

> *Mud and frostbite*[13]
>
> The whole country is soaked in mud and like a sponge .... it is generally impossible to drain the trenches ... when a hard frost sets in at night ... frostbite sets in at once and the man is done for so far as his feet and legs are concerned. Our own British troops have stood it wonderfully well but some of the Indian regiments have suffered pretty severely.

> *Trench warfare*[14]
>
> The war in the western area has reached a pretty disgusting phase. The opposing trenches are very close to each other – in some cases not more than twenty yards apart and there we sit facing each other and killing each other by every possible means ... our own 1st Battalion had a terrible time. The trench they were holding was a very bad one (the water up to the men's waists in some places) ... the hostile trenches are now in many places so close together that the war is almost reverting to continuous hand to hand fighting.

Sergeant Eric Priest: a Seaforth Highlander veteran from 1925–45 on the North West Frontier, Palestine, France and various stalags.

John Singleton Copley's (1738–1815) epic painting 'The Death of Major Pierson', Tate Britain. (*Public domain*)

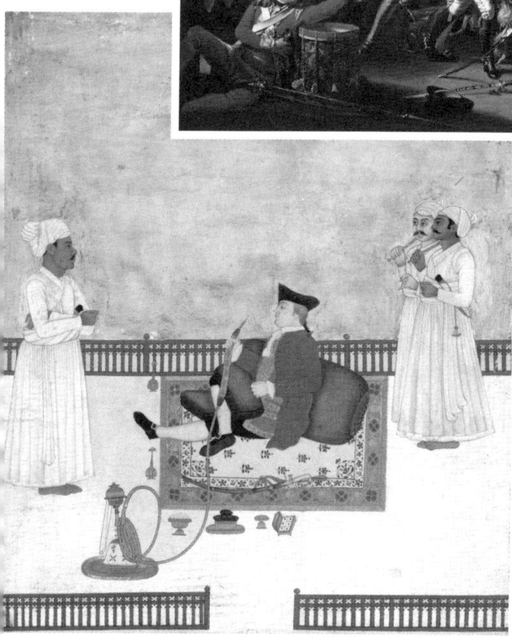

East India Company official negotiating.

Siege of Cuddalore, 1783. During the siege the British Army consisted of the 73rd and 78th [Seaforth] Highlanders, and the 101st Regiment, with a considerable body of native troops, and was subsequently reinforced by a detachment of Hanoverians under Colonel Wangenheim.

Massacre in the boats off Cawnpore. A contemporary engraving of the massacre at the Satichaura Ghat on 27 June 1857 following the Siege of Cawnpore during the 1857 Indian Rebellion. (*Artist: Charles Ball. Image provided by the British Library. Image taken from* The History of the Indian Mutiny. *Originally published/produced in London; New York, London Printing & Publishing Co 1848–1859*)

Crimean War 1854–1856. Portrait of Pipe Major John MacDonald, 72nd Highlanders, with bagpipes. (*Public domain*)

The monument remembering the 1858 Kanpur Well atrocity. (*Public domain*)

The Khan of Lalpura and his Mohmand followers with British political officer Captain Robert Warburton, 1878. (*Photograph by John Burke/NAM 1955-04-39-55*)

Piper George Findlater (1872–1942) of the 1st Gordon Highlanders in the act of winning the Victoria Cross at Dargai in the Tirah, 1897. The Tirah Expeditionary Force was sent to suppress the rebellion and re-secure the pass. The British captured the heights on 18 October, but had to abandon the position because of supply issues. This meant a second attack on 20 October and, during the fierce and prolonged attack by British infantry and Gurkhas, the Gordon Highlanders earned two Victoria Crosses. Findlater was honoured for playing the regimental march despite the fact that he had been shot in both feet and was unable to stand. Under heavy enemy fire, he sat up and played the bagpipes to encourage his comrades in their difficult, uphill attack. (*Oil on canvas by Matthew Hale* (*1852–1942*), *1898/NAM 1957-04-3-1*)

Maxim gun detachment of the 1st Battalion, King's Royal Rifle Corps, Chitral Expedition, 1895. The men are posing with a .303in Maxim machine gun and .303in Lee-Metford magazine rifles. The 1st Battalion were then serving with Lieutenant General Sir Robert Low's Chitral Relief Force. (*NAM 1965-09-137-28*)

Seaforth Highlanders departing Malta for Crete in April 1897.

2nd Seaforth Highlanders during the Boer War.

2nd Seaforth Highlanders during the Boer War. On the reverse is written 'J [or I] Calderwood, Seaforths S. Africa', probably the soldier standing second from right.

Seaforth Highlander in Glengarry bonnet, 1914. (*National Library of Wales*)

Kilted Seaforth Highlanders filling their water-bottles at a town pump before going into the trenches, c.1915. (*NAM 1972-08-67-1-3*)

Seaforth Highlanders helping the locals in a pause in the action in the trenches, 1915.

Seaforth Highlanders rest in a trench, 1915. (*NAM 1972-08-67-1-4*)

An NCO from the Seaforth Highlanders and an officer watch Chinese members of the Hong Kong Volunteer Defence Corps fire a Vickers machine gun at Fanling Camp, 1938. (*NAM 2000-05-111-34*)

Life on the North West Frontier in the 1920s and 1930s.

Fitzroy Maclean (right) was one of only two men who during the Second World War enlisted in the British Army as a private (in the Queen's Own Cameron Highlanders) and rose to the rank of brigadier.

Uganda Battery of King's African Rifles in action against the Vichy-held positions near Ambositra, Madagascar, September 1942.

Men of the 2nd Seaforth Highlanders (The Ross-Shire Buffs, Duke of Albany's), embarking at Sousse, 5 July 1943, en route for Sicily. (*NAM. 1985-11-36-47*)

Universal carriers of 2nd Seaforth Highlanders during Operation VERITABLE in the Reichswald forest, 10 February 1945. **INSET:** Plaque commemorating the 5th Seaforth Highlanders in the Second World War in the Nave of Dornoch Cathedral. (*Brownag via Wikimedia Commons/CC BY-SA 3.0*)

The British Occupation of Java, 1949. Indian troops with four armed Indonesians captured at Bekassi before the village was burnt as a reprisal for the murder of five members of the RAF and twenty Maharatta riflemen whose Dakota transport aircraft crash-landed near the village. (*IWM SE 6054*)

CURRENT AFFAIRS

Daily Worker

EVERY NEW READER A RECRUIT TO SOCIALISM

(6429) 2d ★ ★ ★ SATURDAY MAY 10 1952

Pictures which tell the frightful story of Malaya

THIS HORROR MUST END

You must compel peace

By the Editor

SAVE Britain's honour by ending the war in Malaya and by granting to the peoples of that land the independence they desire. That is the basic lesson to be drawn from the harrowing pictures which we present on this page.

Mr. Lyttelton, in his reply in the House of Commons on Tuesday, seemed to suggest that the pictures which we published of the beheading of the Malayan patriot last week referred to an isolated incident.

The additional pictures which we publish today show only too clearly that this frightful practice was widespread throughout the country.

We present these further pictures, not for reasons of morbid sensationalism, but because we know that the British people will stop such things being done in their name.

Since we published the first pictures, the British Government say they have ordered this practice to cease.

We are not merely pleading for the ending of these barbarous practices, however, but for an end to the whole vile and unnecessary war itself.

Only thus can we establish a new and fruitful basis for co-operation between the peoples of Britain and the peoples of Malaya.

We urge every British citizen, now that the full barbarous and reactionary character of this war is clear, to struggle with all his might to bring our lads home from this nightmare war and so enable the peoples of Malaya to develop their country in independence and peace.

ABOVE: A Dyak headhunter, wearing the beret and badge of the Royal Marine Commandos, cleans out the scalp of a Malayan patriot. In the basket are dismembered parts of the body. A thumb is visible in the corner. Dyaks boast that they can cut off a man's head with two sweeps of a knife.

ABOVE: A British Royal Marine Commando smiles while posing with the severed heads of two Malayan liberation fighters. One belongs to a young woman. Her mouth is bruised. The front teeth have been knocked out.

BELOW: A macabre game to while away long hours in the jungle? The same heads on the ground. A dismembered hand is propped up in between—at the salute.

History behind these pictures

Monday, April 28. The Daily Worker publishes an exclusive picture showing a Royal Marine Commando holding the severed head of a Malayan liberation fighter. We name the date of the incident, and the place.

Tuesday, April 29. Admiralty experts say the picture is "faked." A Lancashire Evening Post "expert" agrees. The Yorkshire Evening Post calls it "a usual Communist trick." A question is tabled in the House of Commons by Tory M.P. Col. Crosthwaite-Eyre.

Wednesday, April 30. We publish another picture and take up the challenge of "fake." The question in the House of Commons is deferred till May 7. There is a muddle in Whitehall. The Colonial Office is not prepared to say the picture is "fake."

The first protests are published in the Daily Worker. A petition calling for a halt to the Malayan war is signed by workers at the British Thomson-Houston factory, Willesden.

Thursday, May 1. Mr. Harold Davies, M.P. (Lab., Leek), tables a question in the House on the activities of Dyak headhunters in Malaya.

Saturday, May 3. The comment of a regular soldier just back from Malaya is published in this paper: "It happens all the time," he says. "I saw worse myself."

Monday, May 5. Colonial Office refuse to answer three questions asked by the Daily Worker on the official sanctioning of head-hunting in Malaya.

Wednesday, May 7. Mr. Oliver Lyttelton, Colonial Secretary, answers questions on the picture in the House of Commons. "Yes," he says, "it is a genuine photograph."

Thursday, May 8. J. R. Campbell, Daily Worker Editor, sends a letter to Mr. Churchill. He demands the end of the Malayan war and refers to Mr. Lyttelton's implication that the atrocity exposed by the Daily Worker was an isolated incident.

Campbell says: "We cannot accept this. For your information, I enclose more pictures of further cases, horrible evidence that this barbaric practice, a gross violation of the rules of war, is widespread."

BELOW: The gory job completed he poses for a picture. According to the Colonial Secretary there are 261 Dyaks in Malaya at the present time.

THIS LEAFLET LASHES THEM

THE first Malayan atrocity photograph, published by the Daily Worker on April 28, and admitted in the House of Commons last Wednesday to be authentic, has been reprinted in leaflet form together with the leading article of protest that accompanied it.

★Order supplies of this leaflet to be distributed in your street, your factory, your trade union branch. (Price 2s per 100, 15s per 1,000 from Publicity Dept., 75 Farringdon Road, London, E.C.1.)

★Follow up with sales of the Daily Worker, especially next Monday's issue in which ARTHUR CLEGG brings to light yet more facts about the inhuman methods being used to suppress the Malayan people.

Union votes against arms drive

Peace Pact call by 865,000 engineers

From GEORGE SINFIELD

BLACKPOOL, Friday.

SPOKESMEN of 865,000 engineering workers, true to the great traditions of organised labour in their industry, today unanimously demanded a Five-Power Peace Pact and prohibition of atomic and germ warfare.

The National Committee of the Amalgamated Engineering Union, by reaching that vital decision, placed its powerful organisation at the head of the struggle for peace.

The move was led in spirited fashion by a Labour councillor, Mr. F. Mansell, of Wolverhampton ...

Quick trial

Thomsons: unions get their case ready

Daily Worker Reporter

SECRETARIES of the print unions were yesterday discussing the case they will present to the Ministry of Labour Court of Inquiry into the causes and circumstances of the D. C. Thomson dispute.

Setting-up of this Court of Inquiry was announced in the Commons yesterday morning by the Minister of Labour, Sir Walter Monckton.

The Minister said he feared there was now "a real risk of an extension which might seriously inconvenience the public and interfere with the supply of news."

This was understood to be a reference to a threat by the wholesalers to stop handling all newspapers if their workers—members of the National Union of Printing, Bookbinding and Paper Workers—continue to treat Thomson publications as "black."

OFFICIALS MEET

Officials of the Printing and Kindred Trades Federation, to which the 17 print unions are affiliated, met representatives of the Newspaper Proprietors' Association at the Ministry of Labour yesterday.

The wholesalers' threat was believed to be among the subjects under discussion.

Composition and terms of reference of the Court of Inquiry, which is being set up under the Industrial Courts Act (1919), are to be announced by the Minister of Labour "as soon as possible." He will lay its report before Parliament.

MIGHT EXTEND

In the meantime he has asked "all concerned" not to take action which might extend the dispute.

The management of the Clyde Paper Mills, Rutherglen, near Glasgow, where 800 workers are on strike over an attempt to get four of them to handle "black" newsprint—destined for Thomsons—yesterday circulated this threat to their employees:

"It must be understood that the management may at any time have to terminate the contracts of employment of those who continue to withhold their labour."

After discussions with union officials, printing workers at the Argus Press yesterday printed the City Press, containing an article supporting D. C. Thomsons.

INJUNCTION

Daily Worker Reporter

AN interim injunction against five prominent trade union officials was granted to D. C. Thomson and Co. in the Chancery Division yesterday. Defendants were Mr. Arthur Deakin, general secretary of the Transport and General Workers' Union; Mr. John Wood, T.G.W.U. trade group secretary; Mr. G. E. Innes, T.G.W.U. regional secretary; Mr. R. W. Briginshaw, general secretary of the National Society of Operative Printers and Assistants; Mr. L. Moncrieff, N.A.T.S.O.P.A. northern district secretary; and Mr. W. A. Morrison, secretary of the National Union of Printing, Bookbinding and Paper Workers.

Mr. Justice Upjohn granted the injunction against all the defendants except Mr. Morrison. The matter will come up in court again on Tuesday.

Holidays a diff

PROGRESSIVE TOURS

Holiday

ITALIAN RIVIERA — SESTRI LEVANTE

PARIS — BASTILLE WEEK

FRANCE — BASTILLE WEEK PLUS WEEK AT GIF-SUR-YVETTE

'This Horror Must End' was a famous news article published by the *Daily Worker* (later renamed *Morning Star*) exposing never before published photographs of British forces and their Iban headhunter allies engaging in atrocities during the Malayan Emergency (1948–1960). The collection of decapitated heads and scalps was a common practice performed by British troops and their allies during the war. The photographs were published by British communist activists in the hopes that they would turn public opinion against the British occupation of Malaya.

Evidence of headhunting. Corpses of Malayan National Liberation Army guerillas killed by British soldiers during the Malayan Emergency. (*Public domain*)

A wounded suspected MNLA supporter being held and questioned after his capture in 1952 during the Malayan Emergency. (*IWM K 13104/Public domain*)

These prisoners, supporters of Indonesian President Sukarno, were captured during an attack by the Queen's Own Highlanders (Seaforth and Camerons) on the Brunei oil town of Seria, December 1962. They are escorted by a Highlander armed with a Sterling sub-machine gun and are being marched into Anduki Airport. (*NAM 2004-12-33-3*)

Two soldiers of the Queen's Own Highlanders on guard in the Seria oilfield in Brunei, January 1963. The troops were in Seria to rescue European hostages who had been held prisoner by rebels for three days in the local police station. (*IWM TR 18603/ Public domain*)

Queen's Own Highlanders First Corporals' Battle Camp in the Falkland Islands, 1982.

Members of W Company Mortar Platoon, 1st Royal Regiment of Fusiliers, prepare to engage enemy targets after an intense evening of incoming fire on the front line just south of Basra, Iraq 2003. (*Photograph by Corporal Paul Jarvis/Wikipedia*)

A member of the IRA in the early 1970s. (*Rare Historical Photos*)

Winning hearts and minds in Bosnia – Royal Regiment of Scotland, 2002.

Around 100 soldiers from The Highlanders, 4th Battalion, Royal Regiment of Scotland were deployed on Saddleworth Moor in the summer of 2018 after wildfires broke out across the moors to support Greater Manchester Fire and Rescue Service. (*UK Ministry of Defence/Wikimedia Commons*)

Royal Regiment of Scotland live-fire training.

Bombardment[15]
But at 7.30 punctually the whole sky was rent by noise – about 400 British guns all opening fire at once in a concentrated bombardment of two hundred yards of German trenches … the whole air and the solid earth itself became one quivering jelly … I was conscious of nothing except the extraordinary sense of security the infantry man gets from hearing artillery fire from his own side.

Birdsong[16]
Through all the bombardment and in fact through all the heavy shelling of that day and the next, the larks mounted carolling up to the sky with shells screaming all around them, as though all that devil's din was only some insane nightmare and as though all that was really true was the coming of spring.

Shrapnel[17]
Just as I got there two shrapnel bursts clanged close behind us. Poor Macmillan got a terrible wound right across the forehead, and Cuthbert fell forward with the blood streaming from his head. I could see it was only a flesh wound … but Macmillan was in a bad state – so bad that the adjutant thought he was dying. I saw that his heart and lungs were still working though part of his brain was laid bare … Appleton was blown to pieces by a shell just as he was getting out of the trench, handsome MacDonald, the piper, was killed stone dead by a bullet through the heart, and Speer through the head, and a dozen or more … were wounded.

The Diary of Captain Walter Bagot-Chester, 3rd Queen Alexandra's Own Gurkha Rifles, delivers the grim news about Lieutenant Tennant:[18]

Toward the last hundred yards or so German 'Woolly Bears' began to burst overhead, and 'Jack Johnsons' close by, but I had only one man hit at this point.[7] We then got into a long communication trench leading up from Lansdowne Post to the Gridiron Trenches … here there was fearful confusion … I presently went onto a trench called the Pioneer Trench. There I had twenty-six casualties from shell. Havildar Manbir had his leg blown off and was in such agony that he asked to be shot. As one got further to the front trench, the place got more of a shambles, wounded and dead everywhere … the ground in front was littered with Seaforth bodies … we had to work at once to try to clear up the trench. It was full of killed and wounded, equipment of all sorts, and the ground in front

> was strewn with dead Seaforths, who made the charge this morning at 5.40 am from this trench.

One of the dead was Lieutenant Charles Tennant who had written his last letter to his 'Darling Lucy'.[19]

To give an idea of how families in general could be gravely affected by the war, we know that the Tennant family had to endure the deaths of nineteen cousins in total, nine of them Tennants, officially recorded as either killed in action, died of wounds or died on active service between October 1914 and August 1917.

More fascinating social-military history is revealed in Boyle[20] where the author painstakingly lists from the regimental Roll of Honour Charles Tennant's comrades in C Company, 4th Battalion – officers and men – on mobilisation, indicating those killed in action or died of wounds up to May 1915. In addition, we see their home addresses and their occupation on enlistment. Of the 132 men listed forty-six were dead or wounded by May 1915 (35 per cent).

The 1/5th (Sutherland and Caithness) Battalion

The 5th Seaforth mobilised at Golspie on the outbreak of war when they were detailed to build defences on the North Sutor at the entrance to the naval base at Cromarty Firth. Training at Bedford followed for eight months after which, in May 1915, they relieved the 1/6th Seaforth in the trenches at Richebourg-St Vaast near la Bassée. The following month they were blooded in the attack mounted by 153 and 154 Brigades at Festubert. After time at Laventie and in the Albert sector, in March 1916 the 51st (Highland) Division took over the 'Labyrinth' near Arras. After the first phase of the Battle of the Somme the 1/5th held the line at High Wood and Mametz Wood. That October they took over the line opposite the wrecked village of Beaumont Hamel and led the 152 Brigade advance. Despite succeeding in taking the German position they lost over 300 casualties but captured over 600 prisoners.

When in April 1917 the 1/5th advanced with 152 Brigade at Arras they lost another 300 casualties but took their objective all the same. German counter-attacks were repelled at Roeux and the Chemical Works. At the third Battle of Ypres they took 700 prisoners and stayed at the salient until 24 September. Cambrai was a successful battle for the battalion with the advent of the massed tank attack. They captured Ribecourt and 300 prisoners, and they took Flesquières. March 1918 saw them straddling the Bapaume-Cambrai road facing a heated gas and shell bombardment from the Germans, which they endured for six days with 377 casualties. Then they returned to the River Lawe sector north of Béthune where they faced another attack which cost them 200 or so casualties.

As with the 1/4th the 1/5th headed south to support the French at Épernay where they encountered some of their heaviest fighting in stopping the German breakthrough at the Marne. At the end of the month they lost 369 casualties in the valley of the River Arde. The following month they went back to the Scarpe, helping to retake the chemical works and Roeux. The end of the war saw the 1/5th taking part in the attack at Thun St Martin where they lost over 400 casualties in sixteen days of intense fighting.

1/6th (Morayshire) Battalion Seaforth Highlanders

Mobilised at Elgin and trained at Bedford the 6th left for France on 1 May 1915 and got their first taste of trenches at Richebourg-St Vaast on the 19th and was relieved by the 1/5th on the 22nd. On 25 June they were detailed to provide small arms covering fire at Festubert, suffering 160 casualties from the heavy bombardment they encountered. In June 1915 they shared the trenches with the 1/5th at Laventie and then the Albert Sector from August to December. The arrangement was typically six days in the line, six in the support trenches, another six days in the line and, finally, six days in billets. On 28 April 1916 the Germans exploded seven massive mines simultaneously under the forward company positions, followed by heavy artillery fire. This caused sixty-seven casualties but they managed to keep the Germans at bay. From July 1916 they accompanied the 5th at Mametz Wood and High Wood, Beaumont Hamel where the Germans lurked in underground bunkers only to re-emerge and attack the British from behind. The battalion was successful in its objectives, losing 277 casualties.

They were part of the highly successful 51st (Highland) Division (along with 9th and 15th Scottish Divisions) attack at Arras in April 1917 which drove the enemy back some four or five miles in places. Then there was fighting at the Roeux chemical factory and Ypres in July. November saw them in the famous tank attack at Cambrai, having been allocated seven tanks to support them. They punctured the Hindenberg Line and took Flesquières with sixty-nine casualties, taking 300 prisoners.

During the March 1918 German offensive, they held the line between Beaumetz and Morchies, enduring five days of artillery bombardment and infantry attack and taking nearly 400 casualties; despite it all they held firm. Having withdrawn, they returned to the line on the River Lawe to face heavy German assaults. In July they were in Épernay with the other battalions; there they stopped the German Marne advance at a cost of 400 killed, wounded and missing. The next month saw them in the Arras area where they attacked the strategically vital Greenland Hill near Roeux. The last operation of the war for the 1/6th was the advance towards Valenciennes, losing over 300 casualties by 28 October.

The 7th (Service) Battalion, Seaforth Highlanders

The 7th (Service) Battalion came into being at Fort George as part of Kitchener's First New Army (K1), training on Salisbury Plain. It landed at Boulogne as part of 26 Brigade in the 9th (Scottish) Division in May 1915 alongside 8th Black Watch, 8th Gordons and 5th Camerons. They took over the trenches near Festubert but their first action was at Loos in September 1915 where the British first used poison gas. They took the German stronghold on the Hohenzollern Redoubt; this and subsequent attacks cost the Seaforth over 500 casualties. Between October and December the Battalion was in the Ypres Salient and from January to May 1916 helped to hold the Ploegsteert (Plugstreet) area. The Battle of the Somme saw the 9th Division attack German positions at Longueval and Delville Wood; this and other actions came at a cost of over 450 casualties.

All the 9th Division battalions were badly depleted and so the 7th Seaforth were withdrawn from the line on 23 July, but returned in August, holding positions on Vimy Ridge and then back to the Somme around Butte de Warlencourt where the mud was worse than ever.

In April 1917 the Battalion was part of the attack on Arras, storming and taking the 'Island' near Blangy with the loss of 181 over six days and considerable gains. Later that year it saw action at Cambrai, Ypres and Passchendaele Ridge. Relentless rain and sucking mud conspired to make these some of the foulest conditions ever.

The March 1918 final German offensive saw the 7th on the Somme facing the full force of the German attack, with the loss of over 300 casualties in a frenetic withdrawal operation. In April they moved up to Flanders, taking Wytschaete from the Germans; by September they were in the line at Ypres. The 9th Division moved from its position on the Frezenburg Ridge outside Ypres to carry the line forward some twenty miles to just outside Harlebecke, costing the 7th 331 casualties.

The 8th (Service) Battalion Seaforth Highlanders

Formed at Fort George as part of Kitchener's Second New Army (K2), the Battalion landed at Boulogne, centred around St Omer and took over a sector in the line at Loos on 6 August 1915. Like the 7th, their first action was at

Loos (with gas) on 25 September, battling through the village with intense house-to-house fighting followed with an attack on Hill 70 which they took, albeit with high casualties, losing most of the 776 who started the battle. This massive loss took a year to restore and required a period of retraining in the Loos sector and Hohenzolern redoubt.

At the Somme in July 1916 the 8th participated in raids on enemy lines, holding the Switch Line against fierce counterattacks in mid-August.

At Arras in 1917 the 8th was held in reserve, kept busy in working parties and carrying ammunition: 27 April brought action again when the battalion attacked the Germans at Guemappe losing over 300 men. A further 203 were lost at the 3rd Battle of Ypres when the 15th Division won 2,000 yards. That August a further 393 casualties brought 8th Seaforth's strength to just over 200 men. That winter they held the line at Arras and Cambrai and there was much retraining of reinforcements. The German March 1918 offensive saw the 8th at Monchy, west of Arras. Eparnay on the Marne was the destination that July; the 8th joined 44 brigade attack and captured Buzancy. The end of the war saw the 8th at Loos again; they finished up at Huissignies.

The 9th (Service) Battalion Seaforth Highlanders (Pioneers)

It all started for the 9th at Fort George in October 1914; the 9th (Service) became the Pioneers of 9th Division. The battalion landed at Boulogne: the first pioneer unit to be formed and the first to land in France. It could boast a number of professional engineers amongst the officers while the men were largely tradesmen – bricklayers, miners and labourers mostly. Training involved infantry skills and engineering; they were tasked with road building, communication trenches, trench mortar emplacements, drainage and field tramways.

The 9th got their first taste of trench life at Bailleul and their first action at the Battle of Loos where they linked up captured German trenches and dug two major communication trenches from the front line to the Hohenzollern Redoubt. At the Somme they were split up with some performing an infantry role at the difficult fighting at Longueval and Delville Wood. Others repaired roads, consolidated strongpoints and captured enemy positions – often under heavy fire and at night. At Arras in April 1917, pioneer work was brought to a halt when the battalion was forced to fix bayonets and repel a German counter-attack.

During the German final offensive of March 1918, the 9th was in a combat role and defended St Pierre Vaast Wood, later fighting a rearguard action at Rancourt and Combles. Finally, in September and October, the 9th took part in 9th Division's advance from Ypres to their last engagement in the war near Harlebecke.

The 1st Garrison Battalion Seaforth Highlanders

Formed at Tillicoultry in July 1916 the 1st Garrison Battalion comprised men who did not quite reach the required standard of fitness for combat due to age or earlier wounds. They landed in Salonika as part of 228 Brigade in 28th Division in August 1916 for service on the Struma front, opposing the Bulgarians for eighteen months. After the armistice the battalion was stationed in Costanza and other Rumanian towns, and Constantinople.

The Victoria Cross

As military awards go, none is higher or more prestigious than the Victoria Cross which is awarded for valour 'in the presence of the enemy' to members of the British armed forces and may be awarded posthumously. It can be awarded to any military rank in any service and to civilians under military command; for example, two were awarded to civilian members of the Merchant Marine in the First World War. The inaugural awards ceremony was held on 26 June 1857 at which Queen Victoria invested sixty-two of the 111 Crimean recipients in a ceremony in Hyde Park, London to honour acts of valour during the Crimean War, and since then two-thirds (nearly 900) of all awards have been presented by the British monarch in person, usually at Buckingham Palace. About 150 awards were either forwarded to the recipient or next of kin by registered post.

The VC has been awarded 1,358 times to 1,355 individual recipients. Only fifteen medals (eleven to members of the British Army and four to members of the Australian Army), have been awarded since the Second World War. Canada, Australia and New Zealand have created their own Victoria Crosses, awards of which have been made to Australian and New Zealand personnel.

Original Warrant, Clause 13 stipulates that a ballot is drawn when an act of gallantry or valour is carried out by a squadron, ship's company or a detached body of men (such as marines) in which all men are deemed equally brave and deserving of the Victoria Cross. The officers select one officer, the NCOs select one individual, and the private soldiers or seamen select two. Overall, forty-six awards have been made by ballot, twenty-nine during the Indian Mutiny. There have been no such awards since the Zeebrugge raid in 1918.

It is generally said that the metal from which the medals are struck comes from a Russian cannon captured at the siege of Sevastopol. However, historian John Glanfield asserts that, through the use of X-ray studies of older Victoria Crosses, it was determined that the metal used for almost all VCs since December 1914 is taken from Chinese guns. Australian research by Creagh and Aston has noted Chinese inscriptions on the cannon, now barely legible due to corrosion.

A likely explanation is that the cannon were taken as trophies during the First Opium War and held in the Woolwich repository.[21] Just one company of jewellers, Hancock & Co., has produced every VC awarded since its inception.

Because of its rarity, the VC is highly prized and the medal has fetched over £400,000 at auction.[22]

A total of seventeen Scaforth battalions were raised during the First World War and sixty battle honours were awarded to the Regiment.[23] An estimated 8,830 men lost their lives.

During the 1920s and 1930s both battalions served as garrison troops across the British Empire, including India, Egypt, Palestine and Hong Kong. The 2nd Battalion served on the North West Frontier of India from 1930.

For a full list of VCs see Appendix 3.

Chapter 7

Striking Miners 1920–1921

The 1st Battalion Seaforth Highlanders returned from Egypt in June 1919 and went on to Glencorse where it connected with elements of the 3rd (Special Reserve) Battalion whose numbers brought it back up to strength. Then back to Fort George. In 1921 the Battalion was deployed to Cowdenbeath and Bridge of Allan to help maintain order during strike action by miners. The average number of workers involved in strikes and lock-outs at this time was 2,108,000, compared with an average of 308,100 between 1927 and 1939. Conflicts in Ireland and India only added to the general unrest.

The 1st Battalion was not alone; it was, of course, working alongside elements of the hastily assembled Defence Force. It moved to Palestine in 1933 and to Hong Kong in 1937 and, in March 1938, was posted to Shanghai.

The Miners' Strike 1921 and the Defence Force

The Defence Force was established by the Government to quell an industrial crisis in the coal-mining industry and associated railways. The crisis originated from the return of control of the mining industry from state control to private owners after the war; the coal industry and railways had been controlled by the state during the war and were not immediately returned to private hands. The coalition government was unwilling to impose wage reductions since that would provoke strike action against the government, with political ramifications. Pay reductions for miners were postponed until the industry was de-controlled on 31 March 1921: the worsening economic slump during 1920 did not help when the mine owners began to propose and impose reductions to miners' wages by 10 per cent to as much as 49 per cent. The so-called 'Triple Alliance' of coal-mining unions called for a strike, creating a crisis which threatened to bring the British economy to its knees. At the same time the government was obsessed with concerns over the spread of Bolshevism. The prime minister, David Lloyd George, was not taking any chances and prepared to mobilise the armed forces.

In 1914 the rail and transport unions had come together with the Miners' Federation of Great Britain to form the Triple Alliance. On 1 April 1921 the Miners' Federation of Great Britain (MFGB) refused the terms of the wage dispute and miners were subsequently 'locked out' of the pits. Their leaders appealed to railwaymen and transport workers for a sympathy strike but, on 15 April 1921, the executives of the NTWF and NUR announced that they would not recommend strike action; this became known as 'Black Friday' and resulted in the end of the unions' 'Triple Alliance'. It left the miners to fight on alone for three months, until they were driven back to work on worse terms than they might have had at the start.

On 4 April 1921 the Speaker of the House of Commons read a Royal Message to the House, as reported in *Hansard*:[1]

> The Emergency Powers Act, 1920, having enacted that if it appears to His Majesty that any action has been taken or is immediately threatened by any persons or body of persons of such a nature and on so extensive a scale as to be calculated, by interfering with the supply and distribution of food, water, fuel, light, or with the means of locomotion, to deprive the community or any substantial portion of the community of the essentials of life, His Majesty may, by Proclamation, declare that a state of emergency exists; and the immediate threat of cessation of work in coal mines having, in His Majesty's opinion, constituted a state of emergency within the meaning of the said Act: His Majesty has deemed it proper, by Proclamation made in pursuance of the said Act and dated the 31st day of March, 1921, to declare that a state of emergency exists.

Four days later Lloyd George announced to the House that efforts to reconcile difference between mine owners and miners' representatives had broken down and that the police force was inadequate in view of the number of places that would require protection against potential acts of 'a concerted plan to suspend the principal services [mines, railways etc] that are essential to the life of the community'. He read a message from the King announcing a National Emergency and the mobilisation of Naval and Military Reserves for active service.

Many men who had served in the military during the First World War elected to re-enlist for a short period of service in the Defence Force, which was established in April 1921.

Accordingly, anyone who had a liability as members of Sections B and D of the Army Reserve, except those resident in Ireland and those already serving in the police, were ordered to report to their normal place of re-joining which was stated on the Protection Certificates they had been issued when transferring to the reserve. The Territorial Force (TF) was not asked to serve, but members of the TF and other ex-servicemen generally were invited to enlist into a new Defence Force from 9 April 1921.

Those men who enlisted into the Defence Force were engaged for 90 days and paid at normal army privates' rates. Recruits had to be between 18 and 40 years of age, and, of course, be medically fit to serve. Separation allowances would be paid in the case of married recruits aged 26 and above. No uniform was issued: men would wear plain clothes and maintain them at their own expense throughout their service, for which they would be paid a £5 grant. Later this was converted into a £5 bounty and uniforms were introduced. For enlistment they reported to their nearest Territorial drill hall. All men would be enlisted as privates: even a brigadier general did so.

Newspapers across Britain reported that enlistment was brisk, with right-wing political parties, the British Legion and the Middle Class Union, all enthusiastically encouraging men to join. For example, the *Western Daily Press* reported fifty men per hour enlisting at the Bristol drill hall used by the 6th Gloucestershire Regiment.

The army formed the recruits into units known as 'Number X Defence Unit', with the number corresponding to the Territorial Force unit to which the nucleus cadre had first been attached.

The newspapers were quick to promulgate a government rebuttal of rumours that the Force had in fact been assembled in order to put down a rising in Germany.

Meetings between the coal owners and miners' representatives resumed on 12 April 1921. The leaders of the 'Triple Alliance' capitulated and the strike was called off on 15 April.

The *Nottingham Journal* of 9 April 1921 reported that the following steps were being taken by the Government:

- A national emergency proclaimed that Army Reserves were to be called up; Special Defence Force to be embodied; appeal issued for special constables and volunteers for administrative services; all military and naval leave stopped;
- Power to: seize land, building and general utility work;
- Seize coal mines and colliery property, tramways and light railways;
- Control Canals railways, shipping and transport generally;
- Close ports and harbours;
- Seize food or forage supplies;
- Fix maximum coal and food process; ration food and coal; prohibit hording; requisition horses and vehicles.
- Prohibit or regulate sale of motor spirit and seize supplies; prohibit sale of fire-arms and ammunition and carrying of arms;

- Refuse transmission of telegrams, prohibit meetings, arrest without warrant any one endangering public safety; search persons and vehicles; close premises.
- It is an offence during a state of emergency to: carry firearms at a meeting; injure any public building; railway, telegraph; bridge, tramway or works; foment mutiny, sedition, disaffection among the forces, impede distribution of food, fuel, water.

The Defence Force was finally demobilised on 9 July 1921.

The 1921 census

The 1921 census in the UK was postponed on account of the strikes and the unrest. It was originally scheduled for 24 April but was delayed until 19 June. The census clearly revealed that many military personnel were surreptitiously deployed to mines around the country. The entry for No. 3 Blackrigg Colliery near Armadale in West Lothian gives only three anodyne words of explanation for why the twenty-six soldiers were there: 'Military protecting Colliery'. They were not listed as soldiers but as electricians, gardeners, labourers, ship riggers and one 51-year-old coal miner named Edward Morgan from Ayrshire. There is no mention of what unit the men were serving in; only ranks were given: one lieutenant, one sergeant, three lance corporals and the rest were privates – probably reservists.

We get the same again at Cowie Colliery in Stirling. This time, the unit was headed by a captain, well-named 30-year-old Edward Armour, an ironmonger from Campbeltown.

The census entry from Pencaitland Colliery in East Lothian gives a variation on this, with twenty-nine naval personnel stationed at the mine. They were all Royal Navy: stokers, seamen and petty officers.

The battalion subsequently served in Ireland during and after partition. The 1st Battalion returned to India in the late 1920s and both battalions served in Palestine in the 1930s.

In 1921 the 1st Seaforth sailed over to Dublin and then on to Belfast. While 1922 was a difficult year in Northern Ireland, life began to return to normal in 1923 and, by 1925, it was normal. In 1923–4 there were only four murders. The Irish Free State suffered a civil war which ended in May 1923 after eleven months of conflict.

In 1926 the 1st was based in Aldershot escorting food supply convoys in London during the 1926 nine-day General Strike. Indeed, the United Press

Archive gives us the situation on 8 May 1926 in a piece titled 'Britain's Army and Navy thrown into strike conflict'.

By 1928 the 1st was back in Dover until 1933. In December that year it assumed the role of foreign service battalion stationed in Jerusalem where the conflict had a definite anti-terrorist flavour to it with escorting, ambush patrols and picqueting. As Sym says[2] 'it was not until the bullet struck, or the bomb burst, that one could differentiate between friend and foe'. It was certainly dangerous work: two lieutenants and three other ranks were killed and nine other ranks wounded.

Unusually, the 2nd Battalion was also in Palestine – in Haifa 100 miles to the north. This, of course, gave opportunity for inter-battalion conviviality and highly competitive sporting contests.

Cairo was the next stop for the 1st Battalion in December 1933 where it acted as a deterrent to a projected invasion by the Italians who had recently attacked Abyssinia. The RAF base at Mersa Matruh in the Western Desert province was also defended.

In May 1936 the 1st was back in Palestine in the state of emergency during the Arab Revolt, providing security against Arab terrorism, sabotage and ambushes. By October they had returned to Cairo.

In 1937 the British colony in Hong Kong beckoned. It was the start of the war between Japan and China and there were fears of Hong Kong being invaded. A typhoon with winds up to 164mph exacerbated things with the battalion deployed cleaning up the damage.

The Japanese, however, continued to be troublesome, so the 1st was sent to Shanghai to protect the British sector of the International Settlement in the Sino-Japanese War. And then it was back to Hong Kong amid the tension generated by the 1938 Munich Crisis in a speedy voyage to Kowloon on HMS *Birmingham*. Then a return to Shanghai until 1940.

Hong Kong and Shanghai 1937–1939

Shanghai was opened up to international trade in 1842 with the Treaty of Nanking. The United Kingdom was one of the countries that took up concessions within the city. To protect British interests, British troops were deployed to Shanghai. With the increased threat from Japanese forces, the British troops were withdrawn from Shanghai in August 1940.

Robert Palmer,[3] explains that British troops in China functioned as a pre-war command reporting directly to Whitehall. Increasing interest in the economic and trade potential offered by China in the nineteenth century was reflected by the various occupations of parts of China. The United Kingdom fought the Opium Wars against China between 1839 and 1942. China, of course, had remained very much isolated as international trade grew from the west. However, Palmer says, 'speculative traders began importing opium from India into China for that country's large population'. This provoked great alarm with the Emperor of China who was more than a little concerned at the social and medical problems ignited by the increased use of high quality opium in his country. Unsurprisingly, he banned the trade.

The United Kingdom, self-righteously, saw this as an attack on free trade (not least on *their* free trade) and against British interests in the area. Canton was the single point of entry to China for British trade and the aggrieved British felt it necessary to resort to military force to pursue their commercial interests. Troops from India were sent to enforce British foreign policy.

On Hong Kong Palmer continues:[4]

> Britain's jewel in the crown, however, was their possession of Hong Kong. They seized the island in 1839, with the cession of the island being confirmed by the treaty of Nanking in 1842. China leased the New Territories to the United Kingdom in 1898 for 100 years. Following the First World War, the British maintained settlements in Tientsin, Shanghai and Wei Hai Wei, as well as their forces deployed to Hong Kong. Tension in China began escalating well before the accepted commencement of the Second World War. The UK sent reinforcements to Shanghai in 1927 due to disturbances in the city, and withdrew from Wei Hai Wei in 1931.

China Command was an independent command responsible for the British possessions of Hong Kong and Kowloon, and the British concessions in the Chinese cities of Shanghai and Tientsin. The garrison of Shanghai and Tientsin in 1930 comprised two British infantry battalions plus supporting services. Hong Kong was the most significant garrison and included the Royal Navy presence. The army deployed two British and one Indian infantry battalions to Hong Kong and Kowloon, with the headquarters of British troops in China located at Hong Kong. Palmer again:[5]

> In 1931, Japan invaded and annexed Manchuria, but the main increase in international tension arose in July 1937, when Japan and China commenced full-scale war. The two British concessions in China were abandoned in December 1939 (Tientsin) and August 1940 (Shanghai). The colony of Hong Kong was seen as isolated and difficult to reinforce in the event of war with Japan. In the event, one Indian battalion was sent to reinforce the

colony in early 1940, and two Canadian battalions arrived in November 1941. This allowed the creation of a second infantry brigade in Hong Kong.

The sad finale was that the Japanese invaded on 8 December 1941 and, despite some heroic resistance, the Governor decided to surrender the colony at 3.15pm on 25 December with 1,045 British and Canadian officers, other ranks and Indian other ranks killed, and 1,068 reported missing. The rest faced the next five years in captivity.

Troops in the Shanghai Area[6]

- Headquarters, Shanghai Area 2nd Bn East Surrey Regiment
- 1st Bn Seaforth Highlanders (Ross-shire Buffs, The Duke of Albany's)
- Detachment, Royal Engineers Shanghai Signal Section, Royal Corps of Signals Detachment, Royal Army Service Corps Detachment, Royal Army Medical Corps Detachment, Royal Army Ordnance Corps, Detachment, Royal Army Pay Corps Shanghai Section, Corps of Military Police, Shanghai Volunteer Corps.

Chapter 8

The Seaforth Highlanders on The North West Frontier

The North West Frontier Province before 1930–31

The Pathans were the largest ethnic group along the frontier. Divided into several tribes, there was much internecine warfare in the region. The largest tribes, the Afridi or Waziris, were further divided into different clans. All were Muslim and had inviolable codes of honour and hospitality. Given that their homelands were inhospitable and barren, the tribes often supplemented their meagre existences by raiding the more prosperous settled areas to the east. Some tribes also controlled important mountain passes and either levied a toll on the trading caravans that travelled to and from Afghanistan or looted them when they refused to pay.

The National Army Museum website tells us 'Many Pathan tribes, such as the Afridis, Orakzais, Mahsuds and Waziris, fiercely resisted British-Indian forays into their territories. Highly mobile, tactically astute and sharp shooters, they were perfectly adapted to their environment. Only experienced and well-trained British and Indian units could match them in frontier fighting'.[1]

In fact, so impressed were the British by the fighting qualities of the various Pathan tribes that they went to great lengths to enlist them into the Indian Army and their various frontier militias.

The Punjab Frontier Force[2]

The National Army Museum goes on to tell us how 'The Punjab Frontier Force (PFF) was formed in 1851 as the Punjab Irregular Force to police and protect the newly acquired frontier. It was called "Irregular" because it was outside the control of the East India Company's army, reporting instead to the Chief Commissioner of the Punjab'.

In later years, PFF regiments were fully integrated into the Indian Army. But their early independence allowed them to reject formal drill and tactics in favour of developing swift-moving soldiers who could live and fight in rough country.

Khaki

The PFF included elite units such as the Queen's Own Corps of Guides raised in 1846, a unique combination of infantry companies and cavalry squadrons.

The Guides were the first unit to adopt khaki uniform: contemporary uniforms were patently impractical, both for ease of movement and camouflage. The Guides' founder, Brigadier General Sir Harry Lumsden, obtained cotton fabric which was dyed with river mud. The result was a loose-fitting uniform which, due to the yellowish dust-colour of the fabric, provided effective camouflage on the frontier.

The etymology is Hindi and Urdu: *khākī* dust-coloured, from *khāk* dust, from Persian; first known use is 1857. However, it is argued that the origin of the word is Irish Gaelic (*cac*) which means 'shit'. Irishmen were responsible for naming the 'colour'. Gaelic has its roots in the Indian sub-continent.

Khasadars

From the late 1890s the British also appointed *khasadars*, who were responsible for maintaining law and order in the tribal areas; they had the power to arrest, call for tribal *jirgas* (councils) or dispense summary justice, if offenders resisted. From 1915 the khasadars and militias were reinforced by the Frontier Constabulary, which guarded the border between the tribal and settled areas.

According to Major George Roos-Keppel[3]

> Every man, woman and child in the clan [the Zakka Khel Afridis] looks upon those who commit murders, raids and robberies in Peshawar or Kohat as heroes and champions. They are the crusaders of the nation. They depart with the good wishes and prayers of all, and are received on their return from a successful raid with universal rejoicings.

The North West Frontier Province was annexed by the East India Company after the Second Sikh War (1848–49). From then on the territories formed a part of Punjab until the province, then known as North West Frontier Province, was created in 1901 from the north-western districts of Punjab Province. The North West Frontier was also divided into a so-called 'settled area' that came under direct British rule and a largely autonomous 'tribal area' directly adjacent to the Afghan border. This latter zone was free from the trappings of colonial rule, such as courts, police and taxation. This region acted as a buffer zone with Afghanistan.

The Jallianwala Bagh (Amritsar) massacre 1919

Also known as the Amritsar massacre, this took place on 13 April 1919. A large peaceful crowd had gathered at the Jallianwala Bagh in Amritsar, Punjab, to protest against the Rowlatt Act and arrest of pro-independence activists Saifuddin Kitchlew and Satyapal.[4]

Acting Brigadier General R.E.H. Dyer misjudged the situation totally and surrounded the protesters with his Gurkha, Baloch, Rajput and Sikh troops from 2nd/9th Gurkhas, 54th Sikhs and 59th Scinde Rifles of the Indian Army. The Jallianwala Bagh had an exit on one side only, as the other three sides were enclosed by ten-foot-high walls and buildings. After blocking this exit with his troops, Dyer ordered them to shoot at the crowd, continuing to fire even as the protestors fled. The troops kept on firing until their ammunition was exhausted. Estimates of those killed range between 379 and 1,500-plus people while over 1,200 others were injured, 192 of them seriously.[5] Responses polarised both the British and Indian peoples and caused many moderate Indians to abandon their previous loyalty to the British and become nationalists, distrustful of British rule. This incident shocked Rabindranath Tagore, an Indian polymath and the first Asian Nobel laureate, to such an extent that he renounced his knighthood.

Britain expressed 'deep regret' for the massacre in 2019.

The National Army Museum tells us that the British had two principal objectives in their pre-occupations with the North West Frontier:[6]

> A. to prevent incursions from the mountains into the settled, law-abiding lowland areas. By punishing recalcitrant tribes, they were able to maintain British prestige and ensure that the subjects of British India would continue to believe in the political will and military power of their rulers.
>
> B. to prevent a Russian invasion from the north-west. All through the nineteenth century, Russia expanded its territories through Central Asia, encroaching ever closer to India. This obviously preyed on the minds of British policymakers.

As time went by the 'Close Border' policy returned. From around 1900 the Indian government became unwilling to continue expending resources on what was a barren and largely unprofitable backwater. Relations with Russia also improved, so the invasion threat receded. In September 1897 a belligerent Lieutenant Winston Churchill epitomised the general view of the situation and how to deal with it: 'After today we begin to burn villages. Every one. And all who resist will be killed without quarter. The Mohmands need a lesson.'

The Third Anglo-Afghan War

The war began on 6 May 1919 when the Emirate of Afghanistan invaded British India and ended with an armistice on 8 August 1919. The Anglo-Afghan Treaty of 1919 resulted in the Afghans gaining control of foreign affairs from Britain and the British recognising the Durand Line as the border between Afghanistan and British India.[7]

Operations in Waziristan (1919–20)

This all started with an incursion by the Mahsud Tribe in the summer of 1917 while British forces were busy fighting in the First World War. The British eventually restored calm; however, in 1919, the Waziris took advantage of unrest in British India following the Third Anglo-Afghan War to launch more raids against British garrisons. One of the reasons fomenting these raids was a rumour spread amongst the Wazirs and the Mahsuds that Britain was about to give control of Waziristan to Afghanistan as part of the peace settlement following the Third Anglo-Afghan War.

> Over 10,000 troops from the Indian Army took part in the campaign to re-establish British control of the border areas and 1,300 men were killed in action or died from their wounds and sickness. Although there was much heavy fighting on the ground, the British bombing of Wazir and Mahsud villages eventually brought the conflict to an end in 1922.[8]

The National Army Museum further tells us how Waziristan was traditionally the most unruly region of the North West Frontier.[9] Inhabited by fiercely independent tribes, including the Mahsuds and the Waziris (or Darwesh Khel), these proud warriors had honed their fighting skills by years of raiding the settled areas to the east, along the Indus, and by attacking the trading caravans that travelled to and from Afghanistan.

The Waziris consisted of the Tochi (or Utmanzai) Waziris who lived along the Tochi and Khaisora valleys, and the Wana (or Ahmadzai) Waziris who lived around Bannu and Wana. In 1919 their fighting strength was estimated at over 20,000 tribesmen. Apart from the Mahsuds, with whom they were frequently at war, the Waziris were the most formidable foes faced by the British on the frontier.

Operations in Waziristan (1921–24)

This was all about road building, conducted from 21 December 1921 to 31 March 1924 by British and Indian forces in Waziristan as part of the new Forward Policy, the aim of which was to reduce and eventually eliminate tribal uprisings and raids into settled districts by stationing regular troops inside Waziristan, who would then be capable of swift reaction to Waziri rebellions. The rebel tribes attempted to harass the British troops but were unsuccessful in stopping the road construction efforts.

> The Mahsud or Wazir is an expert at attacking convoys or small detachments and is assisted by the nature of his country, the ravines being narrow and winding, while the hillsides ... are often thickly covered in bushes. He attacks systematically, with special parties being told off for specific duties, such as the neutralisation of adjacent picquets by fire, support to his advanced parties of swordsmen etc.
>
> Ambushes may sometimes open by a few shots from one side of a nullah. Untrained troops rush to cover on the side from which the fire comes. This is what is waited for. Heavy accurate fire from the other bank then finishes the party.[10]

Pink's War (1925)

Pink's War was an air-to-ground bombardment and strafing campaign carried out by the Royal Air Force, under the command of Wing Commander Richard Pink, against the mountain strongholds of Mahsud tribesmen in South Waziristan in March and April 1925. It was the first independent action by an RAF keen to further establish its military credentials, and remains the only campaign named after an RAF officer. Operations focused on causing disruption to day-to-day activities for the militant tribes, as well as preventing access to safe havens; sorties were flown at night as well as during the day to cause further disruption.

In 1925, the Khyber Pass Railway was opened, running from Jamrud, near Peshawar, to the Afghan border near Landi Kotal, facilitating movement of troops to the frontier districts.

The Afridi 'Redshirt' Rebellion 1930–1931

This was a military campaign fought by the British and Indian armies against the troublesome Afridi tribesmen, 'Ajab Khan Afridi' in 1930–31.

The Afridi are a Karlani Pashtun tribe who inhabit the border area of Pakistan, notably in the Spin Ghar mountain range to the west of Peshawar and the Maidan Valley in Tirah.

The Afridis had often clashed with the British and Indian Armies during India's expansion towards the Afghan border, notably during the Anglo-Afghan Wars.[11]

Brandon Marsh tells us:

> In the spring of 1930, after years of ignoring the growing nationalist movement in the North West Frontier Province (NWFP), the local

> British administration was suddenly confronted with a fullscale rebellion throughout the province. Beginning with a nationalist demonstration and subsequent shooting of Indian civilians by British troops in Peshawar on 23 April, unrest quickly spread throughout the province. Within days the British had evacuated Peshawar city and much of the NWFP was essentially beyond their control. At the beginning of June, the British position was further weakened by an onslaught of Afridi lashkars who descended upon the Vale of Peshawar to fight the Government's forces. Taken by surprise, the British, both in Peshawar and in Delhi, struggled to understand the nature of this opposition and how to beat what was now a major challenge to their rule on the Frontier and in India as a whole.[12]

In the summer of 1930 a rebellion by dissident Afridi tribesmen, known as 'Ajab Khan Afridi' Redshirts, erupted. This threatened the security of Peshawar so two brigade groups were sent to occupy the Khajuri Plain, west of Peshawar and south of the Khyber Pass. Their role was to open up the area by building roads and strongpoints which would help prevent any future tribal infiltration towards Peshawar as well as being a punitive measure, since the Afridis had been accustomed to pasture their flocks on this low ground during the winter months.[13]

On 17 October 1930 the British-led force crossed into the Tirah Valley at Bara, six miles from Peshawar, and advanced a further seven miles to Miri Khel. There a fortified camp was constructed from which operations against the Afridis were conducted. Three months later, on 16 January 1931, the force was withdrawn, having accomplished its objective.

British and Indian Army personnel who took part in the campaign received the India General Service Medal with the clasp 'North West Frontier 1930–31'.

Akbar S. Ahmed's important 1979 article, 'Colonial Encounter on the North-West Frontier Province: Myth and Mystification' reminds us of the dangers of succumbing to the 'romanticisation' and mythologising which embellish some historical accounts of military action, sometimes bordering on propaganda. This is especially true in some of the literature on the North West Frontier. Ahmed says in his abstract to the article:

> The story of colonisation is not a pretty one. To the Pathans living in the North West Frontier Province of Pakistan it meant the destruction of villages, of water-tanks and of grain-stores; it meant electric-fences, blockhouses and an endless series of 'butcher and bolt' raids. The situation was worst in the Tribal Areas: in 1947, when the British left, there were no hospitals, schools, colleges, railways or electricity supplies except, of course, those established within British cantonments and for the exclusive use

> of the British. The institutions the British left behind were instruments of repression and subversion: the Frontier Scouts and Constabulary, blockhouses and barbed wire, political allowances and titles. Today the only remnants of the British cultural legacy are the adjuncts of war: the bagpipes played by the Frontier Constabulary and the shorts still worn as its uniform.

The unspeakable treatment of prisoners of war

According to the British officer John Masters, who was stationed in British India from age eighteen in 1933, Pashtun women in the North West Frontier Province of British India during the Anglo-Afghan Wars would brutally gang-rape non-Muslim soldiers who were captured, especially British and Sikhs.[14] Hiskey adds that 'if they [Pathans] captured any soldiers other than Muslims, and especially if the soldiers were Sikhs or British, they would usually castrate and behead them … frequently done by women. Sometimes they would torture prisoners with the death of a thousand cuts, pushing grass and thorns into each wound as it was made.' Masters says Pashtun women urinated into prisoners' mouths: captured British soldiers were spread out and fastened with restraints to the ground, then a stick, or a piece of wood was used to keep their mouth open to prevent swallowing. Pashtun women then squatted and urinated directly into the mouth of the man until he drowned in the urine, taking turns one at a time. This method of execution was reported to have been practised specifically by the women of the Afridi tribe of the Pashtuns. Hiskey elaborates:

> This kind of cruelty was not confined to war, but was as much a part of the Pathans' normal lives as was their sturdy independence … . If a man suspected his wife of the most minor infidelity, he would cut her nose off … . The Pathans punished an adulterer by forcing a thick and knobbly thorn twig down his penis. They rewarded infringements of lesser laws by tearing a man's tongue out by the roots.

Adding, with no references, it should be pointed out:

> It is still customary among some tribes in Assam (north-eastern region in India) … to punish an unfaithful woman by tying her to a post with her legs apart over a quick-growing kind of bamboo, and leaving her there until the bamboo grows up into her womb and stomach and she dies.

Interestingly, Ahmed would seem to repudiate the military aspects when he asserts:[15]

> Above all, the Frontier represented a male world, and its masculine symbols a system that translated easily into classic British public school life. Women, on both sides, were generally out of sight and, when encountered, honoured. No stories of rapes, abductions or mistresses are told on either side. In any case almost the entire Tribal Area was strictly a 'no families' area for officials. In perhaps the most famous and unique affair of its kind Miss Ellis was kidnapped in 1923 from Kohat by an Afridi, AjabKhan, as revenge for a British raid on his village and what he considered the violation of the Code by exposing his women to the presence of British troops. All accounts of Miss Ellis' treatment corroborate her own statements that her honour was never violated; she found respect and protection at the house of Akhundzada Mahmud among the Orakzai … .

In 1947, following the independence, the North West Frontier region became a part of the newly-formed Dominion of Pakistan. Based upon the recommendations of the Tucker Committee in 1944 the Pakistani government decided to move away from the previous British policy of 'forward defence' in the North West Frontier region and ordered the withdrawal of forces from Waziristan, as it was felt that the presence of a regular military force in the region was provoking tensions with the local tribesmen. This withdrawal began on 6 December 1947 and was completed by the end of the month under the codename Operation CURZON.

After the end of the First World War the regiment was briefly at Fort George and then on to India as the foreign service battalion, arriving in Meerut in November 1919. From Meerut 2nd Seaforth were posted for one year to the North West Frontier at Landi Kotal.[16] Afterwards, they moved to Umbala by train in November 1922. There was then much marching: from Umbala they embarked on a two-month, 500-mile trek back to the Frontier covering an average of twenty-three miles per day accompanied by the Pipes and Drums and the Military Band taking turns. After a year they moved to Nowshera and then, in 1927, were on the road again, marching the 270 miles to Lahore and then Jhansi in 1929, moving to the North West Frontier again in August 1930 to confront the Afridi tribesmen from a base at Miri Khel west of Peshawar. There they helped build roads and strongpoints to deter Afridi infiltration while at the same engaging the tribesmen.

The 2nd Battalion's tour then took it to Palestine, at Haifa. The role was to keep the peace in the face of rising Arab resentment toward increasing Jewish immigration. As we have seen, the 1st Battalion was in Palestine at the same time – in Jerusalem, a rare meeting to say the least.

Chapter 9

Palestine and After

Muddled and inept are two words which spring to mind when examining Britain's policy towards Ottoman-held Palestine in 1917 and explain why Palestine was a posting in the mid-1930s. In order to win Jewish support for Britain's First World War effort, the Balfour Declaration promised to establish a 'Jewish national home' in Palestine.

At the same time, with not a little duplicity, the British had also promised Arab nationalists that a united Arab country, covering most of the Arab Middle East, would be theirs if the Ottoman Turks were defeated.

When the war ended in 1918 with the Ottoman Empire soundly defeated, the Jewish people did not get their promised land, nor the Arabs their Arab Middle East. To put it bluntly, neither promise was delivered. Two years later in 1920, Britain assumed responsibility for Palestine under a League of Nations' Mandate. For the next twenty years, over 100,000 Jews entered and settled in the country, much to the disappointment and chagrin of the native Arabs who, with some justification, felt betrayed and humiliated, and still do to this day.

According to Meser and Metzer,

> The Zionist immigration caused a major demographic shift and naturally alarmed the Arabs. In the 1922 census the population of Palestine was 763,550 of which 89 per cent were Arabs and 11 per cent Jews. By the end of 1947 the Jewish proportion of the population had risen to 31 per cent.[1]

It is no surprise that the British, having alienated both parties in equal measure, found themselves in Palestine struggling against militant Arab groups who were opposed to this mass Jewish immigration. British tactics included curfews and searches while guards were mounted at sensitive locations. Violence reached a peak with the Arab Revolt of 1936–39.

The Arab Revolt 1936–1939

The Arab Revolt, or the Great Palestinian Revolt, is regarded as one of the formative events of Palestinian nationalism. Inflamed by resentment with

British rule and with the Zionist influx into Palestine, the revolt started off as a general strike (*intifada*) but soon erupted into a full-scale insurrection. The British responded with characteristic brutality, reinforcing its military force in Palestine to over 100,000 troops. Imprisonment without charge or trial, harsh curfews, whip lashings, house demolitions and collective punishment against villages and families were just some of the methods employed to suppress the revolt. An estimated 10 per cent of the adult Palestinian male population were killed, wounded, deported, or imprisoned.[2]

In 1933, with the accession of Hitler to power in Germany, the Haavara agreement between the Zionist Federation and the Third Reich facilitated the emigration of German Jews and so Jewish immigration increased significantly during the mid-1930s. In 1935, 62,000 Jews entered Palestine, the highest number since the mandate began in 1920.

At the end of the Second World War, Britain compounded its incompetence when 250,000 Jewish refugees found themselves stranded in displaced persons camps all over Europe. Despite the pressure of world opinion, especially the repeated requests of US President Harry Truman, the British refused to lift the ban on immigration and admit 100,000 Jews to Palestine.

Once again, Britain found itself a superb accidental recruiting sergeant, clumsily bonding disputatious and disaffected groups in opposition to them. The Jewish underground forces came together: the Haganah had held off attacking the British as long as they were fighting Nazi Germany. Now, their fighters allied themselves with Irgun and launched raids against the British.

Unsurprisingly, British soldiers were often targets for attack and kidnap, usually in retaliation for death sentences passed on members of Irgun and Fighters for the Freedom of Israel (LHI). A typical insurgent atrocity was the bombing of the British Officers' Club in Haifa, in which thirty people were killed and injured.

The National Army Museum[3] fills in the detail:

> The main terrorist groups were Irgun Zvai Leumi (National Military Organisation) – ultimately led by future Israeli Prime Minister Menachem Begin – and an even more militant organisation, Lohamey Heruth Israel (Fighters for the Freedom of Israel) or LHI.
>
> The British called LHI the Stern Gang after its leader, Abraham Stern, who was killed in a clash with the Palestine Police in 1942. In November 1944, LHI assassinated the British Minister for the Middle East, Lord Moyne.

On 22 July 1946, Irgun fighters blew up a wing of the King David Hotel in Jerusalem, killing over ninety people, including many civilians. This attack shattered the fragile Haganah/Irgun partnership.

When 3rd Division arrived in Palestine in 1947, the number of British troops deployed there had risen to about 100,000, the majority of them National Servicemen.

In November 1947 the United Nations recommended the partition of Palestine and the establishment of separate Arab and Jewish states. Easier said than done, as news items constantly and, at times, horrifically remind us from 1947 up to January 2025 as this book was being written.

On 15 May 1948, Britain renounced its mandate. The Army departed from Palestine, leaving Jews and Arabs to fight it out amongst themselves in the war that followed. The campaign had cost around 750 British military and police lives.

In 1934 the 2nd Battalion was at Dover Castle, yet again taking over from the 1st Battalion. In September 1937 they went north from Dover to Maryhill Barracks in Glasgow, which is where they were at the outbreak of the Second World War.

Hong Kong 1937

In 1937 the 1st Battalion was in Hong Kong as part of the Hong Kong Infantry Brigade, along with 2nd Royal Welch Fusiliers, 1st Royal Ulster Rifles, 1st Kumoan Rifles and 19th Hyderabad Regiment.

In December 1939 British troops withdrew from Tientsin: 1st Durham Light Infantry moved to Egypt. August 1940 saw British troops withdrawn from Shanghai with 2nd East Surrey Regiment moving to Malaya and 1st Seaforth Highlanders going to Hong Kong, then on to Malaya and, finally, India.

Chapter 10

The 2nd Seaforth Highlanders in the Second World War – The Battle of France

In 1940 the Battalion was an element of the British Expeditionary Force (BEF) and of the reconstituted 152 Brigade of 51st (Highland) Division which found itself attached to the French Tenth Army. After a valiant fighting retreat from the Somme, most of the division was cut off at the coastal town of St Valéry-en-Caux with no option but to surrender. Major General Victor Fortune had taken over command of 51st (Highland) Division in 1937.[1]

The Treaty of Versailles

The Treaty of Versailles, signed on 28 June 1919, ended the state of war existing between Germany and most of the Entente powers. It was signed precisely five years after the assassination of Archduke Franz Ferdinand, which precipitated the war. Germany was excluded from the negotiations but was forced to sign the draft.

The treaty had wide-ranging ramifications for the course of European history for the next twenty years until the outbreak of the Second World War. Significantly, it had a bearing on the re-armament programmes of Britain and Germany. The most critical and controversial provision, however, was:

> The Allied and Associated Governments affirm and Germany accepts the responsibility of Germany and her allies for causing all the loss and damage to which the Allied and Associated Governments and their nationals have been subjected as a consequence of the war imposed upon them by the aggression of Germany and her allies.

This, Article 231, is known as the War Guilt clause and:

- required Germany to disarm
- make territorial concessions: the armistice had demanded an immediate evacuation of German troops from occupied Belgium, France, and Luxembourg within fifteen days. In addition, it established that Allied

forces would occupy the Rhineland. In late 1918 Allied troops entered Germany and began the occupation.
- pay reparations to certain countries. In 1921 the total cost of the reparations was assessed at 132 billion gold marks, then £6.6 billion, roughly equivalent to UK£284 billion in 2023. Because of the way the deal was structured, the Entente powers intended that Germany would only ever pay 50 billion marks. For example, Germany could pay in cash or kind: coal, timber, chemical dyes, pharmaceuticals, livestock, agricultural machines, construction materials and factory machinery were all acceptable. Germany's assistance with the restoration of the university library of Leuven/Louvain, which was destroyed by the Germans on 25 August 1914, was also credited towards the sum. Territorial changes imposed by the treaty were also factored in.

Some economists, for example John Maynard Keynes, considered the treaty too harsh – a 'Carthaginian peace' no less (*Carthago delenda est*) – with the reparations excessive and counter-productive. On the other hand, Marshal Ferdinand Foch criticised the treaty for letting Germany off too lightly. The result was that no one was satisfied while Germany was neither pacified nor conciliated, nor was it irreparably weakened.

The British Army of the Rhine (BAOR)[2]

The BAOR we know from the aftermath of the Second World War was the second such formation. The first was established in March 1919 to facilitate British occupation of the Rhineland under the terms of the November 1918 armistice. The British were joined by occupying armies of the United States of America, Belgium and France. The British Army initially comprised five corps, each of two divisions, plus a cavalry division. Entering Germany on 3 December 1918, it was established as the occupying force in March 1919 with headquarters at Cologne. The *Cologne Post* was its publication from 31 March 1919 to 17 January 1926.

By August 1920 BAOR comprised approximately 13,360 troops, including staff, cavalry, Royal Artillery, Royal Engineers, Infantry, Machine Gun Corps, tanks and the usual ancillary services. The troops were located mainly around Cologne at an approximate cost of £300,000 per month.

When asked in the House of Commons for the total cost for the British Army of Occupation on the Rhine during the twelve months ending 30 June 1923 and the amount of reparations received by the UK during the same period, the reply from Sir W. Joynson-Hicks was as follows:

> The total cost of the British Army of Occupation on the Rhine during the twelve months ended 30 June 1923 was £1,740,000 (exclusive of accommodation and miscellaneous services provided free by Germany). Of this amount, £350,645 was covered by paper Marks supplied by the German Government to meet local expenditure, so that the net cost was about £1,380,000. The amount received by the Treasury on account of cost of occupation and reparation during the same period, apart from the paper Mark receipts referred to above, was £8,287,000.[3]

The British Army left Germany in 1929 and BAOR was disbanded, only to be revived fifteen years later in the hectic and chaotic aftermath of the Second World War. The British Army of the Rhine we associate with the Cold War, as stationed in the British sector of West Germany, had its origins in 1943 with the creation of 21 Army Group which was tasked with the invasion of Europe, Operation OVERLORD, in 1944.

The Ten Year Rule and Caligula's horse

Cabinet papers held at the National Archives give some context relating to defence policy in Britain immediately after the First World War. They tell us that, at the end of the war, Britain had the largest navy in the world, a brand new fledgling Royal Air Force (RAF, the world's first independent air force) and 'an army that had enormously extended its technical, tactical and operational aptitude in warfare'. Sir Eric Geddes was appointed to chair the Committee on National Expenditure which examined all government departments' spending, but the closest scrutiny was, of course, given to the biggest spenders at the time, the armed forces.

Expenditure cuts were the order of the day if Britain was to return to economic levels consistent with those prevailing pre-war, and it was considered very unlikely that the country would be embroiled in another war within the next ten years. So, the Ten Year Rule was born, to ensure that the armed forces would be ready in ten years' time. As we were soon to learn, it had the opposite effect.

General Fortune faced the same intractable problems as all high-ranking British officers in the 1920s and 1930s: after the war military training languished in the doldrums, if it existed at all, and equipment was utterly insufficient and antiquated. Post-eventum revulsion at the carnage and cost, economic and human, of four years of war led to this Ten Year Rule being adopted in 1919, predicated on the myopic view of the future in which the armed forces should draft their estimates 'on the assumption that the British Empire would not be engaged in any great war during the next ten years'. Another global war would not, could not, be contemplated until 1929.

This was all instigated by Winston Churchill who, in 1919, was Secretary of State for War and Air. His boss, Prime Minister David Lloyd George, was intent on selling the Ten Year Rule, and in so doing alluded to recommendations made by the Duke of Wellington following the end of the Napoleonic Wars. However, he proved that we cannot, indeed should not, expect to learn everything from history:

> There is not likely to be great eagerness for war in this generation. I think we might take the lesson of the Napoleonic Wars. As soon as the Napoleonic Wars were over, the greatest soldier we produced in those wars – the Duke of Wellington – advised the Government. He said, 'You need fear no foe – at any rate for a generation. Europe has had enough fighting.' He might have said, 'Russia is stronger, Austria is stronger, Prussia is stronger, and, therefore, you must prepare for some other war.' He did not. He had a great Army, which had done glorious things, but he had the courage and the greatness to say, 'There is no peril that I can see except the financial peril, the social peril, the industrial peril; reduce; cut down.' Lord Castlereagh and all those who had charge of that great war fortunately took his advice, and there was no big war in Europe in which we were engaged until forty years later … .[4]

Opposition came in the shape of former Prime Minister Arthur Balfour and the Committee of Imperial Defence which adopted the rule that 'nobody could say that from any one moment war was an impossibility for the next ten years … we could not rest in a state of unpreparedness on such an assumption by anybody. To suggest that we could be nine and a half years away from preparedness would be a most dangerous suggestion'.

In 1928 Churchill, then Chancellor of the Exchequer, successfully urged the Cabinet to make the rule permanent, so that, according to the Cabinet Papers, each year 'the ten-year clock would be reset back to year one; the armed forces would never get any closer to the ten-year target, so therefore there was no need to spend money on modernising them. The Treasury was satisfied – but the armed forces were deeply worried'.[5]

The Ten Year Rule ushered in scything cuts in defence spending which sank from £766 million in 1919–20, to £189 million in 1921–22, to £102 million in 1932. In April 1931 the First Sea Lord, Sir Frederick Field, claimed in a report to the Committee of Imperial Defence that the Royal Navy had declined not only in relative strength compared to other Great Powers but, 'owing to the operation of the "ten-year-decision" and the clamant need for economy, our absolute strength also has ... been so diminished as to render the fleet incapable, in the event of war, of efficiently affording protection to our trade'.[6] We learn from Corelli Barnett that Field also claimed, even more alarmingly, that the navy was below the standard required for keeping open Britain's sea communications during wartime and that if the navy moved to the East to protect the Empire there would not be enough ships to protect the British Isles and its trade from attack and that no port in the entire British Empire was 'adequately defended'.[7]

The Ten Year Rule was finally abandoned by the Cabinet on 23 March 1932, but not without a caustic caveat: 'this must not be taken to justify an expanding expenditure by the Defence Services without regard to the very serious financial and economic situation' which the country was in due to the Great Depression.

War Office policy was defined as 'limited liability' whereby the thrust of the British response to war would be by sea and by air with only small land forces deployed and operating over the Channel. In December 1937 the Cabinet endorsed and adopted a policy put forward by Thomas Inskip, Minister for the newly-formed Co-ordination of Defence, which, alarmingly, prioritised strategic objectives as follows:

- Defence of the home country against air attack
- Protection of trade routes
- Defence of British territories overseas
- Helping in the defence of territories allied to Britain in a war

Clearly this was the policy of a country anxious to preserve its colonial credentials, to the obvious disadvantage of the mother country. Inskip had an exclusively legal curriculum vitae; his appointment attracted much heated controversy. Winston Churchill was one of the leading advocates of the new ministry, 'supporting' Inskip with not a little satire and irony by asserting that he 'had the advantage of being little known and knowing nothing about military subjects'.[8]

Most commentators had expected Churchill to be appointed. Another priceless reaction was that 'This is the most cynical appointment since Caligula made his horse a consul'.[9] John Gunther, who described Inskip in 1940 as 'the sixty-three-year-old man of mystery', reported the 'cruel story' that Prime Minister Stanley Baldwin was anxious to appoint someone 'even less brilliant than himself'.[10] Collin Brooks described Inskip unfavourably in his diary as 'a second-rate Attorney General'. Most people now view his appointment as a manifestation of caution by Baldwin who wanted to avoid appointing someone more bullish like Churchill. Why? Astonishingly, 'because it would have been interpreted by foreign powers as a sign of the United Kingdom preparing for war'.

Inskip's tenure as Minister for Co-ordination of Defence remains controversial. In early 1939 he was replaced by the former First Sea Lord Admiral of the Fleet Lord Chatfield and moved to become Secretary of State for Dominion Affairs.

Inskip was referred to in the 1940 book *Guilty Men* by Michael Foot, Frank Owen and Peter Howard (writing under the pseudonym 'Cato'), published as an attack on public figures for their failure to re-arm and their appeasement of Nazi Germany.[11]

In February 1939 it finally dawned on the Chiefs of Staff that the security of Britain could not be assured if France was invaded and occupied and they agreed that our defence 'may have to include a share in the land defence of French territory'. Referred to as a 'Field Force' at the time, it was a British Expeditionary Force in effect.

Nevertheless, in 1938 one of the outcomes of Chamberlain's famous visit to Munich had been the decision to double the size of the Territorial Army; alarm bells must have been ringing somewhere. By the spring of 1939 the Highland Division had done well out of the recruitment campaigns. This was in addition to modest increases in the Army budget from 1934 while a five-year re-armament programme was initiated in 1936, but spending was still tightly rationed until after Munich.

While this dithering and indecision may have purportedly been good for the short-term British economy, it left the military in a parlous situation with inadequate supplies, depleted materiel and amateurish training at best. All this while the probability of world war loomed ever closer.

The Germans, however, showed no such hesitancy; they rose to the prospect of what they perceived as a shot at European domination, at least. Re-armament was not the dirty word it had become in Britain. Far from it: Germany expanded its army from 100,000 in 1933 to an incredible two million-plus by the summer of 1939.

The list below gives the make-up of the division at the time of mobilisation: nine battalions divided into three brigades:

51ST (HIGHLAND) DIVISION
Major General V.M. Fortune
152 Brigade – Brigadier H.M.V. Stewart
2nd and 4th Battalions Seaforth Highlanders
4th Battalion Queen's Own Cameron Highlanders
153 Brigade – Brigadier G.T. Burney
4th Battalion Black Watch
1st and 5th Battalions Gordon Highlanders

154 Brigade – Brigadier A.C.L. Stanley-Clarke
1st Battalion Black Watch
7th and 8th Battalions Argyll and Sutherland Highlanders

Source: Ellis, Major L.F., *The War in France and Flanders 1939–40*, Appendix I, UK Military Series.

Certainly, the Highland regiments stood out; not for them the standard khaki but a flamboyant range of headgear comprising tam o'shanters, Atholl bonnets and glengarries. And then there were the kilts. In addition to the successful operation of the reinforcement system under Major General Douglas Neil Wimberley CB DSO MC, this glamour attracted many non-Highlanders to the ranks. However, by 1945 the regiments had fewer than 50 per cent Scots.

Basic training was usually compressed into six months, followed by further training. Of course, many men went to units with inadequate training in the early months of war. Some mortar units had to wait for live ammunition exercises until they got to the firing ranges in France. According to David, universal-carrier crews only took possession of their equipment and ammunition in summer 1939, necessitating dry runs only and leaving no opportunity for operational training and tactics. The first time some mortar platoons fired a live round was in France in 1940. Some 51st Division mortars were issued without firing pins while there were smoke bombs but no high-explosive shells.

As an example of the parlous state of British readiness, Saul David quotes the testimony of a young officer destined to fight with 51st Division:[12]

> I remember going on manoeuvres in 1938 in Suffolk. As soon as the date was announced, all the field officers bar one, and most of the senior captains, found that they were unavoidably unable to attend because of engagements elsewhere and all took their leave. I found myself as a very junior lieutenant commanding C Company consisting of myself, the company sergeant major, the company quartermaster sergeant, one other sergeant, four corporals and about ten jocks.

He then goes on to describe 'the ridiculous sight' of a silhouette standing in for a Bren gun which had yet to arrive and wooden rattles intended to replace the sound of machine-gun fire. He concludes with 'it's amazing to think that only 15 months before hostilities broke out, a Regular was in this state'.

Patently, little progress in weaponry and armaments had been made since 1918. For example, the following were still on issue, or not:

- .303 Short Lee-Enfield rifle with its long knife-edged bayonet. A bolt-action, magazine-fed repeating rifle that was the main firearm of the armies of the British Empire during the first half of the twentieth century, and, through a number of variations and improvements, was the British Army's standard rifle from its official adoption in 1895 until 1957.
- Mills bomb, designed by William Mills (No.36M Mk1 grenade. Fragmentation rifle, hand grenade). They were the first modern fragmentation grenades used by the British Army and saw extensive use in the First and Second World Wars. Mills was a hand-grenade designer from Sunderland who patented, developed and manufactured the 'Mills bomb' at the Mills Munitions Factory in Birmingham.
- Lewis machine gun. First World War era light machine gun, largely replaced with the lighter and better .303 Bren gun. In the disaster of the fall of France, where much of the Army's equipment was lost, stocks of Lewis guns in both .303 and .30–06 design were hurriedly produced, mainly for Home Guard, airfield defence and anti-aircraft use. 58,983 Lewis guns were taken from existing stores, repaired, refitted and issued during the course of the war. Total production of the Lewis gun during the Second World War by BSA was over 145,000 units.
- .303 Bren gun. The Bren was a Czech weapon adapted in the UK – Br, from Brno and En for Enfield. In the British and Commonwealth armies, the Bren was usually issued on a scale of one per rifle section. An infantry battalion also had a carrier platoon, equipped with Universal carriers, each of which carried a Bren gun.
- .303 Vickers medium machine gun
- No standard issue machine pistols or sub-machine guns in contrast to the German army
- .55 Boys anti-tank rifle, nicknamed the elephant gun.
- 25mm anti-tank gun introduced after 1940.

All the while those ominous storm clouds were gathering and war with Germany looked increasingly likely.

Mobilisation of 51st (Highland) Division and Strategy

The 51st (Highland) Division was mobilised on 24 August 1939 to join the BEF in France, travelling from Scotland to Aldershot, arriving by 16 September to receive last-minute equipment and training. Basic training for the infantry, as noted, had been condensed into around six months, included trench digging, camouflage, map reading and signals. Echoes of 1809 and India resonated when

Highland regiments were ordered to wear the standard issue uniform, the War Office having deemed kilts unsuitable for participation in modern mechanised warfare; the kilt was less than practical when riding in a universal carrier, on a motorcycle or in the back of a lorry. Mud was no friend to the soggy kilt wearer, causing endless sores as experienced regularly by their forefathers in the waterlogged trenches of the First World War.

However, it was believed that the kilt did not provide adequate protection to the lower limbs in the event of a gas attack. In a fascinating article by Askival of Strathearn (in relation to the Gordon Highlanders), we learn that one of the many advantages of the kilt was:

> When 'mustard gas' was first used, it was expected that the Highlander would suffer badly from the effects of burning on his bare legs. However, the gas generally attacked the parts of the body where the skin was tender and the Highlander's legs were as tough as his hands or face.
>
> Another common occurrence for burning was when men sat on the ground saturated with 'mustard gas'. The kilt offered protection by being much thicker than trousers, which meant that the gas did not penetrate so easily, and the kilt swinging in the air dispelled the gas more easily.

Gas or no gas, the men were compelled to hand in their kilts before embarking for France. Many were apparently glad to jettison them, but others steadfastly insisted on wearing them to the death, in a manner of speaking. Elements of 1st Camerons were still seen to be sporting kilts as they headed off for their PoW camps, and one was ceremoniously torched by the CO of 5th Gordon Highlanders.

Inadequate as training and equipment was, there was also a major, less obvious, underlying error in terms of general strategy and tactics. Such training was based squarely on the art of defence, which had characterised much of the fighting in the First World War.

In mid-January 1940 many thousands of men departed with 51st Division from Southampton to disembark at le Havre. Some went later, elements of 2nd Seaforth for example, in April. On 28 January the division came under command of I Corps of the BEF, under Lieutenant General Michael Barker whose command also included the 1st and 2nd Infantry Divisions, both Regular Army formations.

The winter of 1940 was cold, very cold. On disembarking, elements of the division moved to transit camps for a meal before entraining for the nearby muster area around Bolbec and Lillebonne, fifteen miles to the east. A short march from there took them to their makeshift billets thrown together in barns and sheds. If the testimony of Company Quartermaster Sergeant Gregor MacDonald with 4th Cameron Highlanders is anything to go by, then accommodation was bleak and grim. He and his comrades were looking forward to 'a nice dry hay shed or barn' to shelter from the driving snow. Instead, they found themselves in dilapidated sheds home to 'lean and hungry cattle' with no effort having been made to clean anything out. The welcome from a 'filthy, unshaven' farmer was just as unpromising. Negotiations in French produced 'a cart of evil-smelling hay'. The manure and mud swilling around the sheds seeped over 'the uppers of our army boots and we had permanently wet and frozen feet. Cattle returning for the night were tethered less than ten feet away 'so we were in constant danger of being spattered in our beds'.

February and March brought a major re-organisation for 51st Division: some of the division's Territorial units were replaced by Regular Army formations in order to strengthen inexperienced Territorial divisions. Mary Tome, in her classic work on the Maginot Line, tells how, on 22 April 1940, 51st Division was detached from the rest of the BEF to come under command of the French Third Army . It was then stationed seven miles to the front (*la ligne de contact)* of the *Ouvrage* Hackenberg fortress of the Maginot Line. Although some believe that Churchill alone sacrificed the 51st to allow the rest of the BEF to evacuate, the fact is that three weeks before Churchill ever entered 10 Downing Street; the division's fate was sealed by the command to move a reinforced divisional group. Before this a British brigade had been detached to the Maginot Line but Gort felt that this could be extended to a division-plus, thus enabling more British troops to obtain battle experience. This was to reinforce the French divisions much further to the east from where the bulk of the BEF was stationed. The 51st was then placed under the command of the French Third Army as it prepared to face off Hitler's Panzers.

There was much soldierly work to be done in the wait for the German attack to begin: digging trenches, establishing command posts, building OPs, laying telephone lines, camouflaging, recce patrols, skirmishing. But, according to David Mowatt of the 4th Battalion Seaforth Highlanders, sniping and shooting generally was *verboten*. 'We didn't have a clue really,' he says.

The inadequate preparation for war and the parlous supply situation soon manifested itself to the troops: indeed, Lieutenant Colonel The Lord Rowallan, commanding 6th Royal Scots Fusiliers, was so concerned that he contacted General Fortune to ask that his men not be involved in any conflict since, as Sean Longden writes in his *Dunkirk: The Men They Left Behind*, they were 'underequipped, undertrained and unready to face the enemy'. When the men of the Royal Northumberland Fusiliers were making ready their Vickers heavy machine guns they noticed 'For drill purposes only' stamped on them.[13]

Discipline was deteriorating with convoys speeding through towns and villages and tail-gating, hair growing uncut and uniforms being discarded. General Fortune had to intervene.

The Maginot Line

The Maginot Line (*Ligne Maginot*) is named after the French Minister of War at the time, André Maginot (1877–1932) who worked tirelessly to secure the funding that would build the line of fortifications that stretched along the Franco-German border in the 1930s to deter invasion by Germany and force them to circumvent the fortifications.[14] The Germans, however, simply invaded through the Low Countries in 1940, by-passing the line to the north. The line, which was initially supposed to be fully extended further towards the west to avoid such an occurrence, was scaled back after demands from Belgium which feared the line would make it the battleground in another German invasion.

The objectives of the Maginot Line included:

- To prevent a German 'blitzkrieg' attack.[15]
- To protect Alsace and Lorraine (returned to France in 1918) and their industry.
- To delay any German attack to permit the mobilisation of the French Army which required between two and three weeks.
- To force Germany to circumvent via Switzerland or Belgium and allow France to fight any war off French soil and avoid a repeat of 1914–1918.
- To be used as a platform for a counter-offensive.

Mary Tome tells us that *Ouvrage* Hackenberg, one of the biggest ouvrages of the Maginot Line fortifications, facing Germany[16] occupied the wooded Hackenberg ridge. Before the war it was a showpiece of French fortification technology. The *gros ouvrage* comprises seventeen combat blocks and eighteen artillery pieces, with just over six miles of galleries. The galleries are between 82 and 98 feet below the surface to protect against bombardment. The main gallery extends 6,181 feet.

In 1940 Hackenberg was never directly attacked; instead, it provided covering fire to neighbouring positions and shelled nearby German forces. Its garrison was one of the last French units to surrender after the June 1940 armistice. After the war it became part of a strongpoint intended to delay any advance by Soviet forces into north-eastern France. Hackenberg is now a museum.

Around 7 April 19-year-old Second Lieutenant John Parnell of 7th Argylls was out on patrol.[17] He and his colleagues had been instructed that patrols were defensive'. Saul David[18] records how Parnell and his comrades were not equipped with 'sub-machine guns like the fighting patrols' and that they didn't 'black their faces or anything sophisticated like that ... we weren't exactly experienced soldiers at this stage'. A patrol seems to have comprised one officer and twelve men. Parnell's bible would have been *Instructions on Patrolling*.

German forces invaded France and the Low Countries on 10 May 1940. In response, the BEF advanced into Belgium to confront them. Stationed as they were at the Maginot Line some 200 miles distant from the English Channel and almost 100 miles from Dunkirk, 51st Division was obviously not involved in operations in Belgium and was thus not subsequently implicated in the famous Dunkirk evacuation and the mythology and propaganda spin which often goes with it.[19] In any event the evacuation from Dunkirk did not end the British Army's role in the Battle for France. What sealed the fate of the Highlanders was the distance between Saarforce and the coast, and Churchill's promise to the French Government that the remaining BEF forces would fight on in France, so anxious was he to keep the French in the war so that Britain did not stand alone against the mighty German war machine.

Dunkirk: the myth and the mess

'The truth of that last day will never be published.'[20]

> Major R.L. Barclay, RASC, 44th Division, in a letter of June 1940 to his wife.

For the new prime minister, Winston Churchill, and his War Cabinet the evacuation was a marvellous political gift and an unmissable opportunity: they could manipulate and repurpose the crushing defeat and humiliating failure of Dunkirk to make it look like a glorious British victory 'snatched from the jaws of defeat' as the cliché goes. After all, the boys were back home, 300,000 of them, and would constitute the British response to Germany's *blitzkrieg* in Churchill's forthcoming Battle of Britain, now that the Battle of France, as far as the War Office mandarins were concerned, was apparently done and dusted. At the very least they would defend Britain against German invasion and annexation, on the beaches, in the fields and so on.

Longden is particularly vocal about this especially British example of smoke and mirrors; how the propaganda people were able to transmogrify the awful truth:[21]

> The public had not yet learnt how the army had been unceremoniously defeated. They did not hear of the failure of BEF officers at all levels. Nor did they read the details of drunken soldiers who refused calls to leave the cellars of Dunkirk and proceed for embarkation. In the mythology there was no room for tales of the failure of a badly trained army, nor for men scrambling to board boats being shot or forced away at gunpoint. Nor was the full story revealed of how the figures for the miraculous Dunkirk evacuation only talked of men who escaped via one port. Forgotten were more than 100,000 men whose escape to the UK came via a host of other coastal towns, from Normandy to the Bay of Biscay.

Longden goes on to cite two books which began the gradual, and no doubt painful for many, writing of the real history of those inglorious days in June 1940. We have the 'chaos, indiscipline and terror' in Richard Collier's 1961 *The Sands of Dunkirk* and Walter Lord's *The Miracle of Dunkirk* and *Dunkirk – The Necessary Myth* by Nicholas Harman to help balance the jingoism and propaganda.[22]

And then there was the abandoned or destroyed materiel, enough, of course to provision a whole army no less:

- 2,472 guns of various sorts
- 75,000 tons of ammunition
- 65,000 or so vehicles
- 20,000 motorcycles
- 416,000 tons of stores
- 162,000 tons of petrol

Add to this the awful fact that 68,111 men of the BEF did not return from France; if this was a victory of sorts for Churchill, then it certainly whiffed of the Pyrrhic variety.[23] Some 40,000 men were taken prisoner, the vast majority of whom would remain so for the next five years, enduring relentless hard labour, a wide range of diseases and injuries, the occasional summary murder or execution, brutal treatment at times, malnutrition, 'stalag mentality' and other psychological disorders, including suicide.

We are reminded that for those left behind, Churchill's 'Battle of France' continued at a furious pace for several more weeks with a second BEF, commanded by Lieutenant General Sir Alan Brooke, landing in France to support French forces in a Brittany Redoubt. However, the decision by the French government to surrender meant that BEF 2 had to be withdrawn. Although 52nd (Lowland) Division and 1st Canadian Division disembarked at Cherbourg on 12 June, they saw no action.

Indeed, as the main force of the BEF embarked in their 'little ships' at Dunkirk in late May 1940, the Highland Division received orders to withdraw west by train and lorry to the defensive line which the French had formed hastily along the River Somme in Picardy, with much of the fighting centred on Abbeville. France, however, was more or less about to give up:

> more widespread evacuations of BEF 2 commenced (OPERATIONS CYCLE and ARIEL), not least in Brittany, but also in the Mediterranean. In total, over 200,000 troops were evacuated from France in the month after Dunkirk, in actions that included the terrible loss of the RMS *Lancastria* to a dive bomber off St Nazaire, the largest loss of British and Commonwealth life in a single engagement during the entire war and the largest ever British maritime loss of life at sea in a single incident.

Until then, 51st (Highland) Division had only endured sporadic attacks in the early days of the German invasion but, on 20 May, it was ordered to withdraw from the *ligne de contact* and join the French reserve. The 7th Argyll and Sutherland Highlanders lost two men with six wounded as they retreated to the *ligne de recueil*; the French 33rd Infantry finally relieved 2nd Seaforth on 23 May. With Operation DYNAMO wound up on 4 June, the Germans swivelled their prodigious firepower on to the French Army and the Highland Division on the Somme.

Two days previously, as the German advance towards the coast continued relentlessly, ad hoc arrangements were hurriedly made to organise opposition south of the Somme. This motley force comprised units from depots and reinforcements in the area; they were consolidated into a formation called Beauman Division. The division was created from lines of communication (LoC) personnel, built on Beauforce, a brigade-size formation under Brigadier Archie Beauman, who commanded one of the districts in the rear area.

As the Germans advanced, the division was drawn back to form a defensive line along the river Somme. According to Mary Tome, with the withdrawal of Allied forces at Dunkirk, the Germans turned their attention to the south.[24]

The British forces in France were now in two groups, with 1st Armoured Division and 51st Division, as noted, attached to the French Tenth Army; they and Beauman Division and other Lines of Communication troops were under command of Lieutenant General Sir Henry Karslake. The total number of British troops in France after the evacuation from Dunkirk was in the region of 140,000.

But, on 30 May, intelligence reports brought the bad news that about 1,000 German troops were massing in St Valéry-sur-Somme. An attack by 152 and

153 Brigades was a costly failure: the former lost 600 men, most of whom were from 4th Seaforth and 4th Cameron Highlanders. This was the first action of the war for the Seaforth Highlanders. Jim Reed tells how, on the eve of the battle, his sergeant gave him the stomach-churning news that they would be advancing with bayonets fixed:

> Then we got some really heavy stuff coming down on us, but having thrown our picks and shovels away we had to try and dig in using our bayonets. The shelling lasted about two hours. We lost about half a dozen men killed from our platoon and quite a few were injured ... I found one of my friends who had his throat torn out. But you soon forget it.

Around this time Gordon Barber, Royal Horse Artillery, was fiddling about with a radio at St Valéry and remembers picking up the BBC: 'This is the BBC' – you know, the old toffee-nosed way of talking – The BEF have been successfully evacuated from Dunkirk. I thought what a load of bollocks'.

On 3 June the Highlanders were deployed as follows:[25]

154 Brigade (who played no active role): holding from the sea to Saigneville, 8th Argylls to the left, 7th Argylls to the right.

- 1st Black Watch: near Miarmay, getting ready to support 1st Gordons.
- 153 Brigade: in control of the Gouy-Miannay valley with 1st Gordons at Cahon; 5th Gordons holding Behen and Moyenneville from where the main French infantry attack was due to begin.
- 4th Black Watch: in Divisional Reserve at le Plouy.
- 152 Brigade: 4th Seaforth was to the right of 5th Gordons in Bainast and Zailleux with 2nd Seaforth just ahead at Bienfay.
- 4th Camerons: just across the Blangy-Abbeville Route Nationale around Huchenneville and Villeurs-sur-Mareuil.
- 1st Lothians: still holding the bluffs of the Somme from Bray to Pont-Remy.

Spread between the three brigades, batteries of the five artillery regiments were taking up positions along with two machine-gun battalions and the pioneers of 7th Royal Norfolks; the other pioneers, 6th Royal Scots Fusiliers, were holding the river Bresle with divisional Royal Engineers.

On 5 June 1940 the German forces along the Somme front stepped up a gear and went on the offensive, launching a series of co-ordinated attacks along the line. The Highland Division and the French 31st Division were given the unenviable task of holding a line near St Valéry-sur-Somme four times longer than that which would normally be expected of a division. The Germans made their breakthrough between Abbeville and Amiens, causing 51st Division to retire behind the Bresle on 6 June. After Abbeville, they tried to repel the Germans at Huchenneville but sustained heavy casualties. By 6 June the division was down to half its fighting strength, with the Argylls having taken the worst casualties in a single day in that regiment's long and illustrious history. The other battalions of 154 Brigade were over-run; what was left was forced to retire to the west. The brigade at that point comprised the following:

- 6th Black Watch (Royal Highland Regiment)
- 7th Argyll and Sutherland Highlanders
- 8th Argyll and Sutherland Highlanders

The Highland Division was strengthened by the addition of A Brigade of Beauman Division, although all three battalions were understrength. As soon as they arrived, they deployed in the front line on the left of the division's positions to allow 152 Infantry Brigade to rest and refit.[26]

The website continues:

> The situation was deteriorating significantly as the 5 Panzer and 7 Panzer Divisions commanded by …Major General Erwin Rommel, were now outflanking the Bresle River line. At dawn on the 8 June, German troops reached Rouen, effectively trapping the 51 Division and French IX Corps in a pocket based around le Havre. They entered the city the next day with opposition leaving the front wide open. With the fall of Rouen, le Havre became the only possible evacuation route for the 51 Division and IX French Corps. The 154 Infantry Brigade and A Infantry Brigade were formed into 'Arkforce' to secure the line of communication back to the port.[27]

Meanwhile, 152 and 153 Brigades, part of the French IX Corps, under Lieutenant General Marcel Ihler, were cut off from the main Allied forces, and had to withdraw toward le Havre in the hope of evacuation by sea. As the force moved back toward the coast, German forces reached the coast near Saint-Valéry-en-Caux first, severing the line of retreat to le Havre. The French and British force pulled back into St Valéry-en-Caux. The plan was for the Royal Navy to evacuate the Division and re-insert them at le Havre with the other British force to continue the fight. In effect, they were walking into a one-way trap of their own making.

St Valéry-en-Caux was the accidental and bewildered host of thousands of fighting British, French and German soldiers, the latter supported in the skies above by dive-bombing screaming and strafing Stukas. David describes it as 'a secluded spot … peaceful, neat';[28] Frinton-on-Sea springs to mind. We shall see below how much of it was soon reduced to rubble. Post-war architecture and an imposing granite war memorial shipped in from Scotland are all there is to remind us that one of Scotland's, no Britain's, finest fighting formations fought and died there to help Britain and France fight another day and to win that fight.

St Valéry-en-Caux

Given the choice, no general would have opted for St Valéry-en-Caux as the place for a major evacuation. But there was no choice for General Fortune. And so Fortune made the decision to evacuate through St Valéry-en-Caux. This news reached the Navy at 0400 hours on 10 June; preparations began.

In the port a box perimeter was set up around the town with the intention of holding it during the day before retiring to the port by night. The 2nd Seaforth, 1st Gordons and 4th Camerons took up positions on the west side while, near the seaside village of Veules les Roses and Fontaine-le-Dun on the east side, were 4th Seaforth, 5th Gordons and 1st Black Watch. The French were allocated the south side of the box but until they arrived the Lothians, Norfolks and 6th Royal Scots Fusiliers filled the gap. The Division was in position early on 11 June. Orders to destroy vehicles were carried out, as evidenced by drained radiators and oil tanks, slashed tyres and smashed batteries. Only Bren-gun carriers were saved – for the last stand.

Longden[29] tells us that 2,000 British and 1,000 French got away from Veules. Numerous groups found themselves wandering around the French countryside hoping to find a way back. One, comprising eight Seaforth Highlanders (an officer and seven men), had slipped through the lines at St Valéry and soon became known as 'Snow White and the Seven Dwarfs' by the local French.

The Germans, under Rommel, sped towards St Valéry-en-Caux and were engaged by the Lothians and Border Horse at Cany, to the west of St Valéry taking the high ground. The Germans pressed the line from the west along the coast and the south-west and in the east 4th Seaforth, 5th Gordons and 1st Black Watch joined battle. The Germans then proceeded to comprehensively destroy St Valéry-en-Caux with, according to Fred Coster of 101st Light Anti-Aircraft Regiment its 'rows of lovely, colourful painted houses … [which were] being lifted up complete then collapsing to the ground in ruins. Then they started machine gunning us ... then they started bombing again … when I looked again the town was an absolute wreck. All within minutes'.[30]

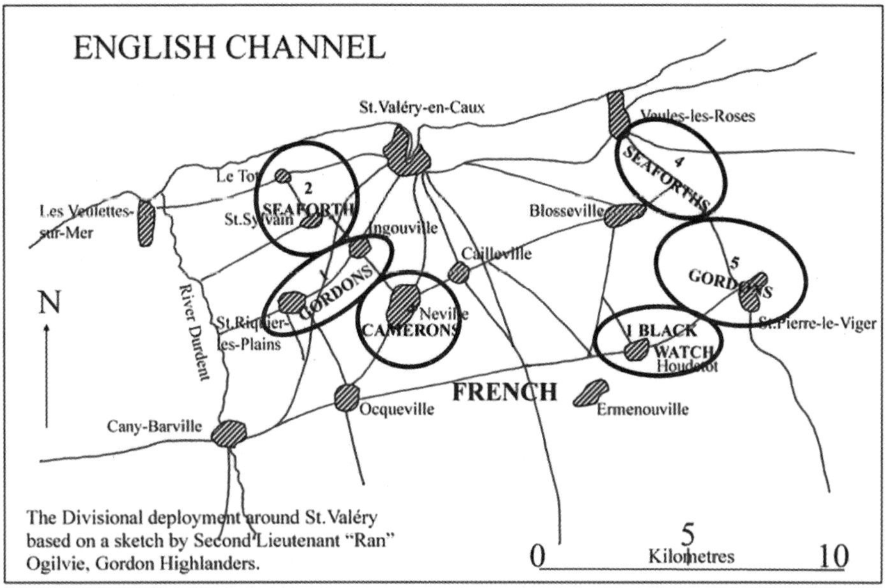

Map of divisional deployment around St Valéry.

Major General Fortune's orders were issued to commanding officers at 10.00am on the 11th:

> The Navy will probably make an effort to take us off by boat, perhaps to-night, perhaps in two nights. I wish all ranks to realise that this can only be achieved by the full co-operation of everyone. Men may have to walk five or six miles. The utmost discipline must prevail.
>
> Men will board the boats with equipment and carrying arms. Vehicles will be rendered useless without giving away what is being done. Carriers should be retained as the final rear-guard. Routes back to the nearest highway should be reconnoitred and officers detailed as guides. Finally, if the enemy should attack before the whole force is evacuated, all ranks must realise that it is up to them to defeat them. He may attack with tanks, and we have quite a number of anti-tank guns behind. If the infantry can stop the enemy's infantry, that is all that is required, while anti-tank guns and rifles inflict casualties on armoured fighting vehicles.

During the afternoon of the same day at St Pierre-le-Viger the 1st Black Watch were assailed by the Germans and by 6.00pm had lost some 500 men wounded or killed. They were supported by French cavalry who dismounted and, tethering their horses in a wood, fought as infantry. The position was finally overrun at dawn the next day.

To the west the perimeter was breached; the 2nd Seaforth were cut off in le Tot, down the present D20 from St Valéry. There the town was ablaze due to relentless bombardment from artillery and air attack.

> In the town the Divisional HQ, the 51st Anti-Tank Regiment, part of the Norfolks and a company of Kensingtons secured the perimeter. An attack into the town was [repelled] in the late afternoon but the town was now surrounded. Final plans were now made for the evacuation, beaches allotted and orders given but these did not reach the 2nd Seaforth cut off in le Tot.
>
> After arriving in the harbour on the 10th and finding no one there the Navy had withdrawn on the 11th and after coming under air attack pulled further out to sea. When the order came to carry out the evacuation it was too late. A combination of fog obscuring the coast, the loss of several boats and the fact that the enemy occupied the cliffs overlooking the town made evacuation impossible.[31]

The Germans demanded that 2nd Seaforth and 1st Gordons surrender but, unsurprisingly, this opportunity was impolitely declined; instead, preparations were made for a defiant last stand. Meanwhile the French capitulated at 8.00am on the 12th.

Given that momentous decision which literally changed the direction of the early part of the war, General Fortune considered all the options open to him: a counter-attack, further resistance, retaking the town. But there was no chance of evacuation or reinforcement, the men were drained and nearly out of small-arms ammunition, and there was no artillery ammunition at all. Shortly before 10.00am on the 12th General Fortune took that most difficult and humiliating of decisions – to surrender.

One of the many intriguing things which come out of Major Grant's diaries is his diminishing confidence in the French troops' enthusiasm for the task at hand, as exemplified by their refusal to allow him to go out on patrol, insisting that he must wait until his 2nd Seaforth had moved up. David says 'his faith in French élan had been shattered' and was only partly restored when a French battle patrol left him 'five Skoda sub-machine guns and some offensive grenades'.

Sergeant John Mackenzie, also of 2nd Seaforth, would also attest to the casual attitude of the French and their laissez-faire philosophy when it came to front-line life and relationships with the enemy. He passed one night with elements of the 102nd French Regiment from whom he learned about the tacit arrangement between the French and the Germans whereby parties of less than six were never fired on and two ration trucks were permitted to move up twice a day between 10.00am and 4.00pm. On another occasion he was in an outside post hoping to gain experience when a group of Germans attacked some Foreign Legion troops nearby; Mackenzie[32] tells us how the Germans

> were a dead easy target from our post, but our French inmates were certainly not going to be looking for trouble on their last night in Tiergarten! I was somewhat startled at this revelation of the 'offensive' spirit amongst our 'Invincible Allies' ... I received lots of advice that night, mainly on how to keep out of trouble. I was advised to remove a vital piece of each Bren so that it could not be fired; never to fire at Jerry patrols unless they were cutting our wire; and never, under any circumstances, to permit firing a mortar. When in January they had fired their mortar, within a few minutes Jerry had shelled the Tiergarten, destroying two posts and killing 15 men!

In 1940 Tom Garside was with the Royal Army Service Corps attached to the 51st under Lieutenant Colonel T. Harris-Hunter TD. Tom had been with the RASC from October 1939 and remained attached to 51st (Highland) Division through North Africa and into Sicily. This personal account of escaping from St Valéry reproduced at https://51hd.co.uk/accounts/tom_garside_st_valery is believed to be the only account Tom ever put into writing, 'kindly sent to us [51hd.co.uk] by Jim Garside, Tom's Son'.

> It was now June 11th and we stayed in an orchard until about 3 o'clock in the afternoon when the drivers were ordered to damage their lorries – but without fire as that would make our position conspicuous – and then evacuate down the road to St Valéry where there was some vague talk about some ships awaiting. I was now a corporal clerk with small military training but was told to take about ten men to St Valéry; presumably where we could then march in good order onto the waiting ships. On an exposed part of this road a flight of aeroplanes came over the rising ground and machine-gunned the road. We dived into the ditch, got out as soon as the scare had passed and proceeded – to another dose of the same. Eventually coming to the outskirts of a small town which we took to be St Valéry, the road forked.

Militarily the topography could not have been worse for the retreating British and French. St Valéry-en-Caux was blessed with steep cliffs around 300-feet high overlooking and dominating the small harbour, allowing the Germans a direct line of fire to confound any attempts at withdrawal. General Fortune could not hold out for long, and concluded that their best and final chance was to be evacuated on the night of 11/12 June, but where were the ships? British destroyers off the coast were bombarded by German artillery on those clifftops overlooking St Valéry. The 51st Division and elements of the French force formed a perimeter around St Valéry in the hope of evacuation. 'The beaches were now raked by machine-gun fire from the area around le Tot.'

The Museum of the Royal Regiment of Scotland archive at Edinburgh Castle tells us that the Commander-in-Chief, Portsmouth, Admiral William James, had mustered ships for such a rescue operation but daytime evacuation was impossible because of the Luftwaffe and, on that final night, fog rendered the flotilla unable to communicate and co-ordinate.[33] On the morning of 12 June the French forces capitulated at 8.30, followed around 10.00 by the British when Major General Fortune ordered a cease fire. At 11.00 says Longden,[34] Fortune received news from England that the previous night's evacuation had been called off due to fog. Yet by that time the news was irrelevant. Half an hour earlier Major General Fortune had already notified the War Office of his intention to surrender. He was one of the most senior British officers to be taken prisoner in the entire war.[35]

The only good news to come out of the debacle was that 2,137 British soldiers and 1,184 French soldiers were evacuated from beaches to the east of St Valéry-en-Caux. The evacuation of le Havre was completed on the 13th.

After the war, General Fortune was knighted by King George VI for his unstinting work in championing the welfare of his men while in captivity; despite suffering a stroke, he had declined an offer of repatriation. From the British point of view, this was the end of the Allied resistance during the Battle of France.[36]

> The final phase of the Battle of France took place between 12 and 18 June 1940. The intention was to concentrate British forces in and around Rennes to form a Second Expeditionary Force under Lieutenant General BROOKE. He was appointed to command a new corps in France on the 6 June, with the first brigade of 52nd (Lowland) Division due to arrive in France on 7 June. By now, the British Army had elements of 1st Armoured Division, Beauman Division, 52nd Division and 1st Canadian Division operating in France.
>
> Just after midnight on 17 June, Lieutenant General BROOKE was informed that the French Government was seeking an armistice with Germany. The evacuation of the remains of the BEF now took priority in terms of British interests. Over 30,000 British troops were evacuated from Cherbourg and 20,000 from St Malo. Lieutenant General BROOKE left Cherbourg on 18 June.

Surrender evokes a wide range of emotions amongst surrendering soldiers. Some feel an irrepressible rage, others weep either with shame or with relief, some are openly defiant as when some Highlanders changed into their dress uniforms to surrender and put on 'a good show', others are astonished by the inappropriateness of this, for example John Christie;[37] some are relieved at still being alive; Fred Coster was numb, and tired, anxious to learn what was going to happen to them now: would they be shot? The author's father, Gunner Eric Chrystal, said, on reluctantly surrendering at the Battle of Arnhem in September 1944, that he never felt so humiliated in all his life.[38]

Not all the troops, however, received news of the surrender at the same time. The 2nd Seaforth were still fighting their own dogged and absolutely determined battle around St Sylvain, a farming village twenty-four miles west of Dieppe at the junction of the D68 and D105 roads, facing, according to Longden,[39] up to 100 German Panzers. And this is when Colour Sergeant Edwin 'Gracie' Fields took on a starring, if reluctant, role. The wily Germans, anxious to secure a capitulation, 'volunteered' Gracie for a front-row seat on the front of a tank which headed towards the Seaforth lines, gun strategically placed in Gracie's back. Whether there was a white flag on show is irrelevant – either the Sutherlands or the Germans were certainly going to shoot him if he tried to run for it. Gracie delivered his woeful message, to the effect that his comrades were surrounded and, if they refused to surrender, the tanks would open up. Characteristically the Seaforth declined the offer of surrender and split up, hoping to make their various ways to the coast, Sergeant Fields included.

Barbed-wire pens were speedily erected to fence in the growing numbers of British captives. Personal effects were left in heaps, men were left dejected in the pouring rain, their protective groundsheets and capes spitefully confiscated. Even at that early stage of a five-year sojourn in prisoner-of-war camps, the troops had a suspicion that they had been forgotten on two levels: their post-Dunkirk battles were not going to be widely reported in case they spoilt the triumphalism back home already surrounding the evacuation; and their plight in captivity for who knows how long was conveniently swept under the plush carpets of Whitehall.

Saul David tells that 'More than 10,000 members of the 51st (Highland) Infantry Division were taken prisoner at St Valéry-en-Caux. They were death-marched to Germany, via Belgium, following the route over which the Germans had advanced against them'. Saul David continues:[40]

> The officers were separated from the men, for most of whom the initial destination was Stalag XX-A at Toruń, about 120 miles (190 km) north-west of Warsaw. Some were loaded into canal barges for part of their

> journey, but all eventually travelled by train in cattle wagons. There were some notable escapes, mostly in the early stages of the march. Of the 290 British Army PoW escapers who had returned to Britain by the end of June 1941, 134 were members of the 51st (Highland) Infantry Division.

Nicholl[41] describes how 'as other camps came into operation, a large proportion of the PoWs were transferred – most to Stalag XX-B at Malbork and Stalag 344 at Lambinowice, but with smaller numbers in many other camps'.

> Early in 1945, the Russian Army had advanced close to these camps, so the PoWs were involved in the *Long March*. Some groups from Stalag XX-A marched around 450 miles (720 km) in the depths of winter to Stalag XIB/357 at Bad Fallingbostel on the Lüneburg Heath, north of Hanover. Others had similar journeys in severe winter conditions, affected by shortages of food and shelter, with many suffering from dysentery and frostbite.

As a postscript, in 1942 French General Charles de Gaulle said:

> I can tell you that the comradeship in arms experienced on the battlefield of Abbeville in May and June 1940 between the French armoured division which I had the honour to command and the valiant 51st Highland Division under General Fortune played its part in the decision which I took to continue fighting on the side of the Allies unto the end, no matter what the course of events.

The following is a summary of the Royal Navy's participation in the aborted rescue off St Valéry.[42]

Admiral Sir William James, commanding the naval evacuation forces, sent a small naval force from le Havre early on 10 June to cover this contingency [the hoped for evacuation], including the destroyers *Boadicea* and *Bulldog*. *Boadicea* having suffered collision damage, had been refitting in Chatham and missed the Dunkirk evacuations. A frantic rush had her ready just in time to be sent straight to the St Valéry operation, under Lieutenant Commander M.D.C. Meyrick, who had assumed command only two weeks earlier.

The website continues:

> Arriving off St Valéry on 10 June, by the afternoon the *Boadicea* had picked up at least 100 evacuees, including 60 soldiers of the Highland Division and a number of French civilians, while further out the *Bulldog* had picked up

> a boatload of soldiers. Then suddenly they came under fire from German artillery and tanks which had reached the edge of the high cliffs bordering St Valéry. Our ships silenced this enemy fire with their main armament, but shortly afterwards both the *Boadicea* and *Bulldog* were fiercely attacked by two waves of German dive-bombers.

It seems that eighteen Ju.87 Stukas attacked the *Boadicea*, delivering three direct hits, two in the engine room and one in the boiler room, causing heavy casualties (including eight killed outright) and severe damage. With her engines out of action, *Boadicea* floundered helplessly just waiting for the next inevitable air attack, while the destroyer *Ambuscade* (herself damaged, but less seriously, by enemy shellfire) approached to take her in tow.

Meanwhile, *Bulldog*, then about two miles from *Boadicea*, was targeted by six more Stukas and also sustained three hits with one boiler being blown up and a second put out of action by an unexploded bomb; a third unexploded bomb lodged between decks. Fortunately, *Bulldog* suffered only minor casualties.

With the two ships thus crippled and sitting ducks for renewed attacks, there came what can only be described as a miracle. Despite being a hot and sunny June afternoon, only minutes after the dive-bombing attacks a thick fog descended and remained for the rest of the afternoon and night.

The website continues:

> *Boadicea*'s Code Books were thrown overboard in a weighted eyeletted canvas bag, but the *Fleet Signal Book* and *Conduct of the Fleet* were both ditched separately in their own lead containers. As the destruction of all signal books was being reported to Captain Meyrick, the Leading Telegraphist arrived on the bridge to report that, thanks to a tray of lead batteries, the wireless transmitter/receiver had power and was serviceable. The Captain was thus in a terrible quandary. Should he report *Boadicea*'s desperate situation in plain language?

Ambuscade miraculously located and then got *Boadicea* under tow despite the dense fog. German bombers could be heard overhead, searching for their 'sitting ducks'. Orders were given on no account to open fire lest their positions should be revealed. *Boadicea* was successfully towed back to Portsmouth. Meanwhile *Bulldog*, 'blessing the same providential fog', managed to raise some steam on one boiler and limped to the Isle of Wight on her own, from where she was also towed to Portsmouth dockyard.

Tragically, the fog on the afternoon of 10 June proved to be a double- edged sword. While it enabled our two ships to reach home, when the fog set in, the Navy had to move out to sea, then could not get back in as the Germans commanded the cliffs above St Valéry. So, at the same time it prevented the rescue ships approaching St Valéry to take on board the beleaguered troops that night. The following night was one night too late.

The Commander-in-Chief Portsmouth filed a detailed report showing the efforts made to evacuate 51st (Highland) Division.

The wounded heroes

The subsequent marches for the captured into Germany and Poland were bad enough for the those sufficiently fit and able, albeit exhausted and shocked, to undergo the atrocious treks through unforgiving terrain and less forgiving weather. Spare a thought, though, for the wounded left behind.

On 12 June 2010, veterans of 51st (Highland) Division attended a commemorative ceremony for the 70th Anniversary of the battle at Saint-Valéry-en-Caux. More recently, in 2021, *The Herald* reported on moves to remember the Battle of St Valéry, at least in Scotland, although the nation as a whole would do well to observe the anniversary of this prodigious act of sacrifice and bravery.

Poppyscotland

Poppyscotland alongside Legion Scotland, the British Army's 51 Brigade, and RCET: Scotland's Armed Forces Children's Charity, are working hard to ensure that future generations learn about the bravery of the men who fought that day.

Gordon Michie, head of fundraising and learning at Poppyscotland said: 'Last year saw the 80th anniversary of St Valéry and we endeavoured to raise public awareness by organising a number of events to commemorate the gallantry of the 'Forgotten 51st'. In addition to the virtual tributes of more than 500 pipers around the world, we launched a suite of learning resources tailored to the Scottish curriculum that could help teachers educate students about the battle.

'Commemorations for the Battle of St Valéry will now take place annually. Ahead of this year's anniversary we're delighted to announce our partnership with Twinkl Scotland and to launch our new collection of St Valéry education resources. The Twinkl Scotland platform allows us to reach an even wider audience of schools and other education providers and means that we can continue to teach the importance of remembering St Valéry and learn from its legacy.'[43]

Chapter 11

Sergeant Eric Priest: One Seaforth Highlander's Journey from the North West Frontier to Stalag 383, 1925–1945

Regimental histories and books on conflict contain many statistics on postings, materiel, commanders, notable soldiers and significant battles with the battle information including casualties, often on both sides. As casualties mount, it is easy to become inured to them. As they reach into the hundreds and thousands the real significance of the figures can become increasingly normalised. The inescapable fact is that each and every casualty is a life lost or wrecked with consequences for family and friends.

The prisoner of war brought his own peculiar problems to those waiting for him or her back home, not least his wife or partner. Florence Priest was one of thousands of such women with her marriage on hold, her husband of five years condemned to a prison sentence with no known end. She shared that sentence from a distance, with no idea of how long their separation might last. Wars are not noted for their predictability and in 1940 no one had a clue when this one would end – Florence would have been quite sure though that Eric was not coming home for Christmas. In the end she and Eric were apart for five long years, linked by sporadic letters and not much else.

We can reflect on one soldier's service with 2nd Seaforth Highlanders, his experience on the unforgiving North West Frontier, with the constant threat of death, injury, capture and torture, and the humiliating surrender and capture of the battalion west of Dunkirk, paid for with a five-year sojourn in German PoW camps with little other than slave labour to pass the time and the subsequent lifelong, life-changing injuries. Sergeant Eric Priest was typical of thousands of Seaforth Highlanders who endured foreign climates, ruthless enemies, anxiety, fear and homesickness. It is a story that is important to tell, lest we normalise even more the wide-reaching impact of war.

Eric Priest, eighteen years and 231 days old, enlisted in the Seaforth Highlanders at 8.40am on 20 November 1925 at West Hartlepool Recruiting Office, seven years after the armistice ending the carnage of the First World War. Of course, he could have had no idea what lay ahead. His attestation was duly signed, as required, by a justice of the peace and the West Hartlepool labourer embarked on a journey in which he saw action against three very different enemies: first, the disaffected and disputatious tribes of India's North West Frontier; second, the Arab and Jewish people of Palestine and, finally, the troops of Nazi Germany as they swept all before them in the invasion of France and the Low Countries.

Eric Priest (Army number 2815950) had never been abroad before joining the Seaforth Highlanders. Naturally, he would have expected overseas postings and conflict in foreign lands, serving his king and defending his country and its empire. His fighting war ended with a ferocious battle and a catastrophic defeat early in the Second World War. Eric's Regular Army Certificate of Service Book tells us that, after enlisting, he was in the UK from 20 November 1925 to 22 December 1926 in basic training before sailing for India and service on the North West Frontier until 9 December 1932. In 1930 he was awarded the India General Service Medal (1908–1935) with North West Frontier (1930–1931) Clasp. He then served in Haifa, Palestine, from 10 December 1932 until 9 December 1933, setting sail for the UK the following day. An entry in *Cabar Feidh,* the Regimental magazine of the Seaforth Highlanders, reveals that 'On expiration of his period of colour service' on 11 December 1933 he transferred to the Army Reserve having in the meantime attained the rank of lance corporal. Eric had served eight years, twenty-two days with the Colours.

Six years later the predicted outbreak of the Second World War became horrible reality. There was a flurry of telegrams around that time, sent to his mother at 101 Murray Street, West Hartlepool from various places: Newcastle-upon-Tyne, where he asked his mother to send his Life Certificate to Fort George – 'I forgot it'; Glasgow; Stanhope Lines, Aldershot; King's Cross in October 1939 and April 1940 – presumably going home on pre-embarkation leave?

As a private in 2nd Seaforth Highlanders, Eric embarked for France in October 1939 with 152 Brigade of 51st (Highland Division) in the British Expeditionary Force (BEF) but was captured with thousands of others at Saint-Valéry-en-Caux during the Battle of France in June 1940.

This calamity was to be followed by nearly five punishing years in two German prisoner-of-war camps, in one of which he endured unrelenting hard labour which left him with lifelong physical injuries, and who really knows with what dreadful memories? Eric was thirty-eight when released in summer 1945. He was discharged from the army on 9 August with the rank of sergeant and returned home to his wife, Florence, in West Hartlepool.

By signing up with the Seaforth, Eric could not have got much further from home – the depot was at Fort George near Inverness, some 311 miles north of West Hartlepool. No Durham Light Infantry (DLI), his local regiment based in Durham City and Barnard Castle, for Eric Priest; we can only assume that the regiment was conducting one of its frequent recruitment campaigns in the north of England at the time, and that he liked the sound of their battle honours, and the look of their Scottish uniform with kilt and Glengarry. Eric did have ancestors, by marriage, in the Western Isles and, if he knew Florence (whose father was born in the Shetlands) before 1925 when he joined up, it may be that he was re-connecting with them.

It was not uncommon for there to be a significant contingent of Englishmen in the Seaforth Highlanders: around 1, 800 or one quarter of the men and officers were English or Irish, and three quarters Highlanders, and 'singular as it may seem, the former were as fond of the kilt and pipes as the latter, and many of them entered completely into the spirit of the national feeling. And, in all the solid essential qualities which form the character of the British soldier, they were perfect'.

Eric Priest's service from the North West Frontier to Stalag 383 sheds light on the Regiment's valiant and self-sacrificing stand and eventual surrender at Saint-Valéry-en-Caux in June 1940 when the greater majority of eyes and ears were, and have been ever since, trained on the evacuation from Dunkirk.

It is quite probable that a number of significant events in the early twentieth-century history of West Hartlepool and Hartlepool had an influence on Eric as he grew up and may have been compelling factors in his decision to join the army. They are the legendary hanging of a French monkey believed to be in the pay of Napoleon; the bombardment of the Hartlepools by cruisers of the German Imperial Navy in 1914; and the locally much publicised award of the Victoria Cross to John Scott (Jack) Youll in 1918, acting second lieutenant in 1st Battalion Northumberland Fusiliers but attached to 11th (Service) Battalion. Jack was born and bred in Thornley, some twelve miles west of West Hartlepool. His story is detailed in the author's *Jack Youll VC.*[1]

However, 14 December 1914 is likely to have had a significant impact on Eric Priest, for that was the morning when unopposed battle-cruisers of the Imperial German Navy remorselessly shelled Hartlepool and neighbouring West Hartlepool, killing sixty-three civilians and nine soldiers in Hartlepool and fifty-six civilians in West Hartlepool; 400 or so civilians were injured and much housing stock was damaged or destroyed.[2]

Eric was a teenager then and it was his first taste of conflict and the destruction caused by war. In forty minutes about 1,000 shells were unleashed on the two towns from the German ships *Blücher*, *Seydlitz* and *Moltke*.

The attack on the east coast caused outrage in Britain, partly because the Royal Navy clearly failed to intercept the Germans, but also because Whitby and Scarborough, unlike Hartlepool, were undefended, open towns; it nevertheless did the Army's recruitment campaign no harm at all. The impact of what was seen in Britain as an atrocity could reasonably be assumed to have influenced the young Eric Priest and may have been a compelling factor in his decision to enlist eleven years later.

The North West Frontier 1919–1930

The 2nd Battalion sailed to India, docking at Meerut in November 1919 en route for the North West Frontier. The region had a reputation for persistent lethal guerrilla warfare, inter-tribal conflict, atrocities a-plenty committed by both British and Pathans (and what are now considered as war crimes). The Pathans were the largest ethnic group along the frontier. Divided into several tribes, there was continual internecine warfare to complicate matters yet further.

British and Indian Army forces that took part in the campaign received the India General Service Medal with the clasp 'North West Frontier 1930–31'. This was awarded to Eric Priest for service during the Red Shirt and Afridi Rebellions on the North West Frontier between 23 April 1930 and 22 March 1931.

The foreign service tour required the 2nd Battalion to finish up in Palestine, at Haifa with the role of keeping the peace in the face of increasing Arab resentment towards Jewish immigration. Some things just never change.

Eric Priest's paybook shows that, from 9 November 1931 to 7 April 1932, he was a caterer in the Sergeants' Mess, and from 10 July 1932 to 9 December 1933 he graduated to steward in the Officers' Mess. More dramatically, he was a machine gunner from 1 April 1927 to 1 April 1930.

Eric was not among the many thousands of men who in mid-January 1940 departed with 5th Division from Southampton and disembarked at le Havre. He would be leaving England in April. On 28 January the division came under command of I Corps of the British Expeditionary Force (BEF), under Lieutenant General Michael Barker whose command also included 1st and 2nd Divisions, both of which were Regular Army infantry formations.

Unsurprisingly, the period immediately before Eric's passage from Southampton to le Havre was marked by a flurry of activity between him and home in West Hartlepool. On 1 September 1939 he sent a telegram from Newcastle-upon-Tyne to his mother at 101 Murray Street, possibly in some panic: 'Send my life certificate at once to me at Fort George, Scotland. I forgot it. Eric'. Two weeks later, on 14 September, he telegrammed Mrs Priest again, this time from Glasgow to advise her that he would be 'home tomorrow'. On 30 September he kept his mother up to speed with developments when he sent her another telegram from Glasgow, telling her he was 'moving Tuesday. letter follows love Eric'. Short of money on 6 October, he telegrammed his mother from Stanhope Lines in Aldershot: 'wire me £2 at once coming home'. The following day at 10.44am he wired again from Aldershot advising his mother 'Home Wednesday letter follows Eric'. At 3.38 pm he was at King's Cross where he thoughtfully updated his mother: 'Be home about 10.30 tonight Eric'. The next telegram we have is dated 4 April and finds Eric at King's Cross again (3.35pm), homeward bound: 'home tonight about 11 love Eric'. Presumably this was leave prior to his departure for France.

By 15 May Eric Priest was in France with the BEF and wrote with optimism to his mother re-assuring her that he was well. It began 'My Dear Mother' and continued:

> Just a few lines to let you know I am quite well and have managed to look after myself so far. Are you keeping alright mother, I know you will be worried to death now that this war has started in full swing, but we can just hope and pray for the best. I don't think it will last that long now and I am looking forward to being back home with you all again.

Eric was clearly anxious to receive news from his mother but the lines of communication between England and France were no doubt less than perfect. His words and his mild rebuke reflects the great value the soldiers placed on letters from home and how important it was to them to hear the family news: 'I have been expecting a letter from you every day but I have not received one. Have you received my letters OK.'

Mrs Priest's dutiful, concerned son, also, no doubt, frightened and anxious about his own situation in his personal war zone, tenderly, and optimistically, ends his letter with:

> Well mother dear how are things going at home. I am always thinking about you, and wondering what you are doing…Now mother let me have a letter from you as soon as possible.
>
> Excuse this short note, but I have not much time to write long letters. But I know you will not mind as long as you know I am alright.
>
> So good night and God bless you my dear mother.
>
> From your dear son Eric xxxxx
>
> P.S Write soon xxx
>
> I'll Be Back

He'll be back: Corporal Eric Priest also left a wife, Florence, and two sons, Eric and Don, back at home at 101 Murray Street, West Hartlepool. We have one letter of the many he no doubt wrote to the boys. This one is to Eric, his elder boy, and the subject of 'missing' letters comes up again, as well as the anticipated assassination of Adolf Hitler:

Dear Eric
I hope you are still being a good lad for your mam, and that you are still playing with our Doni, and lending him your toys. Daddy is still waiting for that letter you said you would write to him.

Have you got another Dicky Bird yet. Tell Doni his daddy will soon be home again, after he has shot Hitler.

Be a good lad and look after mammy and Doni till I come home.

Your loving Daddy.

Meanwhile in Nazi occupied France things had moved on apace and the early history of the Second World War was being rewritten, literally, on a daily basis; a history in which Eric Priest and his comrades played a decisive role. On the morning of 12 June, the French forces in the rearguard west of Dunkirk, our allies, capitulated at 08.30, followed around 10.00 by the British when Major General Fortune ordered a ceasefire. At 11.00 Fortune received news from England that the previous night's planned evacuation had been called off due to fog. Yet by that time the news was irrelevant. Half an hour earlier Major General Fortune had already notified the War Office of his intention to surrender. He was one of the most senior British officers to be taken prisoner during the war.

The only good news to come out of the debacle was that 2,137 British soldiers and 1,184 French soldiers were evacuated from beaches to the east of St Valéry-en-Caux. So near yet so far for the 2nd Seaforth.

Not all the troops, however, received news of the surrender at the same time. The 2nd Seaforth, Eric Priest among them, were still fighting their own dogged and absolutely determined battle around St Sylvain, a farming village twenty-four miles west of Dieppe at the junction of the D68 and D105 roads, facing up to 100 mighty, battle-hardened German Panzers. Characteristically, the Seaforth declined the charitable offer of surrender, split up and tried to make their various ways to the coast.

For Eric's battalion and many others the war was, as they say, conclusively over. How many times must they have heard the increasingly annoying '*Für dich ist der Krieg vorbei*' ?

Seemingly interminable detention in often dreadul conditions was surely bad enough, as was the slave labour endured by PoWs. What no one who has not experienced it can comprehend is the psychological impact years of detention in one of those foreign fields. On release and repatriation many may have suffered (usually un- or mis-diagnosed) what we now term Post Traumatic Stress Disorder; some may not have got quite the welcome home they expected from their wives, some may have found it hard to deal with the reaction of children who did not remember them. We have no evidence of this in Eric Priest's case but there is much testimony that many did.

Surrendering too had its impact – it was the very last thing that many military men and women wanted – they did not join up to fail. A close relative of Eric Priest's was Gunner Eric Chrystal (the author's father) who was forced to surrender after four days of slogging it out near Arnhem Bridge at that other heroic failure beset by Panzers – the Battle of Arnhem in September 1944. Correspondence from Eric Chrystal reveals that never was he so humilated in all his life when he reluctantly responded to the order, *Hände hoch!* that night. It's nice to think that after the was the two Erics might have spent time together comparing experiences and swapping PoW notes, awful as they were.[3]

Barbed-wire pens were erected speedily to fence in the growing numbers of British captives at St Valéry. Personal effects were left in heaps, men were left dejected in the pouring rain, their protective groundsheets and capes spitefully and unnecessarily confiscated. Even at that early stage of a five-year sojourn in prisoner-of-war camps, there was a suspicion that they had been forgotten, on two levels: their particular post-Dunkirk battles were never going to be widely reported in case they spoilt the already mythic triumphalism and positive propaganda circulating back home and already surrounding the main evacuation; and their plight in captivity (for who knows how long) was conveniently swept under the plush carpets of Whitehall.

Saul David tells that 'More than 10,000 members of the 51st (Highland) Infantry Division (of which 2nd Seaforth Highlanders were a part) were taken prisoner at St Valéry-en-Caux. Some were marched to Germany, via Belgium, retracing the route over which the Germans had advanced against them. David continues:

> The officers were separated from the men, for most of whom the initial destination was Stalag XX-A at Toruń, about 120 miles (190 km) northwest of Warsaw. Some were loaded into canal barges for part of their journey, but all eventually travelled by train in cattle wagons. There were some notable escapes, mostly in the early stages of the march. Of the 290 British Army PoW escapers who had returned to Britain by the end of June 1941, 134 were members of the 51st (Highland) Infantry Division.

Corporal Priest was one of those escapees, although his freedom was short-lived. Corporal Priest's capture at St Valéry on 11 June naturally sparked some concern back home amongst relatives and comrades, not least because everyone knew that the usual procedure was for a missing soldier to be initially reported 'missing' until further information became available. That soldier was often subsequently reported taken prisoner of war, but could also have been wounded or killed. Some of that concern was channelled into letters of encouragement to Eric's mother and wife.

When he heard about Eric's 'missing' status, his brother-in-law (Florence's brother) Gunner Magnus Stove wrote a reassuring letter to his sister from his unit, 220 HAA Battery, 56th HAA Regiment RA, stationed at Carkeel Camp near Saltash in Cornwall. Magnus encouraged Florence:

> you won't have to give up hope, as nobody can tell where he might be, in fact he might have been taken prisoner, and if that is so, it will be weeks before you get to know from the War Office. There was one of our men missing for over a month, I know he was alive and well in England, and I am not sure whether he has reported back even yet.

Magnus repeats his encouragement and hope:

> Well Florence you will have to keep on hoping that he will turn up, and I sincerely hope he does, you know there are similar cases in the papers every day.
>
> I hope the bairns [Eric and Don] are keeping well and you keep your heart up as well.
>
> Kindest regards
> From your loving brother
> Magnus

On 2 July 1940 Billy Gooding (Florence's brother-in-law) wrote to Florence from Catterick Camp after receiving news of Eric's missing status from Florence's sister, Lil.

> I am writing these few lines to say how terribly sorry I am. What a wicked world this is, they say 'the Devil looks after his own' and I am sure that is a true saying for I am sure that Eric has done nothing wrong to deserve a fate like that but we must not give up hope, let us hope and pray to God that he is alive and well. Keep that in mind Florry and try and pull yourself together for the kiddies sake. Lil [his wife] has said in her letters that you have been wonderfully patient in the last few weeks of anxious waiting even now when you have got bad news, keep it up. I know it will be hard to do but do not let your feelings get the better of you.
>
> If you ever want anything doing just ask Lil, I know that she will do everything in her power to help you.

Well I am sorry that I cannot say any more but buck-up. I am sure he will come back safe and sound. Love to Eric and Donald.

Yours truly

Billy (Gooding)

On the official side, on 26 June, Florence heard from the Infantry Record Office at Perth that Eric was 'posted as "missing" date unknown'. The record assures recipients that:

> the report that he is missing does not necessarily mean that he has been killed as he may be a prisoner of war or temporarily separated from his regiment. Official reports that men are prisoners of war take some time to reach this country, and if he has been captured by the enemy it is probable that unofficial news will reach you first.

An agonising four months passed before Florence Priest heard, to huge relief no doubt, from the Perth office on 1 November that Eric, her husband, had been reported 'a Prisoner of War at Stalag 8B (Prison Camp in Germany)'.

On 7 December the Joint War Organisation of the British Red Cross Society Prisoner of War Department (JWO) wrote to Eric's mother confirming his camp as Stalag VIIIB and providing some welcome information (PW/A.M.48489). An enclosed circular, 'Communications with Prisoners of War Interned Abroad P2280E', issued by the Postmaster General would have helped enormously. The letter advised that 'no later than one week after his arrival at the prison camp a prisoner may send a postcard to his family telling them of his capture, and state of health. At the same time, it added 'You should not, however, be unduly worried if you do not hear from the prisoner for some time, as this will probably be due to a delay in the post'. The post cards referred to in the Red Cross letter to Florence Priest started arriving on 30 December 1940: this was a Christmas card in effect, sent from Stalag VIIIB to Eric's wife intended for his two boys; it shows a traditional Christmas scene and is signed 'Dad, with love'. It is the first indication that Eric had been promoted to sergeant. Another card on the same date is addressed to his mother, Mrs A.E. Priest at 34 Milton Road, West Hartlepool and signed 'your loving son, Eric'.

It is little surprise that prisoners were anxious to, at least, try to escape. And a number did, mostly unsuccessfully. Sergeant Priest mentioned his escape attempt more than once, but details are scanty and memories have faded. However, the MI9 questionnaire he completed does reveal that, on 16 June 1940, he escaped from the march into Germany and was at large for fourteen days but was, like so many escapees, re-captured. He was then 'questioned by threat'. He answered 'no' to the question relating to any sabotage – 'did you do any sabotage or destruction of enemy factory plant, war material, communications etc. when employed on working-parties or during escape?' You wouldn't say 'yes' would you?

Stalag VIII-B – Łambinowice/Lamsdorf

Łambinowice has a long history of detention and confinement reaching back to Camp Lamsdorf which was a prisoner-of-war camp for French captives during the Franco-Prussian war of 1870. A stay in Lamsdorf was, to a large extent, defined by its working parties. By common consent the worst were the mines of Silesia, a fact to which Eric Priest was to attest, digging coal, salt, copper and lignite.

It would appear that Sergeant Priest (or someone close to him) had contacted the local paper regarding his capture. On 3 December 1941 *The Northern Daily Mail* published a photograph of Eric along with eight fellow prisoners at VIIIB. Soon after, on 22 February 1942, Eric sent a standard *Kriegsgefangenpost Postkarte* to his brother Tom (Shears) and sister-in-law Olive at 59 Brenda Road. He wrote, from VIIIB:

> Just a few lines to let you know I am quite well and I hope you are keeping OK, also Baby June. Please let me have another letter if you can find the time. Give my love to all at home and keep smiling. Your loving brother Eric.

On 13 January 1943 Eric sent a card to his mother, but this time it was from Oflag IIIC, the original number of what was to become Stalag 383; in so doing he was telling us that he had moved the 500 or so miles west from VIIIB in Silesia to Stalag 383 in Bavaria.

A card dated 16 August 1944 from M-Stammlager 383 to his mother in Milton Road is the last correspondence we have from him before release and repatriation one year or so later. The message would suggest that word was getting out that the Allies were progressing towards Germany after 6 June 1944.

We know that Eric, like many other prisoners, suffered ill health for periods during his imprisonment. On 20 February 1941 he was recovering from pneumonia (*Lungenentzündung*) while on the Stalag VIIIB Makoszowy coal mine (*Delbrückschachte*) working party. He was still suffering from it on 14 March and was in the Hindenburg Lazarette (hospital) close to the mine in which he was working. Two years later his Soldier's Service and Pay Book reveal that on 8 June he was in the camp hospital diagnosed with 'congestion of the lungs', possibly a recurrence of his pneumonia, or perhaps bronchitis or heart failure. This is likely to have presented with an uncomfortable, productive cough. In

Stalag 383 he was in hospital and under treatment from 24 October 1943 to 18 February 1944 with an 'injury to his lumbar region'; treatment involved therapeutic massage sessions. On 4 May 1944 he was recorded as 'being in hospital here for '7/52' (seven months in the last year). The only thing giving relief was heat? pad'. Between 15 November that year to 16 January 1945 the doctor wrote 'pain to sacroiliac j[oint] and region and lower Th[oracic] spine. Improved with rest, radiant heat massage'.

The plan in 1945 was that all British PoWs would be interviewed and debriefed by MI9 on release from their camps, and before being permitted to go home or return to their units in Britain. This naturally caused some resentment, particularly amongst those ex-captives who had been languishing in one camp or another for four or five years and just wanted to get home. Accordingly, compliance was not good, and only about one third of liberated PoWs, 2,357, completed the debriefing and the questionnaire. Eric Priest, however, was one of them and his completed form revealed his escape attempt and the inadequate medical treatment he received in his camps on account of the authorities.

Eric answered the question on his MI9 liberation form 'did you receive adequate medical treatment, 'no, could not get x-rayed'. He may well have called on the services of a Sergeant Jamieson, a qualified masseur, whom we knew worked on patients with back problems and partial paralysis in the camp massage room. Jamieson complemented his patient manipulation and manual therapy with training courses for at least six PoW trainee masseurs.

So, we see that Eric spent a considerable amount of time in camp hospitals with serious chest infections, probably exacerbated by the dust inhaled in the mines of Silesia and injuries consistent with the backbreaking slave labour he was subjected to. Obviously, these conditions did not magically disappear with the ending of the war. These injuries, and the pronounced limp he was left with, stayed with him for the rest of his life, requiring him to walk with a stick and wear a brace around his back. Significantly, he never mentioned any of this in his correspondence home, no doubt to minimise anxieties.

After some delay, Stalag 383 was liberated at 4.00pm on 24 April 1945 by elements of the 65th US Infantry Division led by Major General Stanley Eric Reinhart, a First World War veteran. Eric Priest, prisoner number 17459, was finally and officially reported no longer a prisoner on 19 August having disembarked in the UK on 14 May. The MI9 questionnaire he completed on release shows his civilian occupation as an 'electrician (housing)', his address as 105 Welldeck Road, West Hartlepool and his stay in VIIIB extending from July 1940 to July 1942 and in Stalag 383 from July 1942 to April 1945. He was finally discharged from the army on 27 November, 'permanently unfit for any form of military service'.

Chapter 12

1st Battalion Seaforth Highlanders in the Second World War and After

Shanghai

As we have seen, when war was declared the 1st Battalion was in Shanghai under China Command, based at the Racecourse as part of the International Force. In August 1940 evacuations of the garrison began, including 1st Seaforth. After Pearl Harbor the Imperial Japanese Army forced the British to capitulate in December 1941. The remaining British and American troops, taken by surprise, surrendered without a shot being fired; the only exception was the sole British river gunboat in Shanghai, HMS *Peterel*, which declined to surrender; six of the eighteen British crew on board at the time were killed when the ship was sunk after the Japanese opened fire at almost point-blank range. She had been deployed for service on the China station, on the Yang Tse river to protect British commerce and nationals. Japanese marines boarded the *Peterel* to demand her surrender. Captain Polkinghorn attempted to stall for time, to allow the demolition fuses to be lit and the codebooks to be passed down a special chute and burned in the boiler room. When his attempts failed, Polkinghorn told them to 'Get off my bloody ship!' The Japanese disembarked and almost immediately the Japanese cruiser *Izumo*, the accompanying gunboat *Toba* and Japanese shore batteries in the French Concession opened fire. Despite being outnumbered and hopelessly outgunned, the crew of HMS *Peterel* returned fire, using small arms and deck-mounted Lewis machine guns. The crew inflicted several casualties on the Japanese before *Peterel* capsized and drifted from its mooring under heavy fire. The Japanese machine-gunned both the surviving Royal Navy and locally recruited Chinese crewmen in the water.

European residents were required to wear armbands to differentiate them and to attract routine mistreatment. The Japanese sent European and American citizens to be interned at the Lunghua Civilian Assembly Centre, a work camp on what was then the outskirts of Shanghai. Survivors of Lunghua were released in August 1945.

Malaya and India

The 1st Battalion deployed to Malaya on 28 August 1940 where it was stationed in Singapore and then Penang, to defend against possible parachute landings. The 1st Leicestershire Regiment relieved it at Penang on 16 February; it then left the brigade and moved to India, escaping capture when the Japanese took Singapore in February 1942. On arrival in India the 1st was stationed at Akbar Barracks in Agra; it joined 1 Indian Infantry Brigade on 9 May 1942 and remained with that brigade on the Burma/Assam border for the rest of the war.

On 25 February 1942 the Battalion entrained at Agra en route to Kohima. During the day it passed through Etawah and Cawnpore on the train which moved through Mogal Seal, Goya and Asansol on the 26th and Ishundi, Parbatipur, and Lubmanishat the following day. On the 28th the Battalion embarked on the ferry at Amingoan and crossed the Brahmaputra River. From there it continued to Dimapur on the Manipur Road, which was the railhead. The 1st Seaforth left Manipur Road on 2 March and moved by bus to Kohima. The Battalion was located at Shenam on 12 June and was on the border until 15 August 1944, in Shillong until 30 November 1944, and then in Bombay.

The Burma Campaign

Fairrie[1] tells us that long-distance patrols followed into Burma as far as the Chindwin. In the meantime, the Burma Army withdrew to Assam. 'From a battalion defensive position at Shenam the 1st Seaforth patrolled to Tonhe, operating under most difficult monsoon conditions in the flooded Kabaw valley'. Malaria took its deadly toll. In early 1943 the Battalion carried out 'offensive patrolling operations on the Chindwin River', depending on air drops and mules for supplies. The objective was to divert the Japanese from Wingate's first Chindit expedition, Operation LONGCLOTH, in 1943.

According to the Chindit Society, this gave Wingate,[2]

> a chance to prove his Long-Range Penetration (LRP) concept of jungle warfare, based on mobile columns operating behind Japanese lines in North Burma, supplied by air alone and tasked with disrupting the enemy's supply lines.

LONGCLOTH was 'a Brigade-strength foray deep into Japanese territory. While achieving little immediate military return, it led to the eventual destruction of Japanese forces in Burma, as it prompted the enemy to launch the disastrous Imphal/Kohima offensive 12 months later'.

We can do no better than quote the Burma Star Memorial for a general summary of this pivotal campaign; hopefully, its presence here will go a small way to bringing the veterans the recognition and admiration they deserve.

The Story of the Burma Campaign
It was one of the most magnificent, and arduous, feats of arms in military history. A million men, from more than twenty nations, fighting a powerful and implacable foe through thousands of miles of intractable, malaria-ridden jungle, doggedly ploughing on, despite suffering a series of shattering early reverses.

With more than 100 languages and numerous faiths, customs and eating habits, the Fourteenth Army was marshalled together by one man, General Sir William Slim. General Slim was a brilliant leader, loved by his men for his humanity and admired by them for his shrewd military skill. A combination of his leadership and the breathtaking bravery of those under his command ultimately led to a victory that freed millions from tyranny.

This is the story of the Burma Campaign in the Second World War, the story of the Fourteenth Army, the largest Commonwealth army ever assembled. By rights it should be one of the most celebrated stories of that cataclysmic global conflict. Yet Fourteenth Army is known as the 'Forgotten Army'. The long, hard, heroic slog of the Burma Campaign was overlooked at the time and is still very much in the shadow of the better-known campaigns fought in Europe, Africa and elsewhere.[3]

Sym opens his account of the 1st Battalion's action in Burma as follows:[4]

> 1943 saw the 1st Battalion engaged actively on the Chindwin River. One patrol in June, against Japanese positions at Yetagun, achieved particular success, and considerable assistance was rendered to the Chindit Forces during this period. During 1944, the Battalion took part in operations, designed to give the Japanese the impression that our Forces were planning to cross the Chindwin, and to distract attention from General Wingate's second expedition, which was being flown in to Burma. In April the Japanese invasion of Burma developed, and the 1st Battalion, under the command of Lieutenant Colonel J. Jamieson, was engaged in the capture of Kasom and subsidiary engagements to stem the invasion.

Imphal 1944

The Japanese invaded India in early 1944 which necessitated a move for the 1st from the Chindwin to Kunthaung. At the beginning of April, 1 (Indian) Brigade moved to the hills west of Imphal to outflank the Japanese as they advanced along the Ukrhill road. The 1st Seaforth captured the enemy-held villages of Kasom and Lammu. In late 1944 they returned to India to train for the recapture of Malaya.

Here are the accounts of two DCMs and a MM awarded to two men of the 1st Battalion:

2824426 Acting Sergeant James O'Neill DCM, Seaforth Highlanders
A 'Burma Operations' DCM was awarded to 2824426 Acting Sergeant James O'Neill, Seaforth Highlanders.

The original recommendation states:

> When in command of two sections that suddenly encountered a company of Japs at Nampamaung (S.F. 2628) on 20 April 1943, he coolly and skilfully conducted the withdrawal of the two sections, covering their movement with fire and delaying, and inflicting casualties on the Japs.
>
> One of his sections was thus enabled to withdraw southwards along the Chindwin and cross intact at Nanthanyit (S.F. 2321), but he and the other section had to swim the Chindwin – 600 yards wide – at Taungbola (S.F. 2525) under fire. Despite covering fire from the other section and from a patrol on the west bank, three were killed whilst swimming, one drowned and one missing. At least 20 Japs were killed in the engagement.
>
> His placing of his other section in a position whence it could withdraw intact, whilst himself remaining at the point of danger to cover its withdrawal, are in the best traditions of leadership.[5]

The following extracts are from Dunoon's *1st Battalion Seaforth Highlanders, India and Burma 1941–1944*:

> At the time of his award the 1st Seaforth had been moved to Myothat, Burma to patrol the Chindwin River to help the returning Chindits to escape Jap pursuit by drawing off the Japs between Thaungdut and Mawlaik. The survivors were then to be taken back to Tamu where they were to be fed, given baths, fresh clothing and a shave – if they wanted one!
>
> It was on 22 April that a Recce patrol from C Company went out under the Command of Sgt O'Neill and ran into heavy mortar and LMG fire East of the Chindwin. O'Neill withdrew, leapfrogging the sections back to the riverbank. One of his sections provided cover to enable the other to cross the river intact, but O'Neill and the covering section eventually had to swim the 600 yard river under fire. Despite covering fire from the home bank Cpl Heckey and Ptes Wheatly and McColgan were

> killed swimming and Ptes Docherty and Williams were reported missing. O'Neill's exemplary handling of the withdrawal and his cool leadership in very difficult circumstances earned him a recommendation for an MM. He was awarded a DCM.

The original recommendation shows that he was initially recommended for a DCM which was changed to MM and then changed back to DCM.

The Chindits the Seaforth were helping were those returning from Operation LONGCLOTH, the first Chindit expedition which commenced in February 1943.

The 1st Seaforth arrived in Burma in May 1942, as part of 1 Indian Brigade, 23rd Indian Division and it was in the course of the bitter fighting of the First Arakan Campaign that O'Neill gained his DCM. He was invested with his award by Lord Mountbatten on 8 February 1944.

Company Sergeant Major R. Lightfoot, Seaforth Highlanders DCM MM
A Battle of Imphal DCM for being an inspiration to the men of his Company throughout the attacks on Kasom, Lammu and Nippon Hill – during which he rescued a wounded man from 'no-man's land', under mortar fire; and personally stalked and dispatched an enemy sniper.

> At Kasom, Assam on the nights 15/16 April 1944 and 19/20 April 1944, during continuous attacks by the enemy, the conduct of this WO was of the highest order. By his coolness under heavy fire he was an inspiration to all the men of his Coy. When casualties occurred he was immediately on the spot, and personally attended to the wounded until they could be taken over by the MO. During both nights whilst the fighting was at its fiercest, he continued to move from one part of the perimeter to another to encourage the men. Throughout, he showed unflinching courage and devotion to duty.[6]
>
> Throughout the whole of the operations lasting over the period March to July 44, the conduct of this WO has been of an outstandingly high order. He has consistently carried out his duties in the field with ability and succcss. In action he has been cool, brave and at all times showed a complete disregard for danger. At Kasom on the day of 15 April 44, and the night of 15/16 April 44, his Coy was subjected to no less than five persistent and determined counter-attacks by the enemy. Each time they were repulsed with heavy loss and CSM Lightfoot did much by his personal example and devotion to duty to inspire the men to give of their very best. He kept moving from one section to another always ready by deed and word to encourage and urge them on. He gave of his best

> to help the wounded who could be evacuated at the time. Again on the night 18/19 April 44, his Coy took over the defence of the village. Again the JAP made an all-out attempt to capture the village, this time assisted by his 3-inch mortars whose bombs straddled the position. Once more CSM Lightfoot gave his best, steadying and encouraging the men at every point. A man fell wounded by a mortar bomb outside the perimeter, and this WO, at great personal risk immediately went forward and brought him in. At LAM-MU on 24 April 44, his conduct reached the same high standard. An enemy sniper cunningly concealed was giving the Coy advance much trouble, and CSM Lightfoot went forward on his own, located and shot him. In subsequent operations at KHONGJOM on 18 May 44, at MALTA on 30 May 44, at NIPPON on 24 July 44, this WO showed the same high standard of conduct and devotion to duty which were at all times an inspiration to the men of his Coy.[7]

After the war

At the war's end, the 1st Battalion moved to Malaya, as planned, landing at Port Dickson in September 1945. The following year it served in Java before moving back to Malaya where, according to Trevor Royle, from 1948 until 1951, it took part in internal security operations during the Malayan Emergency.[8]

Java

The role of the British Army immediately after the Japanese surrender has long been shrouded in secrecy and rarely sees the light of day. Andrew Roadnight's 2002 paper in *History*, published by the Historical Association, is an exception to this silence.[9] The setting was a series of riots by Indonesian nationalists intent on securing their independence from the Dutch in the post-war period. The British and Dutch were intent on restoring the old hegemonies under the British and Dutch pre-war empires. The 1st Seaforth were among the troops deployed to control this civil unrest.

Roadnight tells how

> between September 1945 and November 1946, up to 35,000 surrendered Japanese troops were assimilated into Lord Louis Mountbatten's South East Asia Command in the Netherlands East Indies. Although under the ultimate control of British officers, the Japanese retained their wartime unit structures, were led by their own officers and remained armed. As a measure of their acceptance by the British, one of them was recommended for the Distinguished Service Order in November 1945, only three months

> after the war's end. The Japanese fought alongside the British despite the anger felt against them as the perpetrators of wartime atrocities and as a former enemy.

The perfidy, Roadnight continues, 'did not prevent senior military personnel and politicians from using the Japanese to assist in the restoration of pre-war European empires in Asia. In this case, the Netherlands East Indies reverting to the Dutch'.

> Crucially, the United States government tacitly supported the use of the Japanese. Aware of the sensitivity of using former enemy troops, the British and Americans tried to conceal the extent of Japanese involvement. Their success in achieving this hid not just their own hypocrisy but also the important part played by the Japanese in securing Allied post-war aims in Asia.

The Malayan Emergency

The Malayan Emergency, or the Anti–British National Liberation War (1948–1960), was a guerrilla war fought in British Malaya between communist pro-independence fighters of the Malayan National Liberation Army (MNLA) and the military forces of the Federation of Malaya, British Empire and Commonwealth. The communists fought to win independence for Malaya from the British Empire and establish a socialist economy, while the Malayan Federation and Commonwealth forces fought to combat communism and protect British economic and colonial interests. Why 'Emergency'? The word was used by the British to describe the conflict to avoid referring to it as a war, because London-based insurers would not pay out for claims relating to civil wars. Three years of jungle warfare followed with 1st Seaforth starting off in Johore and then Pahang where they claimed the lives of 100 or so terrorists.

The war began on 17 June 1948 after Britain declared a state of emergency following attacks on plantations.

In turn, according to Newsinger, there were revenge attacks for the killing of left-wing activists. On 16 June 1948, near the town of Sungai Siput, three European plantation managers were killed by three young Chinese men suspected to have been communists.

The British attempted to starve the MNLA, adopting scorched-earth policies including food rationing, killing livestock, and aerial spraying of the lethal herbicide Agent Orange.[10] Clumsy British efforts to defeat the communists included extrajudicial killings of unarmed villagers, in violation of the Geneva

Conventions. According to Christi Siver[11] 'British efforts to educate soldiers about the Geneva Conventions either did not ever reach units deployed in Malaya or left no impression on them .... All of these regiments went through the introductory jungle warfare course and received the same instruction about 'snap shooting' and differentiating between targets. Differences in training do not seem to explain why some units killed civilians while others did not.'[12] The most infamous example atrocity is the Batang Kali massacre, which has been referred to as 'Britain's Mỹ Lai'. The Briggs Plan forcibly re-located between 400,000 to 1,000,000 civilians into British concentration camps called 'New villages'.[13] Newsinger adds:[14]

> Their homes and standing crops were fired, their agricultural implements were smashed and their livestock either killed or turned loose. Some were subsequently to receive compensation, but most never did. They were then transported by lorry to the site of their 'new village' which was often little more than a prison camp, surrounded by a barbed-wire fence, illuminated by searchlights. The villages were heavily policed with the inhabitants effectively deprived of all civil rights.

The depredations of the Second World War left Malaya economically and socially wrecked, with rising communist party membership, significant labour unrest and endless strikes between 1946 and 1948 with 300 strikes in 1947 alone. Newsinger tells how 'the British used police and soldiers as strike breakers, and employers enacted mass dismissals, forced evictions of striking workers from their homes, legal harassment and began cutting the wages of their workers. Colonial police responded to rising trade union activity through arrests, deportations, and beating striking workers to death'. As a consequence, 'communist militants began assassinating strike breakers, and attacking anti-union estates. These attacks were used by the colonial occupation as a pretence to conduct mass arrests of left-wing activists. On 12 June the British colonial occupation banned Malaya's largest trade union the PMFTU'.

Newsinger continues:[15]

> Malaya's rubber and tin resources were used by the British to pay war debts to the United States and to recover from the damage of the Second World War. Malaysian rubber exports to the United States were of greater value than all domestic exports from Britain to America, causing Malaya to be viewed by the British as a vital asset. Britain had prepared for Malaya to become an independent state, but only by handing power to a government which would be subservient to Britain and allow British businesses to keep control of Malaya's natural resources.

The UK had little in the way of 'war debt' to the USA, having been the recipient of lend-lease from March 1941 onwards. Before that, all purchases were paid for. What Newsinger is presumably referring to is the post-war loans made to the Attlee government, since the UK didn't qualify for Marshall Aid. Those debts weren't paid off until 2006.

According to Hack,[16] 'During the first couple of years of the war, the British forces responded with a campaign of "counter-terror" characterised by high levels of state coercion against the civilian population, such as sweeps, cordons, large-scale deportation, and capital charges against suspected guerrillas.' Hack tells us how:[17]

> At the start of the Emergency, the British had 13 infantry battalions in Malaya, including seven partly formed Gurkha battalions, three British battalions, two battalions of the Royal Malay Regiment and a British Royal Artillery regiment being used as infantry. This force was too small to fight the insurgents effectively, and more infantry battalions were needed in Malaya. The British brought in soldiers from units such as the Royal Marines and King's African Rifles. Another element in the strategy was the re-formation of the Special Air Service in 1950 as a specialised reconnaissance, raiding and counter-insurgency unit.

The Malayan Emergency was, unhappily, the setting for some of the most repellent policies ordained by any British government and the occasion of some of the most repulsive atrocities committed by British soldiers.

Agent Orange

Concentration camps were horrific enough, even though they differed from the Nazi Germany model in a number of respects, but the defoliant Agent Orange features in the list of inglorious British firsts: during the Malayan Emergency, Britain became the first nation in recent modern history to use herbicides and defoliants as a military weapon. It was used to destroy bushes, food crops, and trees to deprive the insurgents of both food and cover, playing a role in Britain's food denial campaign during the early 1950s. A variety of herbicides was used to clear lines of communication and wipe out food crops as part of this strategy. One of the herbicides, brand name Trioxone, was a 50:50 mixture of butyl esters of 2,4,5-T and 2,4-D. This mixture was virtually identical to the later Agent Orange, though Trioxone likely had a heavier contamination of the health-damaging dioxin impurity.[18] It was the British who were actually first to use herbicides in the Malayan 'Emergency' … . To circumvent surprise attacks on their troops the British Military Authorities used 2,4,5-T to increase visibility in the mixed vegetation.

Torture

It has been said that there was 'some vicious conduct by the British forces, who routinely beat up Chinese squatters when they refused, or possibly were unable, to give information' about the insurgents. *The Scotsman* thought this was just what the Chinese needed, praising it as good practice since 'simple-minded peasants arc told and come to believe that the communist leaders are invulnerable'. Worse still, some civilians and detainees were shot, allegedly because they attempted to flee and potentially aid insurgents or simply because they refused to give intelligence to British forces.

Batang Kali Massacre 1948

During the Batang Kali massacre, twenty-four unarmed civilians were executed by the Scots Guards near Batang Kali in Selangor in December 1948. All the victims were male, ranging in age from young teenage boys to elderly men.[19] Many of the victims' bodies had been mutilated and Batang Kali was burned to the ground. On searching the village no weapons were found. The British colonial government orchestrated a cover-up of British military abuses, helping to obfuscate the exact details of the massacre.

Decades of undignified legal battles ensued between the UK government and the families of the civilians executed by British troops. Christi Siver asks an important question in the Abstract to her 2009 paper, 'The Other Forgotten War':

> In the village at Batang Kali, on December 12, 1948, a patrol of the Scots Guards shot twenty-five Chinese villagers. While official reports claimed that they shot the civilians while they were trying to escape, in line with informal British policy, later revelations suggest that the unit shot the villagers without provocation. The war in Malaya often threw British units into dangerous situations; the communists used their knowledge of the jungle terrain and terrorist tactics to secure advantage against the more numerous and well-armed British. Yet Batang Kali is the only recorded case of a British unit killing large numbers of civilians. Why did the Scots Guards decide to kill these villagers while other patrols in similar situations did not?

Internment camps

We have seen how, as part of the Briggs' Plan devised by Lieutenant General Sir Harold Briggs, 500,000 people (roughly 10 per cent of Malaya's population) were forced from their homes by British forces. Tens of thousands of those homes were destroyed, and many people were imprisoned in those British Internment Camps called 'new villages' or concentration camps. During the Malayan Emergency, 450 new villages were created. This practice was prohibited by the Geneva Conventions and customary international law, which stated that the destruction of property must not happen unless rendered absolutely necessary by military operations.

Collective punishment

A key British war measure was inflicting collective punishments on villages whose people were deemed to be aiding insurgents. At Tanjong Malim in March 1952 a twenty-two-hour house curfew was imposed, banning everyone from leaving the village, closing the schools and stopping bus services; the rice rations for 20,000 people were also reduced. The last measure prompted the London School of Hygiene and Tropical Medicine to write to the Colonial Office to note that the 'chronically undernourished Malayan' might not be able to survive as a result. 'This measure is bound to result in an increase, not only of sickness but also of deaths, particularly amongst the mothers and very young children.'[20]

Indeed, it is useful to quote the introduction to Mark Curtis' (editor of *Declassified UK*) *Malaya – Britain's Forgotten War for Rubber*, if only for the context it gives us:

> Between 1948 and 1960 the United Kingdom (UK) fought a counter-insurgency campaign in Malaya, conventionally called the Emergency. A guerrilla war waged by the Malayan National Liberation Army (MNLA) sought to win independence from the British Empire and protect the interests of the Chinese community in the territory. The MNLA was largely the creation of the Malayan Communist Party, most of whose members were Chinese, but also included small minorities of Indians and Malays.
>
> Presented in most British analyses as a struggle against communism during the cold war, the MNLA in reality received very little support from Soviet or Chinese communists. The major concern for British governments was protecting their economic interests in Malaya, which were primarily huge investments in the rubber and tin industries.
>
> Most of the files on the guerrilla war that the British declassified were destroyed, perhaps to cover up crimes. Some files remain, however, at the National Archives in Kew, near London, and reveal that Britain resorted to very brutal measures to defeat the insurgency, including widespread aerial bombing and the use of a forerunner to modern cluster bombs.
>
> British officials also established a vast 'resettlement' scheme that herded hundreds of thousands of Malayan ethnic Chinese into fortified camps

> and that provided a model for the United States' (US) devastating 'strategic hamlet' programmes in Vietnam. They also used chemical agents to reduce the forest cover for the insurgents, from which the US may again have drawn lessons in its later use of Agent Orange in the Vietnam war.[21]

Some people were fined for leaving their homes to use outside latrines. In another episode of collective punishment, at Sengei Pelek the following month, measures included a house curfew, a reduction of 40 per cent in the rice ration and the construction of a chain-link fence 22 yards outside the existing barbed-wire fence around the town. Pamela Sodhy describes how officials explained that the measures were being imposed upon the 4,000 villagers 'for their continually supplying food' to the insurgents and 'because they did not give information to the authorities'.[22]

Deportations
Over the course of the war, some 30,000 people, mostly ethnic Chinese, were deported by the British authorities to mainland China.

Headhunting

During the war British and Commonwealth forces bought the services of Iban (Dyak) from Malayan Borneo as 'native' trackers in the jungle. Infamous for their predilection for head-hunting, they routinely decapitated suspected MNLA members; the official line was that taking the heads was the only means of later identification according to Simon Harrison.[23] To make a repugnant matter even worse, Iban head-hunters were permitted by British military leaders to keep the scalps of corpses as trophies.[24]

After the head-hunting had been exposed to the public, the Foreign Office first tried to deny that any such practice existed and then attempted to justify Iban headhunting and conducted a damage control exercise in the press. Privately, the Colonial Office noted that 'there is no doubt that under international law a similar case in wartime would be a war crime'.[25] But this was not a war, as we have seen; it was an 'emergency'. Skull fragments from a trophy head were later found to have been displayed in a British regimental museum.[26]

Head-hunting exposed
In April 1952 the British communist newspaper the *Daily Worker* (now the *Morning Star*) published a graphic, sickening photograph of Royal Marines in a British base posing with decapitated human heads. At first the government spokespersons from the Admiralty and Colonial Office, characteristically,

claimed the photograph was fake. So, not to be outdone, the *Daily Worker* published another, similar, photograph. Soon the Colonial Secretary, Oliver Lyttelton, had to confirm to parliament that the *Daily Worker* decapitation photographs were indeed genuine.[27] Response? Head-hunting was banned by Winston Churchill not because it was and is repugnant and barbaric but because he feared that any more photographs resulting from head-hunting would fuel communist propaganda.[28]

The *Daily Worker* was the only newspaper to publish such photographs while the hideous practice was virtually ignored by the mainstream British press.

Presumably the whole affair was still thought a fiction despite the statement in the House. The *Daily Worker* obviously had communist sympathies which the British press and establishment, hypocritically, made much of to undermine their editorial integrity.

All in all, during the emergency, security forces killed 6,710 MNLA guerrillas and captured 1,287, while 2,702 guerrillas surrendered during the conflict and approximately 500 more did so at its conclusion. Some 1,346 Malayan troops and police were killed during the fighting, as well as 519 Commonwealth personnel; 2,478 civilians were killed, with another 810 recorded as missing.

1951–1961

On leaving Malaya in 1951 the 1st Battalion returned to Redford Barracks in Edinburgh.

Here is the 1st's journey to 1961:

1952–1954:	Buxtehude, West Germany, BAOR
1954:	Elgin
1954–1955:	The Canal Zone, Egypt, defending against Egyptian terrorists as part of Middle East Land Forces as the British prepared to relocate their Middle East base to Cyprus.
1955:	Aden, supporting Aden Protectorate Levies against troublesome tribesmen.
1955–1957:	Gibraltar, as garrison battalion
1957–1961:	Münster, as part of 6 Brigade in 2nd Division BAOR
1961:	Edinburgh. At Redford Barracks in February 1961 the Battalion amalgamated with 1st Queen's Own Cameron Highlanders to form the Queen's Own Highlanders (Seaforth and Camerons).

Chapter 13

The 2nd Battalion after St Valéry

The 51st (Highland) Division was reconstituted from 9th (Highland) Division. Within the reborn 51st were 152, 153 and 154 Brigades with 152 composed of 2nd Seaforth, 5th Seaforth and 5th Camerons, all of which would be permanent members of the brigade. Other Seaforth battalions would also serve temporarily in the brigade.

Final Battle of El Alamein, 1942, and Tripoli

The final Battle of El Alamein was fought along a line between the railway halt at El Alamein and the Qattara Depression between 23 October and 4 November 1942. It was the climax of the North African campaign in the Second World War. Italy and Germany suffered decisive defeats by the Eighth Army: the 2nd Battalion played a key role.

In August 1942, General Sir Claude Auchinleck was relieved as Commander-in-Chief, Middle East Command by General Sir Harold Alexander. Lieutenant General William Gott was appointed commander Eighth Army but was killed en route to Cairo when his aircraft was shot down by German fighters. In his place, Lieutenant General Bernard Montgomery was appointed to command Eighth Army.

The Allied victory at El Alamein was the beginning of the end of the North African campaign. The battle was a significant morale boost for the Allies, being the first big success against the Axis since Operation CRUSADER in late 1941. (The objective of CRUSADER had been to outflank Axis forces in Libya, defeat the Axis armour forces and relieve the besieged port of Tobruk.) The end of the final Battle of El Alamein preceded by days the Allied invasion of French North-West Africa in Operation TORCH on 8 November, which opened a second front in North Africa.

Despite a serious security breach in which Rommel had been receiving detailed intelligence on the strength and movement of British forces from reports sent to Washington by Colonel Bonner Fellers, the US military attaché in Cairo, the Americans continued using the code until the end of June. Suspicion that the code was compromised was confirmed when 9th Australian Division captured the German 621st Signal Battalion in July 1942.[1]

Thanks to Ultra and various local sources, the Axis order of battle, its supply position and intentions were exposed. Hinsley notes that intelligence identified supply ships destined for North Africa, their location or routeing and, in most cases, their cargoes, allowing them to be attacked. The Italo-German *Panzerarmee Afrika* was soon down to three days' supply of fuel, only two days of which were east of Tobruk. Hinsley writes that 'The Panzer Army ... did not possess the operational freedom of movement that was absolutely essential in consideration of the fact that the British offensive can be expected to start any day'[2]. Submarine and air transport somewhat eased the shortage of ammunition and by late October, there was sixteen days' supply at the front. Eighth Army was ready; 195,000 men and 1,029 tanks began the offensive against the 116,000 men and 547 tanks of the *Panzerarmee*.

We learn from Royle that 2nd Seaforth arrived in Egypt via a 'long and bruising voyage round the Cape of Good Hope which lasted 59 days'. On disembarking the 'division started training for desert warfare and getting used to the heat'.[3]

Fairrie tells us how 2nd Seaforth began the battle in reserve but it was not long before it moved up to attack a German stronghold and form a bridgehead through a minefield which was holding up 2 Armoured Brigade. The Battalion succeeded in holding the bridgehead for thirty-six hours but at the cost of 100 casualties. In Operation SUPERCHARGE, 152 Brigade broke through the enemy lines, thus allowing the armour to operate beyond the minefield.[4]

Royle adds more detail:

> The attacking force moved off shortly after 10pm, each battalion being guided by a navigation officer watching his compass and counting his paces to ensure accuracy. All the first objectives were quickly taken with the follow-up forces passing through the first wave. By dawn the following day the second objectives had been taken and the battle moved into its next phase which Montgomery had promised would be a 'dogfight'.[5]

We also have an account of the battle from Colonel John Sym DSO, who was second-in-command of 2nd Seaforth. On 31 October he was called forward to take over as Brigade Major of 152 Brigade, the BM having been injured by a mine, and held the appointment until mid-December. He later commanded 5th Seaforth in North-West Europe. Extracts were published in the Queen's Own Highlander magazine of winter 1992, commemorating the 50th Anniversary of El Alamein.[6]

On 15 January 1943 the Battalion attacked at Corradini in the Battle of the Hills, reaching Tripoli on 23 January. On 4 February they took part in the victory parade, attended by Churchill. April saw them held up by the Germans on the Djebel Roumana Ridge and linking with the brigade along Wadi Akarit on the right flank. They followed 5th Seaforth and 5th Camerons onto the ridge and mopped up successfully, holding against fierce enemy counter-attacks, but incurring heavy casualties. Their North African campaign cost them 483 casualties.[7]

Operation LIGHTFOOT

With Operation LIGHTFOOT, Montgomery's plan was to cut two corridors through the Axis minefields in the north. One corridor was to run south-west through 2nd New Zealand Division's sector towards the centre of Miteirya Ridge, while the second was to run west, passing two miles north of the west end of Miteirya Ridge across 9th Australian and 51st (Highland) Divisions' sectors.[8] Tanks would then pass through and engage and destroy the mostly Italian armour. Diversions at Ruweisat Ridge in the centre and on the south of the line would keep the rest of the Axis forces from moving northwards. Montgomery expected a twelve-day battle in three stages: break-in, dogfight and final breaking of the enemy.

Operation SUPERCHARGE

This was a revised plan forced upon Montgomery by the failure to break in and through in LIGHTFOOT. His plan was revised on advice from Richard McCreery which was passed on by Alexander. McCreery saw the flaw in Monty's plan for the armour, for which he was never forgiven.

The battle began at 1:00am on 2 November, the aim being to destroy enemy armour, force the enemy to fight in the open, reduce his petrol stocks, attack and occupy his supply routes and effect the disintegration of his army. The intensity and the destruction in SUPERCHARGE were greater than anything witnessed thus far during the battle. The objective of this operation was Tel el Aqqaqir, the base of the Axis defence roughly three miles away.[9]

The initial thrust of SUPERCHARGE was to be carried out by 2nd New Zealand Division. Lieutenant General Sir Bernard Freyberg had tried to free them from this, as they had lost 1,405 men in just three days at El Ruweisat Ridge in July. Along with 5 New Zealand Infantry Brigade and 28th (Maori) Battalion, Freyberg had under his command 151 (Durham) Brigade from 50th (Northumbrian) Division, 152 (Seaforth and Camerons) Brigade from 51st (Highland) Division, 133 (Royal Sussex) Lorried Infantry Brigade and 9 Armoured Brigade.[10]

Despite his significant defeat at El Alamein, Rommel did not give up hope until late in the Tunisian campaign. Churchill was prompted to 'Ring out the bells'.[11] Churchill addressed the Lord Mayor's Banquet at the Mansion House on 10 November 1942. He spoke at length about the victory and made his famous claim that 'This is not the end. It is not even the beginning of the end. But it is perhaps the end of the beginning'.[12]

Reminiscing in 1950, Churchill wrote in his memoirs that 'It may almost be said, "Before Alamein we never had a victory. After Alamein we never had a defeat"'.[13]

Kenneth Mackessack

Kenneth Mackessack was with the Seaforth Highlanders from 1923 to 1948, during which he served on the North West Frontier and at El Alamein where he commanded the 2nd Battalion with the rank of major. He was wounded in the battle and Mentioned in Despatches for his actions. He spent the rest of the war as a military attaché in Washington, for which he was appointed to the Legion of Merit. While in the army he also played cricket for the Army as well as for teams in British India. Following his retirement, Mackessack served as a deputy lieutenant for Moray in 1954.

Major Gilmour had joined the Lovat Scouts in 1937, obtaining his commission and transferring to the Seaforth Highlanders on a regular commission in 1939. From 1942–43 he served with 2nd Seaforth in 51st (Highland) Division in the North Africa campaign. He was awarded the Military Cross for gallantry at El Alamein, with a Bar to the MC for further displays of courage at Wadi Akarit.

The Battle of Wadi Akarit

We have noted above that the Battle of Wadi Akarit (Operation SCIPIO) was an Allied attack from 6 to 7 April 1943, intended to dislodge Axis forces from positions along the Wadi Akarit in Tunisia. By early April

> the Allies reached a bottleneck where the Germans held strong positions on the Djebel Roumana Ridge, and along the Wadi Akarit which connected it to the sea. When the 51st Highland Division attacked on 6 April, 152 Brigade's objective was to dislodge the enemy from the Roumana heights. The task of 2nd Seaforth was to follow 5th Seaforth and 5th Camerons, turn right once astride the ridge and secure the feature at the North-East end of the ridge, referred to as point 112.[14]

The 2nd Seaforth war diary takes up the story:

> The right wing 'A' Coy and part of 'C' Coy under Captain McHardy, had no difficulty in gaining the 112 feature by 0645 hrs, although they arrived on the objective somewhat depleted in strength and ammunition. The Germans were then seen to be approaching up the wadis on the NW side of the ridge and working around the eastern flank of 112. This would not have mattered if the left wing had been able to make good the tops of the ridge overlooking 112. As it was our troops on 112 were under very heavy fire from commanding ground on their left and subject to a counterattack at short range from their front and right. The result was that we lost the feature and suffered heavily in casualties. A few were seen to be taken prisoner, being surprised at very short range. In this attack all Officers and Sergeants of 'A' and 'C' Coys were wounded.

The order was given to withdraw after a number of unsuccessful attempts were made to retake Point 112; it was decided that it was too costly to try and hold the position. There was a firefight as the light faded with each company holding on to what they had gained, but the heights stayed in enemy hands. The diary concludes:

> The day was full of tragic reverses, and it was extremely disappointing to all that we could not secure the objective. Nevertheless, there is no doubt that the Battalion fought hard and did very well to hold on where it did till dark, and to inflict as many casualties as it did. It is impossible to say how many prisoners were taken, but it was literally hundreds. An immense quantity of enemy weapons, ammunition and equipment was left abandoned on the ground.

By first light on 7 April the enemy had evacuated the whole position and the work of clearing the battlefield commenced. A few seriously wounded, which had been in enemy hands all night, were recovered, including Lieutenants Douglas and Payne.

Craig Durham explains how, with the Battalion losing fifty-two killed or died of wounds, 123 wounded and seventeen missing, it was decided to re-form the battalion into two companies, each 100 strong, A and B Companies forming one and C and D the other.[15] Two days after the battle a funeral service was held at the foot of Djebel Roumana to bury the dead in the 'sandy graves without a stone' of the poem's title.[16] The following year they were re-located to the war cemetery at Sfax, where Corporals Eric Bodley and Ebenezer Dick, Privates Danny McKim and James Smith lie today. Captains Lee and Law, and platoon commanders Lieutenants Payne and Gallie, all survived their wounds and the war.

Sicily

The 2nd then trained in Algeria for the invasion of Sicily, eventually sailing from around Sousse in landing craft via Malta. The 2nd Battalion landed in Sicily on 10 July as part of 152 Brigade. Operation HUSKY, the invasion of Sicily, was the largest amphibious assault of the war.

This was the plan:

- Phase 1. Preparatory measures by naval and air forces to neutralise enemy naval efforts and gain air superiority.
- Phase 2. Pre-dawn seaborne assaults, assisted by airborne landings with the object of seizing airfields and the ports of Syracuse and Licata.
- Phase 3. The establishment of a firm base from which to conduct operations for the capture of the ports of Augusta and Catania and the Gerbini group of airfields.
- Phase 4. The capture of the ports and airfields outlined in Phase 3.
- Phase 5. The reduction of the island.

The main amphibious landings involved three British divisions and 1st Canadian Division in the east, and two US divisions in the west, all supported by heavy fire from warships.

On the east side XIII Corps would land two divisions (5th and 50th) to capture Syracusa. Two Divisions of XXX Corps were to land on the south-east corner, 1st Canadian on the left (west) and 51st Highland Division on the right on the Pachino peninsula.[17]

John Sym tells us that:

> Most Landing Craft Assault had cut loose in the rough weather of the crossing from Malta. The brigade advanced inland with little opposition at first.
>
> On 14th July, at about 2.30pm, the first main encounter took place at the village of Francofonte. Here, a battalion of German Parachutists, brought by air from the South of France, put up stiff opposition for nearly 36 hours. The 5th Battalion suffered heavy casualties and it was not until the 2nd Battalion made a full battalion attack, on the evening of 15th July, that the enemy were forced to withdraw, with the loss of half their strength.

This success was followed by fierce fighting on the plain of Catania and in the Sferro Hills at the end of the month with 194 casualties incurred.

By 17 August all German troops had been evacuated to the mainland and the people of Sicily were freed from the brief German occupation. The 2nd returned to the UK in November for training for OVERLORD, as did 5th Seaforth. Only 6th Seaforth went on to fight in Italy, crossing the straits of Messina and landing in Italy on 3 September, with 17 Brigade of 5th Division, including the battalion, being the assault brigade. In November 1943 they moved to the Adriatic front near Ortona but, on 2 January 1944, returned to the west for operations to cross the Garigliano River. Following the Anzio landings on 22 January, 5th Division deployed into the beachhead in February.

We are lucky to have an account of one 6th Seaforth's experience in Sicily before his death as composed by http://www.operation-ladbroke.com/death-gates-augusta-jim-fern-6-seaforths/. Here is a shortened version of Lance Corporal Jim Fern's part in Operation LADBROKE at the Battle of Augusta compiled from the regimental diary and the ten letters he sent home to his sister Violet.

> The town of Augusta in Sicily did not fall easily, despite half its garrison having fled. Lance Corporal Jim Fern of the 6 Seaforth died fighting in the battle to capture it. The young pit worker from Coalville was buried on the battlefield ... On the day of the landings, 10 July, the 6 Seaforth led the landings and the attack on the nearby town of Cassibile, which they captured. Syracuse was then taken by the Northants and Royal Scots Fusiliers, with help from the glider troops of Operation LADBROKE ... Both 15 and 17 Infantry Brigades now entered the town [Priolo], which was soon crammed with British troops and vehicles heading north along the narrow coastal plain. The congestion made a perfect target for enemy artillery, which could fire blind, by the map, and still have a high chance of hitting something. The 6 Seaforth suffered some minor casualties in the crowded streets, although other battalions fared worse. But capturing Priolo town was little in itself. Just north of it was a river that made a natural anti-tank obstacle, and it was covered by enemy troops ensconced on a small ridge or knoll. They were supported by guns firing on the British flanks from the slopes of the foothills of the plateau further inland. It took until nearly 2pm to drive the defenders from the knoll, after a hefty artillery barrage supplemented by naval gunfire, followed by a three-company setpiece attack by the Royal Scots Fusiliers. At this point the 6 Seaforth again took over the lead. They were finally in the open country north of Priolo, and for some miles they met no opposition. However, after crossing the Marcellino River they entered the area behind Cugno Point, which faced the town of Augusta on its peninsula across the bay ... The Italians

> were still deploying to face the sea when the leading company of the 6 Seaforth, presumably preceded by Bren carriers in their reconnaissance role, hit the Italian 'right' flank … Now the 6 Seaforth, deployed in single file along the road north, came under machine-gun fire from both sides. Italian mortars and artillery plastered the road and the approaches south of the Marcellino … So 'A' Company, Jim Fern's company, attacked without support. As a single company facing a whole battalion, progress was slow … we can with some certainty say that Jim probably died between about 4pm and midnight on 12th July 1943, somewhere between the Marcellino River and the area around the seaplane base.

Jim's friend in A Company, Lance Corporal Harold Halford, wrote to Violet on 15 August:

> Jim was lost 2 days after we landed. We were making an attack on a pill box on the outskirts of a town which later fell to us. They got old Jim with machine-gun fire. He died a few minutes after, but I am thankful that he felt no pain.
>
> Jim went into the attack as he had done many times before, with no fear at his heart, his only thought to do his duty as a soldier and obeyed orders to the last ... He died as every soldier likes to die. Fighting.

The Battle for the Sferro Hills, July-August 1943

51st Division was tasked to take the road from Sferro to Catenanuova but to achieve this it was necessary to clear the enemy from the Sferro hills. This was the plan, details of which are in 51st (Highland) Division Operation Order No.76.

The start line and observation post where the GOC made his plan was Mount Turcisi to the south. On the right would be 152 Brigade: 5th Camerons would lead with 5th Seaforth behind and 2nd Seaforth in reserve. Simultaneously 154 Brigade on the left had 7th Black Watch on the right, 1st Black Watch on the left and 7th Argylls in reserve.

> The attack began on 31st July. The 5th Camerons encountered heavy opposition on the ridge and were reinforced by 2nd Seaforth. After a heavy strike by 128th Field Regiment, point 224 was taken. It was held, despite a strong German counter-attack and the fighting continued throughout the day. After a hold up in the gully the 5th Seaforth, following behind 5th Camerons, got to Angelico Farm. The olive grove was full of enemy and the grove continued over the slope. The Camerons got to the base of the

> wood and dug in. They too repelled the tank and infantry counter-attack thanks to the artillery support, which broke it up. 13 Platoon of 1/7th Middlesex also provided important supporting fire.[18]

A list of war dead of the Seaforth Highlanders buried in Syracuse War Cemetery can be found at http://www.wikisicily.com/siracusa/index-rgt.php?Rgt=Seaforth%20Highlanders

Normandy

That November 2nd Seaforth returned to England to train for the Normandy landings. The Battalion landed on 9 June at Courseulles-sur-Mer. For two months they held the bridgehead over the river Orne against fierce German counter-attacks, taking the enemy positions at Tilly-la-Campagne and, not without irony, liberating St Valéry in early September. Operation TOTALIZE had taken place in early August as part of the Battle of Normandy: 51st Division was under command of II Canadian Corps, the objective being to seize the Verrières ridge, which was captured on 8 August. The Highlanders rode into battle in Kangaroo APCs. Operation ASTONIA, the liberation of le Havre, began on 10 September. Liberation of St Valéry took place between these operations, on 2 September; the 5th Battalion and 5th Camerons may well have been granted the honour of entering the town as the first of the Highland battalions although the divisional recce unit, 2nd Derbyshire Yeomanry, preceded the infantry.

The Netherlands and the Ardennes

Their next objective was the Battle of the Maas where victory would open up the strategically important port of Antwerp. Success followed at Schijndel; the land south of the Maas was cleared by 5 November; the 2nd then attacked across the Nederwert canal using assault craft and LVTs, known as Buffaloes. They crossed the Zig Canal via a bridgehead established by 5th Camerons on 17 November and then took Beringen. That hard winter they helped against the German offensive in the Ardennes, taking Ronchampey on 11 January and Laroche the next day.

Germany

The Battalion crossed into Germany on 9 February 1945 with close-quarter fighting in the Reichswald as the Germans fell back towards the Siegfried Line. It was in 153 Highland Brigade, one of the assault formations, on the banks of the Rhine by early March. The Battalion crossed the Oudi Issel river using the wreckage of a bridge the retreating Germans had blown up. The Reichswald and subsequent conflicts came at a cost of 120 casualties. There were actions at Adelheide and Ganderksee before taking Bremervorde two days before the German surrender on 4 May.

Chapter 14

The Territorials in the Second World War

As in the First World War, Seaforth territorial battalions served with determination and valour in many theatres.

4th (Ross-shire) Battalion Seaforth Highlanders TA

The 4th sailed with the BEF on 26 January 1940, later taking up defensive positions on the Maginot Line in the Saar Valley. Along with 4th Camerons, 4th Seaforth took part in the counter-attack on the German bridgehead over the Somme at Abbeville. With the 2nd and other elements of 51st (Highland) Division they were forced to retreat to St Valéry-en-Caux where they were surrounded and had no choice but to surrender on 12 June 1940.

5th (Sutherland & Caithness) Battalion Seaforth Highlanders TA

As we have seen, the 5th joined 2nd Seaforth and 5th Camerons in the reconstituted 152 (Highland) Brigade. They sailed for Egypt in June 1942 where they served alongside the 2nd Battalion and 5th Camerons in 51st (Highland) Division at El Alamein, losing 177 casualties in Operation SUPERCHARGE, in which they made it possible for the armour to get through the minefields. In February 1943 the Highland Division was faced with the German tank obstacle that was the Wadi Zigzaou on the approach to Mareth. The 5th Seaforth took possession of the tank ditch during the assault on the Mareth Line while April saw them at Wadi Akarit. North Africa cost the 5th Battalion 472 casualties. Like the 2nd they saw heavy fighting in Sicily at Francofonte and the Plain of Catania with Sicily costing them a further 132 casualties. With Sicily taken, the 5th returned to Britain to prepare for the Normandy landings where they joined with the 2nd in the fierce fighting for Caen and then Tilly -la-Campagne in Operation TOTALIZE. As we have seen the liberation of St Valéry-en-Caux on 2 September was a big day for the 5th: the Battalion and 5th Camerons were probably granted the honour of entering the town first of the Highland battalions.

That autumn saw the 5th in the Netherlands at the river Maas and then in the Ardennes in January 1945. Their progress mirrored that of the 2nd all the way to the Rhine that March. Then they were assigned to dock duties at Cuxhaven before guarding the SS concentration camp at Sandbostel, from where they moved to Hanover in February 1946. The Battalion was disbanded on 3 September 1946.

6th (Morayshire) Battalion Seaforth Highlanders TA

A second-line TA unit that was transferred to 17 Infantry Brigade, part of 5th Division, 6th Seaforth crossed to France with the BEF on 20 January 1940. There was change in the air as a Regular battalion was to be attached to each Territorial brigade. The effect of this on the Seaforth meant that the 6th was replaced by the 2nd in 152 Brigade with the 6th replacing 2nd Seaforth in 17 Brigade, joining them at Hallouin.

Madagascar

While the Germans were overrunning the Netherlands the 6th were in Belgium and then on the Scarpe near Arras and, later, at Ypres. When the Belgians surrendered, the 6th retreated to Dunkirk where they were evacuated on 1 June 1940. The Battalion was re-formed at Turiff in Aberdeenshire and remained in the UK until March 1942 when they were in for a complete change of scenery. On 6 March, having embarked for Madagascar with 17 Brigade, they were part of the force that captured that island on 6 May. The Battalion lost three officers and fourteen soldiers in the attack on Antisirane, including the Adjutant, Captain J.K. McCall, and the Intelligence Officer, Captain S.B. Black, both of whom were killed. Attacking alongside 2nd Northampton, the Seaforth were reinforced by a company of Royal Welch Fusiliers from 29 Brigade.

Why was French Madagascar strategically important? Firstly, occupation would help secure the vital convoy route around the Cape of Good Hope, safeguarding Allied supply lines Also, Madagascar, as the name suggests, was a French colony at the outbreak of the war, having been under French administration since 1885. It boasted important harbours, Malagasy troops and, after the fall of France, became a flashpoint between the UK and Vichy France and the scene of fighting between Allied and Vichy French forces in 1942. Operation IRONCLAD was launched to deny any chance of the island falling to the Imperial Japanese Navy.

Tens of thousands of Malagasy men had been conscripted into the French army: 34,000 of them were in France when it capitulated in summer 1940 with 72,000 more languishing in Madagascar waiting to be transported to Europe.[1] Malagasy troops captured by Germany during the invasion were treated abominably: many were massacred in summary executions or murdered when they reached prisoner-of-war camps.[2] German propaganda showed black French troops to be savages who fought to the death and took no prisoners.

Charles de Gaulle naturally urged Malagasy troops to join the Free French, but the colonial administration under Governor General Armand Annet pledged allegiance to Vichy France. This disturbed de Gaulle and the British command who were concerned lest French Madagascar's allegiance to Vichy would open the door to Axis bases on the island. Japanese (as we have seen) German and Italian vessels, particularly merchant raiders and submarines, were already operating in the Indian Ocean, attacking Allied shipping and inflicting numerous losses.[3]

In 1940 the Nazi regime believed that Madagascar might offer a solution to the Jewish Question, the Final Solution: they proposed deporting Europe's Jewish population en masse to the island. There they would be under strict control by the *Schutzstaffel* (SS) who would manage Madagascar much like a police state. This was to be Germany's 'Final Solution' to their Jewish Question: a massive forced exodus of millions to a remote island where they would live, in effective quarantine, ostracised from the rest of the world. Over a period of four years, the plan was to despatch a million Jews each year to the island in the hope that conditions would be unsurvivable and many would perish.[4]

This hideous apocalyptic scheme, the Madagascar Plan, never got off the ground. Germany's defeat in the Battle of Britain meant that the mad plan to capture and commandeer the British merchant fleet to transport millions of Jews became unfeasible. In any event, in 1942, Madagascar was, of course, invaded and captured by British forces in the Battle of Madagascar. The Madagascar Plan was binned and instead the Nazis decided at the January 1942 Wannsee Conference that the Jewish population would have to be exterminated by what we now call the Holocaust.[5]

The island was officially handed over by the British to Free France in 1943 under whose control it remained for the rest of the war.

After four weeks in Madagascar the 6th Battalion was relieved by Rhodesian forces and sailed to Bombay to assist in the defence of India against the Japanese. They moved by rail to Ranchi where they helped quell civil disturbances.

Iran and Iraq

With German forces advancing towards the Caucasus and the Caspian Sea with a greedy eye on oil reserves, Iran and Iraq were increasingly vulnerable.

The 5th Division, including 6th Seaforth, was ordered to northern Persia, landing at Basrah and moving to Kermanshah via Baghdad. Internal security operations with two Russian battalions followed in Tehran during the bread riots and famine of the winter 1942–1943. A platoon of 6th Seaforth was part of the operation to kidnap the pro-German General Fazlollah Zahedi.

Fazlollah Zahedi and Fitzroy Maclean

Zahedi was an Iranian lieutenant general and statesman who replaced the Iranian prime minister, Mohammad Mosaddegh, in a coup d'état supported by the United States and the United Kingdom. But in 1941 the British suspected that Zahedi was planning a revolution in co-operation with German forces, and were concerned that, as one of the worst grain-hoarders, he was attracting much animosity. He was arrested in his own office by Fitzroy Maclean, who describes the escapade in his 1949 memoir *Eastern Approaches*.[6] On searching Zahedi's bedroom, Maclean wrote that he found 'a collection of automatic weapons of German manufacture, a good deal of silk underwear, some opium, an illustrated register of the prostitutes of Isfahan', and correspondence from a local German agent. Zahedi was flown out of the country and interned in Palestine. According to Hermione Ranfurly, Maclean was 'allotted a platoon of Seaforth Highlanders and instructed to kidnap' General Fazlollah Zahedi, the commander of the Persian forces in the Isfahan area.[7] This incident led Hitler's government to withdraw support from its network in Persia.

Maclean was one of only two men who, during the Second World War, enlisted in the Army as a private (in the Queen's Own Cameron Highlanders), and rose to the rank of brigadier, the other being future fellow Conservative MP Enoch Powell.

The *Iran Digest* records how during the final months of 1942 and in 1943, the streets of Kermanshah were full of semi-naked and hungry people with fifteen deaths attributed to hunger and poverty occurring every day. In February 1943 typhus broke out and the hospital was closed because of widespread infection among doctors and staff.[8] Only in 1943 did the Soviets release 25,000 tons of grain to help the situation.[9]

The famine rarely features in academic papers. C. O'Sullivan tells us that 'The British government blamed the situation on hoarding, inefficient distribution and an inadequate transport system', but Washington suspected that the British had deliberately manipulated the food supply to further their own political objectives.[10] Mohammad Gholi Majd seems to be the only author to have written about the famine. Majd has concluded that three to four million Iranians, a quarter of the population, died of starvation and disease during the

Allied occupation, citing US State Department population figures for 1941 (15 million) and 1944 (10–12 million).[11]

Between 28 November and 1 December 1943, the leaders of the 'Big Three' met in Tehran to discuss military strategies against Germany and Japan and the post-war era. They also signed the 'Declaration of the Three Powers Regarding Iran', which provided economic assistance to Iran during and after the war. They also agreed on 'desire for the maintenance of the independence, sovereignty, and territorial integrity of Iran'. British and US troops withdrew from Iran in January 1946. The Soviets withdrew in May 1946, but only after pressure from the United Nations.

Sicily and Italy

In July 1943 the 6th Battalion took part in Operation HUSKY, the invasion of Sicily. From Persia, it had travelled overland to Syria for training and intensive exercises before moving to Egypt to prepare for embarkation as an element of Eastern Task Force which took a circuitous route intended to deceive the enemy into believing it was headed for Greece and the Greek islands. The Division was involved, as part of XIII Corps, in the capture of Syracuse, Augusta and Catania from Axis forces.

On 3 September, 17 Brigade crossed over into Italy; the landings, Operation BAYTOWN, were made north (5th Division) and south (1st Canadian Division) of Reggio. They later encountered opposition from the Germans before they relocated to the Adriatic front at Ortona. In January 1944, 5th Division transferred from Eighth Army to Fifth Army and participated in the first attack on the Gustav Line along the Garigliano river, making the first break in the German line.

Soon after, 5th Division was transferred to the Anzio beachhead as part of VI (US) Corps. Relieving 56th (London) Division, 5th remained in the beachhead, enduring German bombardments and attacks; 17 Brigade, including 6th Seaforth, was responsible for the area known as the 'Lobster's Claw'. With the opening of 15 Army Group's Operation DIADEM against the Gustav Line on 11 May, VI Corps was on notice to break out of the Anzio beachhead and advance on Rome. The British element of VI Corps played its part in that advance as German forces made a fighting withdrawal to and beyond Rome which was liberated on 4 June.

After twelve months in Italy, 6th Seaforth returned to Egypt to rest and refit and then, in March 1945, sailed to Marseille from where they moved north to join the Allied advance through Belgium and into Germany. The Battalion finished the war at Lübeck.

7th (Morayshire) Battalion Seaforth Highlanders TA

Originally serving with 26 Infantry Brigade, part of 9th (Highland) Division, the Battalion was posted to garrison the Shetland Islands as part of the Orkney and Shetland Defences, OSDEF. In October 1941 it moved to Northumberland to join 46 (Highland) Brigade in 15th (Scottish) Division with whom it was to stay for the duration of the war. The Battalion remained in the UK until 1944, deploying to France on 16 June and seeing action in Operation EPSOM, the operation to seize the crossings over the river Odon in preparation for the attack on Caen. This involved two attacks by 7th Seaforth, at Cheux and le Valtru. On crossing the Odon, they attacked positions on the Eterville Ridge, suffering 300 casualties in some of the hardest fighting encountered by the Battalion.[12]

That July 15th (Scottish) Division moved into the American sector and 7th Seaforth took part in Operation BLUECOAT, the breakout from Caumont, capturing Quarry Hill against fierce opposition as the advance guard at Lassy.

The 7th then crossed the Seine south of Rouen and led the 46 Brigade advance, capturing Grand Rocherelles by night and then les Andelys. Continuing into Belgium and the Netherlands through Courtrai and Loos, they established the bridgehead over the Wilhelmina canal allowing 15th (Scottish) Division to clear the area around Best near Eindhoven. They protected the Nijmegen corridor and helped capture Liesel and Slot, advancing to the Maas and then taking part in the attack on Blerick. In January 1945 the 7th saw action at Hasselt, Schloss Moyland and Schloss Kalbeck through the Siegfried Line and on to the Rhine.

Their engagement at Best was particularly significant as this was an important action in the MARKET part of Operation MARKET GARDEN which was the Allied attempt to shorten the war by capturing the bridges along the Rhine in the Netherlands. The bridge at Arnhem is the most famous and is remembered as the 'bridge too far'.[13]

The 7th crossed the Rhine at Xanten on 24 March 1945 after training in river crossing. The Elbe was next on 29 April making 15th (Scottish) the only division to cross the Seine, Rhine and Elbe. Like the 6th Battalion, the 7th finished the war at Lübeck before going on to occupy Kiel and disbandment in January 1946.

The 8th and 9th Battalions, raised early in the war, served in a home defence and reserve capacity. In December 1941, the 8th was re-designated 30th Battalion Seaforth Highlanders.

Chapter 15

1945 and Beyond

This is what the 2nd Battalion did after the war:

1945–1946:	keeping the peace in Neustadt near Hanover (BAOR).
1946:	moved back to the UK, stationed first at Knook Camp near Warminster and then Bicester.
1948:	amalgamated with the 1st Battalion Seaforth Highlanders.[1] This was part of a process whereby Line regiments were reduced to single-battalion units. A few were restored to twin-battalion status in the course of the Korean War but only temporarily.

As we have seen above, post-war, the 1st Battalion served in Java before moving to Malaya where, from 1948 until 1951, it engaged in security operations during the Malayan Emergency. After this, postings included Edinburgh (1951–2), BAOR (1952–4), garrison postings in the inhospitable and reviled Suez Canal Zone, then Aden, similarly hot and dusty (1954–5), to protect the Aden Protectorate Levies against disaffected tribesman spurred on by Nasser's truculence in Egypt and finally Gibraltar (1955–7), before going back to Germany (Münster, 1957–61).[2]

1961 saw them in Singapore at Selarang Barracks as the British Battalion of 99 Gurkha Brigade in 17th Gurkha Division.

Post-war, the regiment retained one Territorial Army (TA) unit, 11th Battalion Seaforth Highlanders.[3]

The TA battalions amalgamated in 1967 to form the 3rd (Territorial) Battalion Queen's Own Highlanders.[4]

1st Queen's Own Highlanders

In 1961, at Edinburgh's Redford Barracks, the regiment was amalgamated with the Queen's Own Cameron Highlanders to form the single-battalion Queen's Own Highlanders (Seaforth and Camerons) which merged, on 17 September 1994, with the Gordon Highlanders to form the Highlanders (Seaforth, Gordons and Camerons) as part of the Options for Change defence review.[5]

Established by the amalgamation of the Seaforth Highlanders (Ross-shire Buffs, The Duke of Albany's) and the Queen's Own Cameron Highlanders, the Queen's Own Highlanders (Seaforth and Camerons) recruited mainly in Orkney, Inverness, Caithness, Ross and Cromarty, Sutherland, Moray and Nairn. Their first overseas deployment found the regiment in Singapore in 1961. From there, it was posted to Brunei for the next three years where the Highlanders assisted in suppressing a revolt by the North Kalimantan National Army and released European hostages in December 1962.

The Brunei Revolt

The northern part of the island of Borneo comprised three British territories: the colonies of Sarawak and North Borneo (to be renamed Sabah) and the protectorate of the Sultanate of Brunei. Brunei had been a British protectorate since 1888.

The Brunei Revolt is also known as the Brunei rebellion of 1962, a December 1962 insurrection in the British protectorate of Brunei by opponents of the established sultanate and its proposed inclusion in the Federation of Malaysia which wanted to establish a republic. The insurgents, 4,000 under Yassin Effendi, were members of the TNKU (North Kalimantan National Army), a militia bankrolled by Indonesia and linked to the left-wing Brunei People's Party (BPP), which favoured a North Borneo Federation. The TNKU began co-ordinated attacks on the oil town of Seria (targeting the Royal Dutch Shell oil installations), on police stations and government facilities around the protectorate. The revolt began to break down within hours, having failed to achieve key objectives such as the capture of Brunei Town, and Sultan Omar Ali Saifuddien III. The Battalion had a significant role in retaking Anduki airfield, having been shipped in on HMS *Cavalier*; six days later the revolt evaporated.

The revolt influenced the Sultan's 1963 decision not to join Malaysia. It was one of the first stages of the Indonesia/Malaysia confrontation and the formation of modern Malaysia.

In 1964, the Queen's Own Highlanders moved to Mercer Barracks in Osnabrück in what was then West Germany, remaining there with the British Army of the Rhine as part of 12 Infantry Brigade in 2nd Division for much of the next thirty years, including eight operational tours in Northern Ireland.[6]

In August 1966 they were in Berlin as part of the Berlin Infantry Brigade. From 1968 to 1971 they were at Redford Barracks, taking in a nine-month stint in Sharjah, the Trucial States, training in the mountains and deserts of Sharjah and Oman. It was Germany again from 1971 to 1976, at Belfast Barracks in Osnabrück, and then Kirknewton near Edinburgh from 1976 to 1980. Subsequently, the Regiment was posted to Belize, formerly British Honduras, in 1976 to defend against invasion by Guatemala, supported by detachments from the Life Guards, 3rd Royal Horse Artillery and the RAF; it returned in 1985. From 1977 to 1979 it was in Edinburgh and Northern Ireland with Gibraltar in 1978 and Hong Kong in 1980–1981 where the role was to deter illegal immigration from China. Nine thousand immigrants were arrested. Sadly, the Commanding Officer, Lieutenant Colonel D.N.A. Blair, and his signaller, Lance Corporal Victor MacLeod, were among the nineteen killed at Warrenpoint in 1979; that tour saw three other Highlanders killed. In 1981 the Battalion returned to the UK, to Tidworth.

The Queen's Own Highlanders (Seaforth and Camerons) also sent detachments on the MV *Norland* to the Falkland Islands, arriving after their liberation in June 1982 to restore some kind of normality. From 1982 until 1988 they were at Tidworth (1982–1983), Northern Ireland (1983–1985) and Fort George (1985–1988), interrupted by that second tour in Belize in 1987. From March 1988 to 1993 Münster was their home, with training in Canada and two tours in Northern Ireland.

The whole Regiment deployed to the First Gulf War (1990–91) in January 1991, to recover Kuwait from Iraq, remaining in the Persian Gulf until November 1992. During that time three of their soldiers were killed in a friendly fire incident when their Warrior APC was hit by a missile fired by a US jet.

The 1st Battalion The Highlanders (Seaforth, Gordons and Camerons)

As noted, on 17 September 1994 the Seaforth amalgamated with the Gordons and Camerons at Dreghorn Barracks in Edinburgh to form The Highlanders. One year later the new regiment completed that two-year deployment to Northern Ireland, moving to Ebrington Barracks in Londonderry from 1994 to 1997 as province reserve battalion. In April 1997 they were in Catterick Garrison's Somme Barracks as part of 19 Mechanised Brigade, deploying to Kosovo and then Bosnia on peacekeeping duties in 2002–03.[7] The Regiment then joined the Bergen-Hohne Garrison, Bad Fallingbostel at St Barbara's Barracks in BAOR in 2004 as part of 7 Armoured Brigade, formerly part of 7th Armoured Division, the Second World War's famous Desert Rats, equipped with Warrior IFVs.

In 2006 they joined the Royal Scots Borderers, Black Watch, Royal Highland Fusiliers and Argyll and Sutherland Highlanders to form the present Royal Regiment of Scotland.

Territorials

The contribution made to the Territorial Army on its re-establishment in 1947 came in the form of 11th Seaforth Highlanders TA which flourished from 1947 to 1967. The battalion was part of 152 (Highland) Brigade in 51st (Highland) Division. The 11th was organised into six companies: A to D, Battalion HQ and S Company. In 1967 this changed to:

B (Seaforth) Company, 51st Highland Volunteers (T&AVR II)
B (Seaforth) Company, 3rd Queen's Own Highlanders (T&AVR III)
C (Seaforth) Company, 3rd Queen's Own Highlanders (T&AVR III)

The Royal Regiment of Scotland

Nemo Me Impune Lacessit (*No one assaults me and gets away with it*)

> Since its formation the regiment has deployed to almost every theatre of operations the British Army has been involved in; conflicts in Afghanistan, Iraq, Bosnia and Northern Ireland, supporting peace operations in Cyprus, West and North Africa, disaster relief in the Caribbean and giving support to UK Civil Authorities to deal with wild-fire, flooding and the COVID-19 pandemic. In recent years, SCOTS soldiers have had key roles in NATO Response Forces, partnered US forces in training in the US and Europe.[7]

As with the other Scottish regiments involved, the Highlanders were permitted to retain their former name as the new battalion's primary title, with the battalion number as a subtitle. They therefore became The Highlanders, 4th Battalion The Royal Regiment of Scotland, or 4 Scots. Currently, 2nd and 3rd Battalions serve in a light infantry role, the 4th as mechanised infantry and 5th Battalion as a rifle company.[8]

In September 2015 the battalion moved from Germany to Bourlon Barracks in Catterick Garrison, where they became a heavy protected mobility battalion forming part of 20 Armoured Infantry Brigade.[9]

As a result of *Army 2020 Refine* restructure, the battalion joined the Strike Experimentation Group in 2020.[10]

Since 2006 the regiment's soldiers have seen multiple tours including several during Operations TELIC in Iraq (2005–08) and HERRICK in Afghanistan (2008–13), as well as service in Germany, Belize, Sierra Leone and Cyprus.[11]

Incidentally, the Battalion is the backbone of the Army's only shinty team, The Scots Shinty Club. Due to the 4th Battalion's regular placements abroad, the team only plays in cup matches.[12]

Battalions; Regimental HQ Staff

- 2 SCOTS, The Royal Highland Fusiliers, 2nd Battalion The Royal Regiment of Scotland is a light role infantry Battalion at Penicuik.
- 3 SCOTS, The Black Watch, 3rd Battalion The Royal Regiment of Scotland at Perth.
- 4 SCOTS, The Highlanders, 4th Battalion The Royal Regiment of Scotland, a mechanised infantry battalion at Cameron Barrracks, Inverness.
- 5 SCOTS, Balaklava Company, 5th Battalion The Royal Regiment of Scotland, a rifle company of The Royal Regiment of Scotland at Stirling.
- 6 SCOTS, 52nd Lowland, 6th Battalion The Royal Regiment of Scotland at Glasgow
- 7 SCOTS, 51st Highland, 7th Battalion The Royal Regiment of Scotland at Perth.

Regular Battalions/Company

- Royal Highland Fusiliers, 2nd Battalion Royal Regiment of Scotland, at Glencorse Barracks, Penicuik (Light Infantry) – 4 Infantry Brigade and Headquarters North East
- The Black Watch, 3rd Battalion Royal Regiment of Scotland, at Fort George, Inverness (Light Mechanised Infantry) – 51 Infantry Brigade and Headquarters Scotland
- The Highlanders, 4th Battalion Royal Regiment of Scotland, at Bourlon Barracks, Catterick Garrison (Mechanised Infantry) – 1 Armoured Infantry Brigade
- Balaklava Company, Argyll and Sutherland Highlanders 5th Battalion The Royal Regiment of Scotland, at Redford Barracks, Edinburgh (Public duties) – 51 Infantry Brigade and Headquarters Scotland

The Museum of the Royal Scots (The Royal Regiment) and the Royal Regiment of Scotland is in Edinburgh Castle.

Lineage

<table>
<tr><th>1880</th><th>1881 Childers Reforms</th><th>1921 Name changes</th><th>1957 Defence White Paper</th><th>1966 Defence White Paper</th><th>1990 Options for Change</th><th>2003 Delivering Security in a Changing World</th></tr>
<tr><td>1st (The Royal Scots) Regiment of Foot</td><td>The Royal Scots (Lothian Regiment)</td><td colspan="4">The Royal Scots (The Royal Regiment)</td><td rowspan="14">The Royal Regiment of Scotland</td></tr>
<tr><td>25th (King's Own Borderers) Regiment of Foot</td><td colspan="5">The King's Own Borderers renamed in 1887: The King's Own Scottish Borderers</td></tr>
<tr><td>21st (Royal Scots Fusiliers) Regiment of Foot</td><td colspan="2">The Royal Scots Fusiliers</td><td rowspan="3" colspan="3">The Royal Highland Fusiliers (Princess Margaret's Own Glasgow and Ayrshire Regiment)</td></tr>
<tr><td>71st (Highland) (Light Infantry) Regiment of Foot</td><td rowspan="2" colspan="2">The Highland Light Infantry renamed in 1923: The Highland Light Infantry (City of Glasgow Regiment)</td></tr>
<tr><td>74th (Highlanders) Regiment of Foot</td></tr>
<tr><td>42nd (Royal Highland, The Black Watch) Regiment of Foot</td><td rowspan="2" colspan="5">The Black Watch (Royal Highlanders)</td></tr>
<tr><td>73rd (Perthshire) Regiment of Foot</td></tr>
<tr><td>72nd (Duke of Albany's Own Highlanders) Regiment of Foot</td><td rowspan="2" colspan="2">Seaforth Highlanders (Ross-shire Buffs) renamed on 22 November 1881: Seaforth Highlanders (Ross–shire Buffs, The Duke of Albany's)</td><td rowspan="3" colspan="2">The Queen's Own Highlanders (Seaforth and Camerons)</td><td rowspan="3">The Highlanders (Seaforth, Gordons and Camerons)</td></tr>
<tr><td>78th (Highlanders) (Ross-shire Buffs) Regiment of Foot</td></tr>
<tr><td>79th (Queen's Own Cameron Highlanders) Regiment of Foot</td><td colspan="2">The Queen's Own Cameron Highlanders</td></tr>
<tr><td>75th (Stirlingshire) Regiment of Foot</td><td rowspan="2" colspan="5">The Gordon Highlanders</td></tr>
<tr><td>92nd (Gordon Highlanders) Regiment of Foot</td></tr>
<tr><td>91st (Princess Louise's Argyllshire Highlanders) Regiment of Foot</td><td rowspan="2">Princess Louise's (Sutherland and Argyll Highlanders) renamed on 2 June 1882: Princess Louise's (Argyll and Sutherland Highlanders)</td><td rowspan="2" colspan="4">The Argyll and Sutherland Highlanders (Princess Louise's)</td></tr>
<tr><td>93rd (Sutherland Highlanders) Regiment of Foot</td></tr>
</table>

Appendix 1

The British Army Formations and Units 1939–1945

ARMY: Two or more Corps formed an Army, and two or more Armies formed an Army Group.

CORPS: a main sub-division of an army in the field, consisting of two or more divisions.

DIVISION: the main formation in an army, the division is both the highest tactical formation and the lowest operational formation. Numbering between 12,000 and 18,000 men, it was an 'All-Arms' formation, comprising armour, infantry, artillery, engineers and signals, although divisions did have a predominant role as armoured, infantry, anti-aircraft or airborne. A division is commanded by a major general. In most armies a division is composed of several regiments or brigades; in turn, several divisions typically make up a corps.

BRIGADE: a smaller formation, typically consisting of a number of infantry battalions and/or other units and forming part of a division. The role of a brigade was to command three battalions or three regiments, with three brigades forming a division. A brigade could operate independently and comprise all arms, i.e. armour, infantry, artillery, engineers and signals. A brigade including all-arms was described as a brigade group. However, most brigades had a functional organisation and formed part of a division. A brigade or brigade group was commanded by a brigadier.

152 Infantry Brigade	03.09.1939–12.06.1940 & 07.08.1940–31.08.1945
4th Seaforth Highlanders	03.09.1939–12.06.1940
6th Seaforth Highlanders	03.09.1939–30.03.1940
4th Queen's Own Cameron Highlanders	03.09.1939–12.06.1940
152 Infantry Brigade Anti-Tank Company	28.01.1940–12.06.1940 & 01.09.1940–14.12.1941
2nd Seaforth Highlanders	30.03.1940–12.06.1940 & 04.09.1940–31.08.1945
4th/5th Seaforth Highlanders	07.08.1940–04.04.1941
7th Seaforth Highlanders	07.08.1940–23.08.1940
5th Queen's Own Cameron Highlanders	07.08.1940–31.08.1945
5th Seaforth Highlanders	05.04.1941–31.08.1945

Source: https://www.unithistories.com/units_british/units_british.html
https://www.unithistories.com/units_british/51InfDiv.html

The smallest unit was a **battalion**, or a cavalry/armour, artillery, engineer regiment or RAMC medical regiment/field hospital. Anything smaller, i.e., squadron, company, battery, troop, section was a sub-unit. The **Section** in infantry battalions in 1939 comprised eight men but by 1944 had increased to ten. A section was usually commanded by a corporal, although in the Parachute Regiment a sergeant was usually in command.

Three sections formed a **Platoon**. The equivalent of a platoon was a **Troop** in armoured regiments, artillery regiments and engineer companies. A platoon or troop was usually commanded by a subaltern (a captain, lieutenant or second lieutenant). Early in the war, due to the shortage of officers, a rank of platoon sergeant major (warrant officer class III) was introduced to command platoons where no officer was available.

Three platoons formed a **Company**, or three troops formed a **Squadron** in armoured regiments or a **Battery** in an artillery regiment. A company or squadron was usually commanded by a major or, sometimes, a captain. Most infantry battalions comprised four rifle companies, as well as a support company (by 1944) and headquarter company. Three squadrons usually formed an **armoured regiment** and three batteries an **artillery regiment**, although there were exceptions for medium and heavy regiments.

Source: https://web.archive.org/web/20220928024917/https://www.britishmilitaryhistory.co.uk/documents-units-formations-1930-1956/

Appendix 2

Seaforth Highlanders

Battle honours

- *72nd Highlanders*: **Carnatic, Hindoostan, Mysore, Cape of Good Hope (1806), South Africa 1935, Sevastopol, Central India, Peiwar Kotal, Charasiah, Kabul 1879, Kandahar 1880, Afghanistan 1878–80**
- *78th Highlanders*: **Assaye, Maida, Java, Koosh-ab, Persia, Lucknow, Afghanistan. 1879–80**
- *Seaforth Highlanders (1881–1902)*: **Tel El-Kebir, Egypt 1882, Chitral, Atbara, Khartoum, Paardeberg, South Africa 1899–1902**
- *The Great War*: Le Cateau, Retreat from Mons, **Marne 1914 '18,** Aisne 1914, La Bassée 1914, Armentières 1914, Festubert 1914 '15, Givenchy 1914, Neuve Chapelle, **Ypres 1915 '17 '18,** St Julien, Frezenberg, Bellewaarde, Aubers, **Loos, Somme 1916 '18,** Albert 1916, Bazentin, Delville Wood, Pozières, Flers-Courcelette, Le Transloy, Ancre Heights, Ancre 1916, **Arras 1917 '18, Vimy 1917,** Scarpe 1917 '18, Arleux, Pilckem, Menin Road, Polygon Wood, Broodseinde, Poelcapelle, Passchendaele, **Cambrai 1917 '18,** St Quentin, Bapaume 1918, Lys, Estaires, Messines 1918, Hazebrouck, Bailleul, Kemmel, Béthune, Soissonnais-Ourcq, Tardenois, Drocourt-Quéant, Hindenburg Line, Courtrai, Selle, **Valenciennes,** France and Flanders 1914–18, Macedonia 1917–18, Megiddo, Sharon, **Palestine 1918,** Tigris 1916, Kut al Amara 1917, **Baghdad,** Mesopotamia 1915–18
- *The Second World War*: Ypres-Comines Canal, Somme 1940, Withdrawal to Seine, **St Valéry-en-Caux,** Odon, Cheux, **Caen,** Troarn, Mont Pinçon, Quarry Hill, Falaise, Falaise Road, Dives Crossing, La Vie Crossing, Lisieux, Nederrijn, Best, Le Havre, Lower Maas, Meijel, Venlo Pocket, Ourthe, **Rhineland,** Reichswald, Goch, Moyland, Rhine, Uelzen, Artlenberg, North-West Europe 1940, '44–45, **El Alamein,** Advance to Tripoli, Mareth, Wadi Zigzaou, **Akarit,** Djebel Roumana, North Africa 1942–43, Landing in Sicily, Augusta, Francoforte, Adrano, Sferro Hills, **Sicily 1943,** Garigliano Crossing, **Anzio,** Italy 1943–44, **Madagascar,** Middle East 1942, **Imphal,** Shenam Pass, Litan, Tengnoupal, **Burma 1942–44**

Source: https://en.wikipedia.org/wiki/Seaforth_Highlanders

Appendix 3

Victoria Cross Recipients

The following soldiers serving with the Seaforth Highlanders and its antecedents were awarded the Victoria Cross:

78th Highlanders
Andrew Bogle, 1857, Indian Mutiny, 78th
Joseph Crowe, 1857, Indian Mutiny, 78th
Herbert Macpherson, 1857, Indian Mutiny, 78th
Surgeon Joseph Jee, 1857, Indian Mutiny, 78th
Valentine McMaster, 1857, Indian Mutiny, 78th
Stewart McPherson, 1857, Indian Mutiny, 78th
Henry Ward, 1857, Indian Mutiny, 78th
James Hollowell, 1857, Indian Mutiny, 78th

72nd Duke of Albany's Own Highlanders
Aylmer Cameron, 1858, Indian Mutiny
George Sellar, 1879, Afghanistan

Seaforth Highlanders
John Mackenzie, 1900, Ashanti
Sidney Ware, 1st Battalion, 1916, First World War
Walter Ritchie, 2nd Battalion, 1916, First World War
Thomas Steele, 1st Battalion, 1917, First World War
Donald Mackintosh, 2nd Battalion, 1917, First World War
Alexander Edwards, 6th Battalion, 1917, First World War
Robert McBeath, 5th Battalion, 1917, First World War
John Meikle MM, 4th Battalion, 1918, First World War

Source: https://en.wikipedia.org/wiki/Seaforth_Highlanders

Notes

Introduction

1. That said, however, three excellent books describe the regiment in detail: John Sym (ed), *Seaforth Highlanders* (1962); Angus Fairrie, *Queen's Own Highlanders (Seaforth and Camerons) An Illustrated History* (1998) and Trevor Royle, *Queen's Own Highlanders: A Concise History* (2007). Fairrie's book is impressively detailed, comprehensive and well illustrated.
2. The 1881 the Childers Reforms were a radical re-organisation of the infantry regiments of the Army under the auspices of Secretary of State for War, Hugh Childers. General Order 41/1881 created a network of multi-battalion regiments. In England, Wales and Scotland, each regiment was to have two regular or 'Line' battalions and two militia battalions. In Ireland, there were to be two Line and three Militia battalions. This was done by renaming the numbered regiments of foot and county militia regiments. In addition, the various corps of county rifle volunteers were to be designated as volunteer battalions. Each regiment was associated by headquarters location and territorial name to its local 'Regimental District'.

   From 1881, regimental seniority numbers were officially abolished and battalions came to be known by their number within the regiment and the regimental district name. Unofficially, regiments were still referred to by their numbers by their officers and men, as tradition, and several regiments, such as The Buffs (Royal East Kent Regiment), Cameron Highlanders, and Black Watch, lobbied to keep their distinct names as part of their battalion titles.

   Raugh and Skelley tell us that, at the same time, short service was increased to seven years with the Colours, and five with the reserve of the twelve-year enlistment period that the Cardwell Reforms had introduced. He also introduced the ability for time-served soldiers to extend service in the reserve by four years, albeit classed as the second division, or Section D, of the First Class Army Reserve (Regulation of the Forces Act, 1881. Provision for Supplementary Reserve – via JustisOne.)

   The Cardwell Reforms were a series of reforms and re-organisation of the Army introduced by Secretary of State for War Edward Cardwell between 1868 and 1874 which were all about efficiency. In 1870, he pushed through Parliament major changes in Army organisation. Observing the German Empire's victory over the Second French Empire in the Franco-Prussian War he concluded that the Prussian system of professional soldiers with state-of-the-art weaponry was far superior to the traditional system of gentlemen-soldiers on which Britain depended.

   Albert Tucker in his 'Army and Society in England 1870–1900: A Reassessment of the Cardwell Reforms' (*Journal of British Studies*, 1963) Vol. 2, No. 2 pp.110–14 tells us that 'The goal was to centralise the power of the War Office, abolish the purchase of officers' commissions, and create reserve forces stationed in Britain by establishing short terms of service for enlisted men. Ending the purchase system was controversial.

The families of officers had invested millions of pounds in the commissions and when a man was promoted he sold his junior commission to help pay for the more expensive senior commission. Legislation in the Commons would reimburse the officers for their full purchase price but the measure was defeated, whereupon the government announced that all purchases were abolished, thereby destroying the value of those commissions. The House of Lords passed the remedial legislation and the final expenditure made by officers was reimbursed'.

3. Paul, *The Scots Peerage. Vol. 7*, pp.512–13.
4. Fairrie 1983, p.13; https://www.armynavyairforce.co.uk/seaforth_highlanders.htm tells us that:

 The Duke of Albany's Own Highlanders, which forms the 1st battalion of the present regiment, and which formerly ranked as the 72nd Regiment of the Line, has had several ancestors bearing the same title. When, in 1758, the 2nd battalions of the fifteen Line Regiments were formed into separate regiments, the second 33rd became the 72nd, and was disbanded in 1763. The Royal Manchester Volunteers, formed in 1778, and reduced in 1783, next took the number; and this very reduction led to the re-numbering of the Line, so that in 1786 the former 78th became the 72nd, and was the third of the name.

5. War Office Memorandum, *London Gazette, No. 25040,* HMSO, 22 November 1881, p.5713.

Chapter 1: Early Seaforth: The 78th (later the 72nd) 1778–1793

1. halifaxcitadel.ca/history/the-78th-highland-regiment.html
2. Royle, *Queen's Own Highlanders. A concise history*, p.17.
3. Brander p.56.

The Battle of Jersey 1781

1. Porter, *History of the Corps of Royal Engineers*. pp.207–8.
2. *London Gazette*, 13 January 1781; Lempriére, *History of the Channel Islands*, pp.131–2
3. See http://www.guernsey-society.org.uk/donkipedia/index.php5?title=Baron_de_Rullecourt
4. *British War with France and Spain, 1778–1783.* 13 October 2007.

India 1781–1802

1. Fairrie, p.6.
2. Sym, pp.2–3.
3. Ibid., p.4.
4. Succession spats in both the Carnatic and Hyderabad opened the door for European intervention in support of various rival Indian claimants. At first the French, under Joseph-François Dupleix, governor of Pondicherry (now Puducherry) from 1742 to 1754, were successful both in the Carnatic and in Hyderabad, which the French officer Charles-Joseph Patissier, marquis de Bussy-Castelnau, controlled for seven years. Dupleix, however, was checked by forces of the East India Company under soldier and first British administrator of Bengal, Robert Clive, in 1751 and the French claimant was defeated the next year. In the Seven Years' War (1756–63), both the French and British sent armies to south India; the French were defeated at Wandiwash (1760) and the British captured Pondicherry (1761). Thenceforth, the British controlled the Carnatic

through its nawab, who became deeply indebted both to the East India Company and to its individual officers. https://www.britannica.com/event/Carnatic-Wars

The 72nd in India

1. https://electricscotland.com/history/sketches/highlandsketches69.htm
2. *Short History of the Seaforth Highlanders*, p.12.
3. Quoted in Cannon, *Historical Record of the Seventy-Second Regiment, or the Duke of Albany's*. https://www.gutenberg.org/files/66993/66993-h/66993-h.htm
4. The Fencibles (from the word *defencible*) were British regiments raised in the United Kingdom, Isle of Man and the colonies for defence against the threat of invasion during the Seven Years' War, the American War of Independence, French Revolutionary Wars, Napoleonic Wars and the War of 1812 in the late eighteenth and early nineteenth centuries. Generally temporary units, composed of local recruits and commanded by Regular Army officers, they were generally confined to garrison and patrol duties, freeing Regular Army units to perform offensive operations. Most fencible regiments had no liability for overseas service.

   They included naval forces known as River Fencibles, made up of sailors on the Thames and other southern English towns and cities, as well as Sea Fencibles, who, among their other duties, crewed small commercial vessels converted to coastal defence.
5. Fairrie, p.8.

Cape Colony and the Kaffir Wars

1. Quoted in Cannon, op. cit.
2. The Treaty Tree has a bloody history. It is a 500-year-old white milkwood tree on Treaty Road in Woodstock, Cape Town. Peace was made under the tree on 10 January 1806 after the Battle of Blaauwberg, thereby starting the second British occupation of the Cape and leading to the permanent establishment of the Cape Colony as a British possession. Until 1834 slaves were sold and convicts hanged under it. See *The Treaty Tree: The Battle of Blaauwberg 200 Year Anniversary, Battle of Blaauwberg Heritage Society.*

   In 1509 a massacre by Khoikhoi of sixty-four Portuguese sailors under the command of Dom Francisco de Almeida took place close to the tree.
3. 'Kafir' was, and is, a disparaging and insulting term for a black African. Kafir is an Arabic and Islamic term which, in the Islamic tradition, refers to a person who disbelieves in God as per Islam, or denies his authority, or rejects the tenets of Islam. The term is often translated as 'infidel', 'pagan', 'rejector', 'denier', 'disbeliever', 'unbeliever', 'non-believer', and 'non-Muslim'.
4. One of a long series of Kaffir Wars stretching from 1779 until 1879. See, for example, Tylden, G. 'The Third Kaffir War, 1799–1802', *Journal of the Society for Army Historical Research* 37, no.150 (1959): 72–82; Tylden, G. 'South Africa, 1877–78: The Ninth Kaffir War', *Journal of the Society for Army Historical Research* 20, no.80 (1941): 226–32; Smithers, A.J. *The Kaffir Wars, 1779–1877.*

Rioting in Lancashire 1840

1. See Chrystal, *Factory Girls: The Working Lives of Women and Children.*
2. Murder of PC in 1840s Colne Riots, *Lancashire Telegraph.*
3. See Chrystal, *History of the World in 100 Pandemics.*

Crimea

1. Biddulph, The Expedition to Kertch 1855, pp.128–35.
2. *Hansard* Volume 139: debated on Tuesday 26 June 1855 The Expedition To Kertch
3. Kinglake, *The Invasion of The Crimea,* Chapter IV, 'The Renewed Expedition to Kertch'.
4. https://collection.nam.ac.uk/detail.php?acc=1971-02-33-491-3 relating to 'Kertch from the North', 1855, Coloured tinted lithograph, 1855. One of 41 lithographs from 'The Seat of War in the East – Second Series', after William Simpson. Published by Paul and Dominic Colnaghi. Printed by Day and Son.

India 1857–8: The Indian Mutiny

1. See *The Revolt in Central India, 1857–59,* Army Intelligence Branch 1908 Action at Kota-ki-Serai archive.org. See Ali, A. (2012) 'The Uprising of 1857 in Bhopal as gleaned through Persian and Urdu documents', *Proceedings of the Indian History Congress,* 73, 573–577.
2. *Indian History Congress* 73 (2012), pp.573–7.
3. *London Gazette,* 11 November 1859.

The Second Anglo-Afghan War 1878–1881.

1. *London Gazette,* No.25027, 18 October 1881, p.5140.

Chapter 2: The 78th Highlanders 1793–1881

1. Quoted at https://www.waterlooassociation.org.uk/2018/06/27/maida-the-lucky-battle/
2. Hopton, *The Battle of Maida 1806,* p.111.
3. Quoted at https://www.waterlooassociation.org.uk/2018/06/27/maida-the-lucky-battle/
4. Smith, *The Napoleonic Wars Data Book.*
5. Harrison, p.25.
6. Grant, *The Story of Thomas Keith.*
7. Brett-James, *'The Walcheren Failure'. History Today, 13 (12): pp.811–20.*
8. Feibel, 'What Happened At Walcheren: The Primary Medical Sources', *Bulletin of the History of Medicine,* 42 (1): pp.62–79; Howard, 'Walcheren 1809: a medical catastrophe', *BMJ,* 319 (7225): pp.1642–5.
9. www.napoleon-series.org/military-info/battles/1814/c_lowcountries1814.pdf
10. [source: https://www.clash-of-steel.co.uk/conflicts/entry/1042

The Calton Riots and the Scottish Radical Rising 1820

1. *Lundy,* 'Friends set to bring city's Calton Weavers back to life', *Evening Times, 17 May 2007.*
2. *Calton Weavers' Gate* (PDF). *City of Glasgow.*
3. *Currie.* 'WEAVERS STRUGGLES ... THE CALTON WEAVERS MASSACRE', *Media Matters.*
4. Gibbs/O'Neill, *The Calton Weavers, the 1820 Radical War and Scotland's first working-class martyrs* – Glasgow Live.
5. Gibbs/O'Neill, *The Calton Weavers, the 1820 Radical War and Scotland's first working-class martyrs* – Glasgow Live.
6. Prebble, pp.9–10, 17, 364

India 1842 and Kabul

1. See Chisholm, ed. 'Ellenborough, Edward Law, Earl of', *Encyclopædia Britannica.* Vol. 9 (11th ed.), pp.289–90.

2. Dalrymple, *Return of a King; the Battle for Afghanistan.*
3. Dalrymple *(8 May 2010). 'The Ghosts of Gandamak' New York Times.*

The cholera pandemic 1817–1828

1. Chrystal, *History of the World in 100 Pandemics.*

Aden 1848–1853

1. Garston, 'Aden: The First Hundred Years,' *History Today* (Mar 1965) 15#3 pp.147–58. Gavin, *Aden Under British Rule: 1839–1967*; *Kou, The History of Aden 1839–1872.* Roxani, *Aden and the Indian Ocean Trade: 150 Years in the Life of a Medieval Arabian Port*; *Thoman, 'Aden'. In Olson (ed), Historical Dictionary of European Imperialism.*

The Battle of Khushab

1. Hunt, p.215.
2. Raugh, *The Victorians at War, 1815–1914: An Encyclopedia of British Military History* 2004, p.89. *Christie and Kidson, Britain: losing and gaining an empire, 1763–1914. p.150.*

Siege of Cawnpore

Much of the following is sourced on https://www.britishempire.co.uk/forces/armycampaigns/indiancampaigns/mutiny/cawnpore.htm

1. Saxena, 'Revolt and Revenge; a Double Tragedy' (delivered to The Chicago Literary Club, February 2003); Moody, *History of the Cawnpore Cup.*
2. Wright, *Historic Incidents and Life in India,* p.239.
3. Pratul Chandra Gupta (1964). *Nana Sahib and the rising at Cawnpore.*
4. Thompson, p.150.
5. [https://www.britishempire.co.uk/forces/armycampaigns/indiancampaigns/mutiny/mutiny.htm]
6. 'Echoes of a Distant War', Hibbert, *The Great Mutiny: India,* p.194.
7. Nayar, *The Great Uprising.*
8. Sen, *Eighteen Fifty-seven, p.145.*
9. Williams, 'Memorandum', printed with Narrative of the Events in the NWP in 1857–58, section on Kanpur (hereafter Narrative Kanpur), p.20: 'A man of great influence in the city, and a government official, has related a circumstance that is strange, if true, viz. that whilst the massacre was being carried on at the ghat, a trooper of the 2nd Cavalry, reported to the Nana, then at Savada house, that his enemies, their wives and children were exterminated ... On hearing which, the Nana replied, that for the destruction of women and children, there was no necessity and directed the sowar to return with an order to stay their slaughter.' See also Kaye, *History of the Sepoy War in India, 1857–58*, 3 vols. ii, p.258. (This reprint of Kaye's work carries the title *History of the Indian Mutiny of 1857–58.*)
10. Brock, *A Biographical Sketch of Sir Henry Havelock, KCBI,* pp.150–2.
11. https://www.britishempire.co.uk/forces/armycampaigns/indiancampaigns/mutiny/cawnpore.htm describes the carnage.
12. Mowbray, *The Story of Cawnpore.*
13. English, 'The Kanpur Massacres in India in the Revolt of 1857'. *Past & Present,* pp.169–78.
14. Saxena, op. cit. pp.150–2.
15. English, op. Cit., pp.169–78; Mukherjee, *'The Kanpur Massacres in India in the Revolt of 1857: Reply', Past & Present, pp.142: 178–89.*

16. Hibbert, op. cit., *The Great Mutiny: India, 1857*, p.212.
17. 'India Rising: Horrors & atrocities.' National Army Museum.
18. Extract from the diary of Major George Bingham, 1857. (NAM. 1959-03-105); the exhibit apparently also includes (sickeningly to my mind) a lock of hair taken from Cawnpore and mounted on velvet board.
19. Gupta, p.145.
20. https://www.britishempire.co.uk/forces/armycampaigns/indiancampaigns/mutiny/mutiny.htm

The Siege of Lucknow 1857

1. Holmes, *Sahib*, p.393. Surgeon Anthony Holme was with HM 90th Foot diverted to India while en route to China and arrived with Havelock's column. Quotations from his *Service Memoirs*, p.124.
2. Germon, *Journal* pp.97–8.
3. Field Force Orders of the late Major General Havelock, 17 October 1857, *London Gazette*, No. 22154, 18 June 1858, p.2957.
4. Extract from Field Force Orders of the late Major General Havelock, dated 17 October 1857. *London Gazette*, No. 22154, 18 June 1858, p.2957.
5. *London Gazette* No 22248, 12 Apri 1859, p. 1483.
6. Extract from Divisional Orders of Major-General Sir James Outram GCB, dated 27 October 1857. *London Gazette, No. 22154*, 18 June 1858, p.2958.

The experience of women in the Indian Mutiny

1. https://www.thesocialhistorian.com/siege-of-lucknow/
2. See, among others, Chrystal, *Roman Military Disasters*; *Women at War in the Classical World*.
3. Germon, R.C., *A Lady's Diary During the Siege of Lucknow*, Google Books. 1870.
4. Fairrie, p.31.

Chapter 3: Seaforth Highlanders 1st and 2nd Battalions: 1881–1899

The International Occupation of Crete 1897

1. [http://www.britainssmallwars.co.uk/international-occupation-of-crete-1897.html; 2013].
2. McTiernan, Mick, *Crete: A Very Bad Place Indeed For a Soldier*, pp. 2021.
3. The National Archives, WO33 149. Telegram No.6. General Officer Commanding in Chief Malta to Secretary of State for War, 18 March 1897.
4. WO 33/150. *Correspondence Relative to the Occupation of Crete*. No. 1. Chermside to Secretary of State for War, 14 April 1897.
5. National Army Museum, NAM 6807. Egerton Papers 1968-07-171. *Diary of the Detachment 1st Bn. Seaforth Highlanders at Canea Crete During the early days of the International Occupation 1897.*
6. WO 33/149. No.30. Secretary of State for War to Commander in Chief Malta, 29 March 1897.
7. WO 33/150. *Correspondence Relative to the Occupation of Crete*. No.1. Chermside to Secretary of State for War, 14 April 1897.
8. Brucellosis is a highly contagious zoonosis caused by ingestion of unpasteurised milk or undercooked meat from infected animals, or close contact with their secretions. It is also known as undulant fever, Malta fever, and Mediterranean fever. See Chrystal, *A History of the World in 100 Pandemics, Plagues & Epidemics*.
9. https://britishinterventionincrete.wordpress.com/2016/07/

10. Quoted in https://britishinterventionincrete.wordpress.com/category/european-intervention-crete/british-army-in-crete/seaforth-highlanders/

Sudan 1898

1. The Mahdist War was a war between the Mahdist Sudanese of the religious leader Muhammad Ahmad bin Abd Allah, who had proclaimed himself the 'Mahdi' of Islam (the 'Guided One'), and the forces of the Khedivate of Egypt, initially, and later the forces of Britain. Eighteen years of war resulted in the nominally joint-rule state of the Anglo-Egyptian Sudan (1899–1956), a *de jure* condominium of the British Empire and the Kingdom of Egypt in which Britain had *de facto* control over the Sudan.
2. Dominic Green, *Three Empires on the Nile: The Victorian Jihad, 1869–1899*, p.252
3. A zareba is a thorn fence fortifying a camp or village.
4. Churchill, Winston (1899) *The River War: An Account of the Reconquest of the Soudan, Vol II*, pp.66–7.
5. Collins, *A History of Modern Sudan*, pp.30–1.
6. Ellis, *The Social History of the Machine Gun.*
7. During the 19th century the region was home to the Dum Dum Arsenal, a British Artillery facility. It was there that, in the early 1890s, Captain Neville Bertie-Clay developed a bullet with the jacket cut away at the tip to reveal its soft lead core, the hollow-point bullet, known also as a dum-dum or more correctly as an expanding bullet. The previous name of Dum Dum was 'Domdoma'. See First World War.com – Encyclopedia – Dum-Dum Bullet". www.firstworldwar.com; *"BlackHammer CyberPunk Project: F.I.D. AmmoList"*. www.ambient.ca. *Retrieved* 30 December *2019. "303 British". 3 January 2008;* 'Ordnance Factory Dum Dum'. *History – Dum Dum Story*. OFDD.
8. Nicoll, Fergus (last updated 2020) Finial of the Mahdī's qubba. *Making African Connections.*The tomb was reconstructed in 1947 under the direction of the Mahdī's son, al-sayyid ʿAbd-al-Raḥman al-Mahdī.
9. A *qubba,* also transliterated as ḳubba, kubbet and koubba, is a cupola or domed structure, typically a tomb or shrine in Islamic architecture.
10. Gordon, 'Viewing Violence in the British Empire: Images of Atrocity from the Battle of Omdurman, 1898'. *Journal of Perpetrator Research 2.2*, 2019, p.81; ibid, *Viewing Violence in the British Empire: Images of Atrocity from the Battle of Omdurman, 1898* , also at http://uu.diva-portal.org/smash/get/diva2:1318055/FULLTEXT01.pdf
11. The Guardian Research department (2011) '21 February 1899: Treatment of the Mahdi's body condemned'. *The Guardian*. Nicoll, Fergus op.cit.
12. Moorehead, *The White Nile*, p.335.
13. Churchill, op. cit., p.211.
14. See Harrison, 'Skulls and Scientific Collecting in the Victorian Military: Keeping the Enemy Dead in British Frontier Warfare'. *Comparative Studies in Society and History*. p.291
15. It would be hard to believe that the looting would not be accompanied by rape of civilians.
16. Daly, p.3.
17. 'Fuzzy-Wuzzy' is a poem by Rudyard Kipling, published in 1892 as part of *Barrack Room Ballads*. It describes the respect of the ordinary British soldier for the bravery of the Hadendoa Beja warriors who fought the British Army in the Sudan and Eritrea. The term 'Fuzzy Wuzzy Angels' was used by Australian soldiers during the Second World War to describe Papua New Guinean stretcher-bearers. The term was not generally thought to be problematic when used by Kipling and by British soldiers during the Sudan Campaign or by Australian soldiers in the 20th century; however, more recently

some have deemed it to be a racial slur. See The meaning and origin of the expression: Fuzzy wuzzy *The Phrase Finder;* Nelson, '8 words, phrases and terms you didn't know had racist links and origins', *The Scotsman*; Eubanks, 30 July 2020 'Here are some commonly used terms that actually have racist origins', *ABC News*. The Ansar are a Sufi religious movement in the Sudan whose followers are disciples of Muhammad Ahmad, the Sudanese religious leader based on Aba Island who proclaimed himself Mahdi on 29 June 1881. His followers won a series of victories against the Egyptians culminating in the capture of Khartoum in January 1885.

18. Daly, *Empire on the Nile: The Anglo-Egyptian Sudan, 1898–1934.*
19. Ali Mohamed, Abdelrahman (2017) 'Sudanese Cultural Heritage Sites'. UNESCO.
20. 'Imperial trophies collecting on campaign during the reconquest of Sudan', *The National Army Museum*, 2018. Retrieved 23 December 2020. Nicoll, , Material related to the Mahdīa.
21. See Harrington, *British Artists and War.*
22. Powell, Munroe, Hall, Banks, *What will they say in England? A story of the gallant 21st.*
23. See McGonagall.van Wyk Smith, p.28; Moore, pp.7–22.
24. See Sharkey, *Mahdist Oral Praise Poetry.*
25. See Henty, *With Kitchener in the Soudan: A Story of Atbara and Omdurman*. Library of Alexandria.
26. Bottomore, p.6, Ch. IV.
27. Croft, David; Perry, Jimmy; Webber, Richard *(2003). Dad's Army: The Complete Scripts: Scripts 1–8. Orion Publishing Group.* . See eg Series 4 Episode 8 *The Two and a Half Feathers.*

The Hazara Expedition 1888–1891 and The Chitral Expedition 1899

1. https://www.britishbattles.com/north-west-frontier-of-india/black-mountain-expedition-1888/
2. https://www.britishbattles.com/north-west-frontier-of-india/black-mountain-expedition-1888/
3. Field Marshal Lord Roberts, *Forty-one Years in India 1897*, p. 524.
4. Harris, *Much Sounding of Bugles: The Siege of Chitral. Hutchinson*. p.26.
5. Official despatch of the affair *London Gazette.*
6. https://www.britishbattles.com/north-west-frontier-of-india/siege-and-relief-of-chitral/
7. Younghusband, George John; Younghusband, Sir Francis Edward, *The Relief of Chitral, p.132.*
8. Fincastle, The Viscount; Eliott-Lockhart, P.C. (2 February 2012). *A Frontier Campaign Narrative of the Operations of the Malakand and Buner Field Forces, 1897–1898*. p.55; Churchill, *The Story of the Malakand Field Force*, p.61.

Chapter 4: The 2nd Seaforth Highlanders in the Second Boer War 1899–1902 and after

1. https://www.britishbattles.com/great-boer-war/battle-of-paardeberg/
2. Hewlett, *Operations Against the Zakka Khel Afridis 1908.*
3. Intelligence Branch, Division of the chief of the staff, army headquarters, India; Official account of the Bazar Field Force, a punitive expedition against the Zakka Khel Afridis in February/March 1908, led by Major-General Sir James Willcocks. Intelligence Branch Amy Headquarters India. 'INDIA—NORTH-WEST FRONTIER POLICY'. (Hansard, 26 February 1908). Hansard.millbanksystems.com. 26 February 1908.
4. A *jirga* is a tribal council.

5. Bewsher, *The History of the 51st (Highland) Division, 1914–1918.*
6. Other nicknames included: *First World War:* from the Germans – Ladies from Hell. *Second World War:* Highway Decorators, after the insignia of the Division.

Chapter 5: The Seaforth Highlanders in the First World War

1. SMS *Emden* was the second and last member of the Dresden-class of light cruisers built for the German *Kaiserliche Marine* (Imperial Navy). SMS *Konigsberg* was the lead ship of her class of light cruisers built by the German *Kaiserliche Marine.*
2. Sym, p.180.
3. Fairrie, p.90.
4. Hastings, pp.218–19.
5. *Ibid.,* p. 21.
6. *Historian, IR 93.*
7. Sym, p.151.
8. Fairrie, p.10.
9. Sym, op. cit.
10. Sym, op. cit.
11. Source: https://www.theworldwar.org/learn/about-wwi/spotlight-first-usage-poison gas#:~:text=On%20April%2022%2C%201915%20at,a%20new%20form%20of%20weapon].
12. *The First Day of the Somme* p.166.
13. Middlebrook, op. cit, pp.169–70.
14. Stewart & Buchan, *The Fifteenth (Scottish) Division 1914–1919.*
15. https://www.firstworldwarglasgow.co.uk/index.aspx?articleid=11605 tells.
16. 'Mudlife' in *Catastrophe*, p.516.

Chapter 6: The Territorials in the First World War

1. Mitchison, p.11.
2. 2011, pp.200–03.
3. pp.175–6.
4. National Army Museum: the yeomanry, a mounted force drawn from the upper classes, was created at the peak of the fear of French invasion and used extensively in support of the civil authority to put down riots and disturbances .... Troop shortages and patriotic zest during the imperial crises and expansion of the British Empire in the second half of the nineteenth century prompted the creation of other volunteer and yeomanry units, such as the Volunteer Force, with a far less distinct role, as well as the permanent embodiment of the militia in vulnerable British towns.
5. https://www.longlongtrail.co.uk/army/the-territorial-force/
6. Report of the Royal Commission upon the Volunteer Force ([3053] HC (1862) xxvii, p.89).
7. Chappell & Edmonds, *History of the Great War: Military Operations, France and Belgium, 1914.* Vol. II: Antwerp, La Bassee, Armentieres, Messines, and Ypres, October-November 1914.
8. Imperial War Museum. '*Seaforth Highlanders*'. The Long, Long Trail; 'Seaforth Highlanders 1st Btn during the Great War'. *The Wartime Memories Project.* Seaforth Highlanders 2nd Btn during the Great War'. The Wartime Memories Project.
9. Kitchener fought off opposition to his plan and attempts to water it down including piecemeal dispersal of New Army battalions into existing regular or Territorial Force divisions (the view of the Commander-in-Chief of the British Expeditionary Force

(BEF), Field Marshal French). Kitchener declined to use the existing Territorial Force (set up by Lord Haldane and Douglas Haig as part of the Army reforms of the Edwardian period) as the basis for the New Army, as many of its members had volunteered for Home Service only, and because he was suspicious of the poor performance of French 'territorials' in the Franco-Prussian War 1870–1871. Simkins, *Kitchener's Army: The Raising of the New Armies 1914 – 1916* tells how, In the early days of the war, the Territorial Force could not reinforce the regular army, as it lacked modern equipment, particularly artillery. In addition, it took time to form First-Line units composed only of men who had volunteered for 'General Service'. 'Kitchener's motives for a massive early expansion were probably due as much to the politics of the Liberal Government as to Kitchener's own autocratic methods. Following Asquith appointing the Conservative Kitchener as Secretary of State, Asquith relied on Kitchener's prestige to help him retain the confidence of the country'[www.westernfrontassociation.com/world-war-i-articles/did-kitchener-s-decision-to-raise-his-new-armies-carelessly-wreck-the-pre-war-plans-to-achieve-smooth-and-effective-british-].

10. Medlicott, *Contemporary England 1914–1964*, p.21.
11. https://www.iwm.org.uk/memorials/item/memorial/80456 © WMR-80456 www.warmemorialsonline.org.uk/memorial/239235
12. MacDonald, p.18.
13. Ibid., pp.34–5.
14. Ibid., p.92.
15. Ibid., p.93.
16. Ibid., p.120.
17. Ibid., pp.306–7.
18. Ibid. p. 306n: explains that 'Woolly Bears' were shrapnel shells which burst in a cloudlike explosion. 'Jack Johnsons', nicknamed after a famous negro boxer of the time, were HE shells which burst with a thick black cloud.
19. Tennant's body was never identified. He is commemorated on the le Touret Memorial to the Missing and in his home village of Fairlie.
20. 2019, pp.19–22.
21. Davies, (28 December 2005). 'Author explodes myth of the gunmetal VC'. *The Daily Telegraph. London.* Glanfield (2005) pp.24–35. Creagh, *Charles Barrett (ed.). Advances in X-ray Analysis Vol. 35. Plenum. pp.1127–32.* Creagh, *Energy Dispersive X-ray Spectrometry. Editrice Compositori. pp.299–305.* Stewart, Ian, *'The Victoria Cross ... awarded to Captain Alfred Shout have been sold at auction'.* Victoria Cross.org; Raugh, Harold E., *The Victorians.*
22. The VC recipients are:
    - Sidney Ware, 1st Battalion, 1916.
    - Walter Ritchie, 2nd Battalion, 1916.
    - Thomas Steele, 1st Battalion, 1917.
    - Donald Mackintosh, 2nd Battalion, 1917.
    - Alexander Edwards, 6th Battalion, 1917.
    - Robert McBeath, 5th Battalion, 1917.
    - John Meikle, MM, 4th Battalion, 1918.

Chapter 7: Striking miners 1920–1921

1. Hansard, *House of Commons*, 5th Series, vol. 195, col.35.
2. Sym, p.230.
3. In his *British Troops in China History & Personnel,* p.3.

4. Ibid.
5. Ibid.
6. source https://www.britishmilitaryhistory.co.uk/wp-content/uploads/sites/124/2018/07/British-Troops-in-China-History-Personnel.pdf

Chapter 8: The Seaforth Highlanders on The North West Frontier

The North West Frontier before 1930–1931.

1. https://www.nam.ac.uk/explore/north-west-frontier-india
2. https://www.nam.ac.uk/explore/north-west-frontier-india#:~:text=The%20Punjab%20Frontier%20Force%20(PFF,Chief%20Commissioner%20of%20the%20Punjab.
3. Major George Roos-Keppel , *Political Agent in the Khyber,* 1901.

The Amritsar Massacre 1919

4. The Anarchical and Revolutionary Crimes Act of 1919, popularly known as the Rowlatt Act, was a legislative council act passed by the Imperial Legislative Council in Delhi on 18 March 1919, indefinitely extending the emergency measures of preventive indefinite detention, imprisonment without trial and judicial review enacted in the Defence of India Act 1915 during the First World War. It was enacted in the light of a perceived threat from revolutionary nationalists of re-engaging in similar conspiracies as had occurred during the war which the Government felt the lapse of the Defence of India Act would enable.
5. For the wide divergence in casualty figures see, among others, Collett, *The Butcher of Amritsar: General Reginald Dyer. Committee on Disturbances in Bombay, Delhi, and the Punjab, Report; disorders inquiry committee 1919–1920. pp.xx–xxi, 44–5, 116–17; Narain, The Jallianwala Bagh Massacre.* No.29509, *London Gazette (Supplement). 14 March 1916, p.2902.*; 'Punjab disturbances, April 1919; compiled from the Civil and military gazette'. *Lahore Civil and Military Gazette Press 1921.*
6. https://www.nam.ac.uk/explore/north-west-frontier-india
7. The Durand Line forms the Afghanistan-Pakistan border, a 2,670-kilometre (1,660 mile) international land border between Afghanistan and Pakistan in South Asia.[1] The western end runs to the border with Iran and the eastern end to the border with China.

   The Durand Line was established in 1893 as the international border between India and the Emirate of Afghanistan by Mortimer Durand, a British diplomat of the Indian Civil Service, and Emir Abdur Rahman Khan, the Afghan Emir, to define the limit of their respective spheres of influence and bolster diplomatic relations and trade. The British considered Afghanistan to be an independent state at the time, although they controlled its foreign affairs and diplomatic relations. It did not take long for the Afghans to repudiate the agreement. They continued to claim parts of the province as their own, as they indeed had been prior to Sikh rule. In the years that followed, they regularly interfered in tribal affairs on the British side of the line, hoping to regain lost influence there.
8. Holdich, 'Tirah'. Khyber.ORG. 2009.
9. https://collection.nam.ac.uk/detail.php?acc=1989-03-28-2
10. Pamphlet issued by HQ Waziristan District, 1924.

The Afridi 'Redshirt' Rebellion 1930–1931

11. Thomas, *Beyond Khyber Pass.*
12. From the abstract of Marsh, 'These Infernal Khudai Khidmatgaran': Defining and Repressing Frontier Nationalism, 1930–1931 in *Ramparts of Empire – Britain and the World.*

13. Sym, p.229.
14. Hiskey, *The Curious Practice of Execution by Golden Shower.*
15. Ahmed, *'Colonial Encounter on the North-West Frontier Province: Myth and Mystification,'* p.295.
16. Fairrie, p.125.

Chapter 9: Palestine and after

1. Meșer & Metzer, p.15.
2. See *Kabahā* (2014), *Kabha* (2014) *and Khalidi* (2006).
3. https://www.nam.ac.uk/explore/conflict-Palestine

Chapter 10: 2nd Battalion Seaforth Highlanders in the Second World War – The Battle of France

1. Smart tells us that lowlander Major General Sir Victor Morven Fortune KBE CB DSO DL (1883–1949) was educated at Winchester and the Royal Military College, Sandhurst; he was commissioned as a second lieutenant in the Black Watch (Royal Highlanders) in 1903. In 1927, as lieutenant colonel, he was promoted CO of the 1st Battalion Seaforth Highlanders and subsequently commander of 5 Infantry Brigade in 1930. He became General Officer Commanding (GOC) of 52nd (Lowland) Division in 1935 and GOC of 51st (Highland) Division in 1937.
2. See Chrystal, *British Army of the Rhine 1945–1993.*
3. Idem p.10.
4. Prime Minister's Review: Reduction in Armaments, of, Commons Debate, 18 August 1919. [https://www.nationalarchives.gov.uk/cabinetpapers/themes/10-year-rule-disarmament.htm].
5. See also Ferris, 'Treasury Control, the Ten Year Rule and British Service Policies, 1919–1924.' *The Historical Journal* 30, no.4 pp.859.
6. Kennedy, *The Rise and Fall of British Naval Mastery*, p.273.
7. Barnett, p.297.
8. Inskip was Baldwin's first Minister for Co-ordination of Defence. His appointment in 1936 was highly controversial. Winston Churchill, who had long campaigned for the creation of such an office, expected to be appointed to run it. When Baldwin named Inskip, a lawyer, Churchill famously observed that Inskip 'had the advantage of being little known and knowing nothing about military subjects'. Inskip also had no real powers and few staff. In early 1939 he was replaced by the former First Sea Lord, Admiral of the Fleet Lord Chatfield, and moved to Secretary of State for Dominion Affairs.
9. This quote has been used for many occasions while the original source remains unclear. The highly influential polemic *Guilty Men* (the relevant chapter is 'Caligula's Horse') attributes it to a 'great statesman' (p.74), whom some have surmised was Churchill. However, Stewart, *Burying Caesar: Churchill, Chamberlain and the Battle for the Tory Party* (London; Phoenix, 1999), p.487 attributes the originator of the quote to Churchill's non-politician friend Professor Frederick Lindemann. For Caligula's horse, see Suetonius, *Caligula,* and Camus', *Caligula.*
10. Gunther, *Inside Europe.* Harper & Brothers. p.348. Bouverie, *Appeasement: Chamberlain, Hitler, Churchill, and the Road to War*, p.94.
11. Cato, *Guilty Men*. London.
12. David, *After Dunkirk: Churchill's Sacrifice of the Highland Division, France 1940,* p.6.
13. Longden, *Dunkirk: The Men They Left Behind,* p.128. See also David, *After Dunkirk: Churchill's Sacrifice of the Highland Division, France 1940;* Ellis, *The War in France and*

Flanders 1939–40, Appendix I. *UK Military Series;* '51 Infantry Division 1939' (PDF). *British Military History.*

Tenth Army was reformed in the Second World War after service in the First World War. This, the first new Tenth Army, was disbanded between 7 and 8 June 1940, when IX Corps was encircled at Saint-Valéry-en-Caux. The rupture of the Somme front, on 5 and 6 June 1940, marked the beginning of the last phase of the Battle of France. For the Allies it was essential to regroup on the Seine to prevent the Germans from crossing. This explains why a new Tenth Army was then formed to hold the front at the Lower Seine under command of General Robert Altmayer (1875–1959). His troops were not yet in place when the Germans arrived at the Seine on 9 June and immediately crossed it in the Portejoie, Saint-Pierre-du-Vauvray and Venables sector. The Weygand Line had been broken.

14. André Maginot (1877 –1932) was an NCO in the First World War who had been injured severely in the conflict leaving him with a limp for the remainder of his life. He was later French Minister of War. The line was given his name after his death.
15. *Blitzkrieg* wasn't in use at the time and first appeared in a German military journal in the late 1930s. Even then, it wasn't part of the German military vocabulary but was popularised by the UK and American press. The term seems to have been rarely used in the German military press before 1939, and recent research at the *Militärgeschichtliches Forschungsamt*, at Potsdam, uncovered it in only two military articles from the 1930s. Both used the term to mean a swift strategic knockout, rather than a radically new military doctrine or approach to war. In English and other languages, the term had been used since the 1920s. The term was first used in the publications of Ferdinand Otto Miksche, first in the magazine *Army Quarterly,* and in his 1941 book *Blitzkrieg,* in which he defined the concept.
16. Tome, p.99. This is the first volume in a series of four books about the history and characteristics of the French Maginot Line. It is the standard work on the Maginot Line.

    The book is divided in 3 parts. The first part of the book describes the political and military situation between 1919 and 1939 and the circumstances that led to the decision to build the Maginot Line. It also describes the design and construction of the Line. The second part of the book describes the infantry troops who manned the Maginot Line – units, uniforms, equipment, armament, etc. The third part of the book describes the troops, their officers and men. The book is written in French and illustrated with numerous photos, plans, drawings and maps.

    Tome 3, pp.100–1 and Kaufmann J.E. and Kaufmann, H.W. *Fortress France: The Maginot Line and French Defenses in World War II.* Tome 3, pp.100–1 and Kaufmann, J.E. and Kaufmann, H.W. *Fortress France: The Maginot Line and French Defenses in World War II.*
17. 7th Battalion Argyll & Sutherland Highlanders. *Wartime Memories Project.*
18. David, p.32.
19. For example: http://www.gengriz.co.uk/lothians.htm. *The Heroes of St Valéry.* In a masterpiece of propaganda, this horrendous military disaster was quickly turned into a political rallying point, twisted almost to the point of victory and establishing forever the myth of 'The Dunkirk Spirit'.
20. IWM pp/mcr/373
21. 2008, pp.10–11.
22. Richard Collier's 1961 *The Sands of Dunkirk,* Walter Lord's *The Miracle of Dunkirk* and *Dunkirk – The Necessary Myth* by Nicholas Harman.

23. See Chrystal, *Wars & Battles of the Roman Republic*, pp.66–71; Plutarch, *Pyrrhus* 21.
24. Tome 3, pp.100–01 and Kaufmann, J.E. and Kaufmann, H.W. *Fortress France: The Maginot Line and French Defenses in World War II.*
25. David, p.97.
26. https://www.britishmilitaryhistory.co.uk/docs-france-norway-1940-british-forces-south-river-somme/
27. 'British forces south of the river Somme', *British Military History.* 154 Brigade (part of 51st (Highland) Division) was raised in 1908, on the creation of the Territorial Force, as the Argyll and Sutherland Brigade and was later redesignated as 154 (3 Highland) Brigade. 154 Brigade was more fortunate than its sister brigades of the 51st Division (152 and 153). It was detached in June 1940 to form the mobile battlegroup 'Arkforce' and able to escape from Northern France while the rest of the division was forced to surrender at St Valéry-en-Caux. However, the brigade was severely depleted by the time it returned to Britain, and in August 1940 it was re-organised and merged with 28 Brigade of 9th (Highland) Division to form part of the new 51st Division. In this capacity it went on to serve in North Africa, Sicily and North-West Europe. See https://51hd.co.uk/tag/154_brigade
28. Saul, p.13.
29. Longden, p.246.
30. IWM has the private papers of Private Frederick Coster: https://www.iwm.org.uk/collections/item/object/1030007443

    'Detailed memoir (174pp) with few dates recording his career with the TA in 44 Battery, 101st LAA Regiment RA (Finsbury Rifles), 1st Armoured Division, UK and France, and as a PoW in Poland, March 1938-July 1946, including: volunteering, March 1938; his training, March – September 1939; mobilisation in Kent, ?September 1939; service in Dover, winter 1939 – March 1940, and Blandford St Mary, March – May 1940; active service in France, May – June 1940, and the subsequent retreat to St Valerie en Caux where, now attached to the 51st Highland Division, he was captured by the Germans, June 1940'.
31. Saul, p.33.
32. Sergeant J.A. Mackenzie, 'Forty Years Ago – with the 78th to St Valéry', Part III, *The Queen's Own Highlander*, Summer 1980.
33. *'Action off Saint-Valéry-en-Caux', Museum of the Royal Regiment of Scotland.*
34. Longden p.189.
35. One of perhaps 14 or 15 in the rank of major general or lieutenant general, including a VC holder.
36. *'Heroes of St Valéry'.*
37. In Longden, p.191; John Forbes Christie, IWM 88/47/1.
38. Chrystal, *Gunners from the Sky*, pp.143, 159.
39. Longden, p.192.
40. Saul, *Churchill's Sacrifice of the Highland Division, France 1940.*
41. Nicholl, *The Last Escape.*
42. https://51hd.co.uk/accounts/action_off_st_valery. Compiled from personal accounts by the following participants: Commander M.D.C. Meyrick DSO OBE RN (Rtd), Lt Commander H.D. Howse MBE DSC FSA (Rtd), Mr F.G. Bull, and A. Hales from HMS *Boadicea*, and from HMS *Bulldog*, Commander F.J.G. Hewitt DSC & Bar RN (Rtd), and Lt Commander R.S. Bryden DSC MBE RN (Rtd).
43. 'Council supports Saint Valéry en Caux Battle commemorations' Archived 5 March 2012 at the Wayback Machine The Highland Council, 11 June 2010.

The Herald (25 May 2021) reports on some important initiatives which ensure the 51st Highland Brigade is restored to the school curriculum, the national memory and consciousness. The article is titled *'Bravery of 51st Highland Division at 'forgotten Dunkirk' will be remembered'*.

Chapter 11: Sergeant Eric Priest: One Seaforth Highlander's Journey from the Northwest Frontier to Stalag 385, 1925–1945

1. Chrystal, Paul; Youll, Nina, *Jack Youll VC*, Barnsley 2025.
2. Chrystal, Paul, *Old Hartlepool and West Hartlepool,* Catrine, 2019.
3. Chrystal, Paul; Chrystal, David, Major retd, Mention in Despatches, BEM, *Gunners from the Sky: 1st Airlanding Light Regiment RA in Italy and at the Battle of Arnhem, Barnsley*, 2023.

Chapter 12: 1st Battalion Seaforth Highlanders in the Second World War and after

1. Fairrie, p.267.
2. https://thechinditsociety.org.uk/operation-longcloth. Brigadier (later Major-General) Orde Charles Wingate, DSO.
3. https://burmastarmemorial.org/history
4. Sym, p.278.
5. DCM: *London Gazette*, 30 September 1943.
6. *London Gazette*, 8 February 1945.
7. MM *London Gazette*, 28 June 1945 (originally recommended for the DCM).
8. Royle, 2007.
9. Roadnight, A. (2002). Sleeping with the Enemy: Britain, Japanese Troops and the Netherlands East Indies, 1945–1946. *History, 87*(286), 245–268.
10. There were experiments with using Agent Orange to defoliate possible ambush sites but it was found that hand clearing was more effective. See Hughes, pp.4–5; 580–90.
11. Siver, pp.2–8, 19–20, 57–90.
12. Deery, Phillip. 'Malaya, 1948: Britain's Asian Cold War?', *Journal of Cold War Studies 9,* No. 1 (2007): pp.29–54; Siver, Christi L. 'The other forgotten war: understanding atrocities during the Malayan Emergency' In *APSA 2009 Toronto Meeting Paper*, 2009, p.36; Newsinger 2013, p. 217.
13. See Keo, Bernard Z. (March 2019). 'A small, distant war? Historiographical reflections on the Malayan Emergency', *History Compass.* 17 (3). 'Despite their innocuous nomenclature, New Villages were in fact ... concentration camps designed less to keep the communists out but to place the rural Chinese population under strict government surveillance and control.'
14. Newsinger, John (2015), *British Counterinsurgency* (2nd ed.), p.50.
15. Ibid., (2015), pp.41–2, 43.
16. Hack, 2012, 682–4.
17. Hack, 2000.
18. See Hay (1982) and Jacob (2021), pp.169–74.
19. Hack (2018), p.210.
20. CO1952f. CO 1022/54/SEA/10/409/01. 'Punishment of the Malayan Town of Tanjong Malim for non-cooperation with the Administration: Reconciliation with the town after the visit of the High Commissioner, General Sir Gerald Templer in August 1952' in *Letter to Colonial Office*. Kew: The National Archives.
21. Malaya – Britain's forgotten war for rubber by Mark Curtis, Editor, *Declassified UK.*

22. See also Sodhy, P. (1987). The Malaysian Connection in the Vietnam War. *Contemporary Southeast Asia*, *9*(1), 38–53.
23. Harrison, pp.157–8.
24. Hack, p.317.
25. Harrison, pp.157–8; Hack (2022), p.317.
26. Fujio Hara (2002). *Malaysian Chinese & China: Conversion in Identity Consciousness, 1945–1957.* University of Hawaii Press. pp. 61–5. Mark Curtis (15, 1995). *The Ambiguities of Power: British Foreign Policy Since 1945.* pp. 61–71. Hack, *The Malayan Emergency: Revolution and Counterinsurgency at the End of Empire.* Cambridge p.316.
27. Chin Peng, *Miraflor, Alias Chin Peng: My Side of History.* p.302.
28. Harrison, *Dark Trophies: Hunting and the Enemy Body in Modern War*, p.158. *'Signs of the Times – Trophy Skulls'* George.loper.org. August 8, 1996.

Chapter 13: 2nd Battalion Seaforth Highlanders after St Valéry

1. https://www.historynet.com/intercepted-communications-for-field-marshal-erwin-rommel/? By Will Deac, 12.6.2006.
2. Hinsley, F. H. et al (1981). *British Intelligence in the Second World War: Its influence on Strategy and Operations.* Vol. II. London; p. 427.
3. Royle, p.163.
4. Fairrie, p.268.
5. Royle, p.164.
6. https://51hd.co.uk/accounts/colonel_john_sym_dso
7. Fairrie, p.138. See below for more details.
8. Playfair.
9. Ibid., Map 10.
10. Ibid., pp.64–5.
11. *Autumn 1942. International Churchill Society.*
12. 'Winston Churchill's Speech at the Mansion House', 10 November 1942. *Imperial War Museum.*
13. Churchill p.603.
14. https://www.thehighlandersmuseum.com/?p=31048#:~:text=Soon%20after%20El%20Alamein%2C%20the,connected%20it%20to%20the%20sea
15. Craig Durham, The Highlanders Museum (Queen's Own Highlanders Collection) https://www.thehighlandersmuseum.com/?p=31048
16. *The Graves at Akarit*, written by Private John Smart, of 'A' Company 2nd Seaforth Highlanders, in memory of his comrades who fell at Wadi Akarit, in Tunisia, on 6 April 1943. See https://www.thehighlandersmuseum.com/?p=31048#:~:text=Soon%20after%20El%20Alamein%2C%20the,connected%20it%20to%20the%20sea
17. https://51hd.co.uk/history/sicily_landing
18. https://51hd.co.uk/history/sicily_sferro

Chapter 14: The Territorials in the Second World War

1. Grehan, *Churchill's Secret Invasion: Britain's First Large Scale Combined Offensive* 2020. Barnsley.
2. Scheck, *Hitler's African Victims: The German Army Massacres of Black French Soldiers in 1940.* 2006 Cambridge.
3. Osborne, *World War II in Colonial Africa: The Death Knell of Colonialism*, p.74.

4. See Browning, *The Origins of the Final Solution: The Evolution of Nazi Jewish Policy, September 1939-March 1942*. Comprehensive History of the Holocaust.
5. Longerich, *Holocaust: The Nazi Persecution and Murder of the Jews.*
6. Maclean, *Eastern Approaches.*
7. Ranfurly, *To War with Whitaker. The wartime diaries of the Countess of Ranfurly 1939–1945*, p.160.
8. O'Sullivan, *FDR and the End of Empire: The Origins of American Power in the Middle East.*
9. *Iran Press Digest* 1985.
10. Foran, *Fragile Resistance: Social Transformation In Iran From 1500 to the Revolution.*
11. Majd, 'The Three Famines and the Makings of a Malthusian Catastrophe in Iran, 1869–1944' (PDF). *Journal of Iranian Islamic Period History.* 12 (27): pp.99–101.
12. Fairrie, pp.150–1.
13. See Chrystal, *Gunners from the Sky*, Chapter 6: 'We need to explain how and why the 1st Airlanding Light Regiment, after a period of enforced inactivity, found themselves in a hastily-planned operation hundreds of miles behind enemy lines, in some cases 7 miles from their objective, with temperamental radios and up against two German Panzer regiments lurking nearby that had, until the last minute, apparently remained invisible to and undetected by British Army intelligence'.

Chapter 15: 1945 and beyond

1. Fairrie, p.103.
2. Royle, pp.194–8; Chrystal, *British Army of the Rhine 1945–1993.*
3. Fairrie, p.106.
4. Ibid., pp.116–17.
5. Queen's Own Highlanders (Seaforth and Camerons), Regiments.org.
6. Lesley-Dixon, Kenneth, *Northern Ireland: The Troubles, from the Provos to the Det.*
7. https://www.theroyalregimentofscotland.org/about/our-history
8. *The Highlander: The Regimental Journal of The Highlanders (Seaforth, Gordons and Camerons),* Winter 2003, Vol., No.2.
9. 'Turning Catterick Into A "Super Garrison"'. Forces TV.
10. Information on the Army 2020 Refine exercise (PDF). Marlborough Lines Andover, Hampshire United Kingdom: Ministry of Defence (UK), 2017. Army 2020 Refine was the name given to the restructuring of the British Army in the 2010s, in light of the Strategic Defence and Security Review 2015. A December 2016 written statement stated that the first Strike Brigade to form would consist of:
    - Household Cavalry Regiment
    - King's Royal Hussars
    - 1st Bn Scots Guards
    - The Highlanders, 4th Bn Royal Regiment of Scotland.
11. Regular Army Basing Announcement' (PDF), Ministry of Defence.
12. '*SCOTS Camanachd – Armed Forces Shinty Club*'.

Further Reading

To help the reader, Further Reading suggestions are given here in a General section followed by books and papers specific to individual chapters.

General

Addison-Smith, Lt Col CL, *10th Battalion Seaforth Highlanders in the Great War*, Edinburgh 1927

Allen, Charles, (2000), *Soldier Sahibs: The Men Who Made the North-West Frontier*, London

Barthorp, Michael, *Afghan Wars and the North-West Frontier 1839–1947*. London, 2002

Bird, Derek, *The Spirit of the Troops is Excellent: The 6th (Morayshire) Battalion, Seaforth Highlanders in the Great War 1914 – 1919,* Librario Publishing, 2008

Blampied, H. John, *With a Highland Regiment in Mesopotamia* (the 2nd Battalion, The Black Watch in Iraq During the First World War, 1916–1917; WWI Centenary Series), Legare Street Press, 2015

Bloomer, William Henry, *Badges of the Highland and Lowland Regiments: Including Volunteers and Territorial Battalion*s, W.H.& K.D.Bloomer, 1982

Borthwick, Alastair, *Battalion: A British Infantry Unit's Actions from the Battle of El Alamein to the Elbe, 1942–1945.* Kindle Edition (5th Seaforth Highlanders)

——, *Sans Peur: 5th Battalion Seaforth Highlanders in World War II,* Stirling 1946

Boyle, Fergus D., 2019, *CHUM: A Memoir*, Independently published

Brander, Michael (1971). *The Scottish Highlanders and their Regiments. London*

Campbell, Colin, *Pipe tunes of WW1- Part 4 The Seaforth Highlanders,* Piping Press, https://pipingpress.com/pipe-tunes-of-ww1-part-4-the-seaforth-highlanders/

Cannon, Richard, *Historical Records of the 72nd Regiment*, Parker, Furnival & Parker, 1848

Chrystal, Paul; Youll, Nina, *Jack Youll VC*, Barnsley 2025

Chrystal, Paul, *Biowarfare and Bioterrorism: Disease as a Weapon of War*, Barnsley, 2023

Chrystal, Paul; Chrystal, David, Major retd, BEM MiD, *Gunners from the Sky: 1st Airlanding Light Regiment RA in Italy and at the Battle of Arnhem, Barnsley*, 2023

——, *A History of the World in 100 Pandemics, Plagues & Epidemics*, Barnsley, 2022

——, *British Army of the Rhine: The BAOR 1945–1993*, Barnsley, 2018

Collier, Richard, *The Sands of Dunkirk*, Glasgow. 1961

Collins, Norman, *Last Man Standing: The Memoirs, Letters and Photographs of a Teenage Officer,* Barnsley, 2002

Craster, H.H.E., 'The Seaforth Highlanders, August 1914 to April 1916', *The Scottish Historical Review*, Vol. 16, No. 64, 1919, pp.309–24

Davidson, Hugh Major, *The Seaforth Highlanders in South Africa 1899–1902*, W. & A.K. Johnson, 1904

Davidson, Hugh Major (ed), History and Service of the 78th Highlanders – 2 Volumes, Edinburgh 1901

Denoon, Brian, *1st Battalion Seaforth Highlanders, India and Burma, 1941–1944,* 2000

Egerton, Major General Granville, *With the Seaforth Highlanders in the Sudan Campaign*, London 1909
Fairrie, Lieutenant Colonel Angus *'Cuidich'n Righ' A History of the Queen's Own Highlanders (Seaforth and Camerons), Inverness, 1983*
——, *Queen's Own Highlanders, Golspie 1998 – second edition of Fairrie (1983)*
Frank, Adam, *The Clans, Septs and Regiments of the Scottish Highlands*, Famedram Publishers, 2005
Haldane, M.M., *History of the Fourth Battalion The Seaforth Highlanders With Some Account of the Military Annals of Ross, the Fencibles, the Volunteers, and the Home Defence and Reserve Battalions 1914–1919*, Naval & Military Press Ltd, 2003
Henderson, Diana M., *Highland Soldier: A Social Study of the Highland Regiments, 1820–1920*, John Donald Publishers Ltd, 2001
Holdich, T.H. 'Tirah'. PDF *Khyber.ORG.* 18 December 2009, https://en.wikipedia.org/wiki/Afridi_Redshirt_Rebellion,_Indian_North_West_Frontier_1930%E2%80%931931
Holland, James, 2016, *Burma '44 The Battle that Turned Britain's War in the East,*
Holmes, Richard (2005) Sahib: *The British Soldier in India* 1740–1914
Illustrated History of the First Battalion Seaforth Highlanders, Peshawar, India 1909
Joslen, H.F. (2003) [1960]. *Orders of Battle: Second World War, 1939–1945.* Uckfield, East Sussex: Naval and Military Press
Kaufmann J.E. (2006) H.W. *Fortress France: The Maginot Line and French Defenses in World War II*, Stackpole Books
Kennedy, Jonathan, *Pathogenesis: How Germs Made History* (Torva, London, 2023
Lord, Walter, *The Miracle of Dunkirk*, London, 1982
Mackintosh, Col George, 1909, *A Short History of the Seaforth Highlanders*, St Catherine Press Ltd
Marsh, Brandon. *Ramparts of Empire: British Imperialism & India's Afghan Frontier 1918–1948*, 2016
Masters, Robert E.L, *Perverse crimes in history: evolving concepts of sadism, lust-murder, and necrophilia from ancient to modern times. Julian Press, 1963*
McLynn, Frank, 2011, *The Burma Campaign: Disaster into Triumph 1942–1945*, London
McVeigh, James (1887). *The Jubilee Memorial. The Historical Records of The 78th Highlanders Or Ross-shire Buffs, (Now 2nd Battalion Seaforth Highlanders) From 1793 to 1887. From Official and Authentic Sources.* Dumfries
Miller, Charles, *Khyber, British India's North West frontier: the story of an imperial migraine.* Macdonald and Jane's, 1977
Moreman, Tim, *The Army in India and the Development of Frontier Warfare 1847–1947.* Macmillan, 1998
Nairne, Col C.S., *A Short History of the Seaforth Highlanders*, Ross-Shire Printing & Publishing Co
Neave, Airey, *The Flames of Calais*, London, 1972
Nevill, Capt. H.L., *Campaigns on the North-West Frontier*, 1912. Reprinted by Battery Press, 1999
Nixon, Paul, https://armyservicenumbers.blogspot.com/2009/09/seaforth-highlanders-1st-2nd-battalions.html *Army Service Numbers 1881–1918*
Oatts, Lewis Balfour, *The Highland Light Infantry* (Famous Regiments Series) Leo Cooper, 1969
Official History of Operations on the N. W. Frontier of India 1920–35 Parts I, II and III. Naval & Military Press in association with the Imperial War Museum

Pratt Paul, W., *Highland Regiments: Tigers in Tartan*, 1971
Richards, Donald Sydney, *The savage frontier: a history of the Anglo-Afghan wars. Macmillan, 1990*
Roger, Alexander, *Battle Honours of the British Empire and Commonwealth Land Forces 1662–1991*. Crowood Press, 2003
Royle, Trevor, *Queen's Own Highlanders. A concise history*. Mainstream Publishing, Edinburgh, 2007
Snyder, Timothy, *Bloodlands, Europe between Hitler and Stalin* (London 2010) *175–182*
Stewart, David, 1825, *Sketches of The Character, Manners, and Present State of the Highlanders of Scotland with details of The Military Service of The Highland Regiments*
Stewart, Jules, *The Savage Border: The Story of the North-West Frontier*, Stroud, 2007
Stiles, Richard G. M., *The Story of the India General Service Medal 1908–1935*. Terence Wise. Knighton, Powys, 1992
Stockman, Jim, *Seaforth Highlanders: a Fighting Soldier Remembers,* Crecy Publishing, 1987
Sumner, Ian, *The Indian Army 1914–1947*. Osprey Publishing, 2001
Sutherland, Colonel John, War Diary of the *5th Battalion Seaforth Highlanders,* London 1920
Sym, John, *Seaforth Highlanders*, Gale and Polden, 1962
Thomas, L. *Beyond Khyber Pass*, London, n.d. (ca. 1925)
Thompson, Julian, *Forgotten Voices of Burma: The Second World War's Forgotten Conflict,* London, 2010
Thompson, Julian, *The Imperial War Museum Book of the War in Burma 1942–1945*
Todd, Andrew, *The Elephant at War: The 2nd Battalion Seaforth Highlanders*, Bishop Auckland 1998
Van Emden, Richard, *Last Man Standing: The Memoirs, Letters and Photographs of a Teenage Officer*, Barnsley 2012
Walker, F.W., *The great deeds of the Seaforth Highlanders (The story of the regiments)*, Dent, 1915
Watson, Frederick, *The Story of the Highland Regiments,* London, 1925
Watt, Lauchlan MacLean, *The Seaforth Highlanders,* 1915
Wilkinson-Latham, Robert, *North-West Frontier 1837–1947*, Osprey Publishing, 1977

ADDITIONAL FURTHER READING BY CHAPTER

Chapter 1: Early Seaforth: the 78th (later the 72nd) 1778–1793

Balakrishna, Sandeep, *Tipu Sultan, The Tyrant of Mysore,* Rare Publications
Biddulph, H., 'The Expedition to Kertch, 1855. A Contemporary Account by Lieut. Robert Biddulph, R.A.' *Journal of the Society for Army Historical Research*, vol. 21, no. 83, 1942, pp.128–35
The Cambridge History of the British Empire, 1929
David, Saul (2003), *The Indian Mutiny: 1857*, London
Dodwell, H.H. (ed), *Cambridge History of India*, Vol. v
Harris, John (2001), *The Indian Mutiny*, Ware
Hasan, Mohibbul (2009), *History of Tipu Sultan (Reprint ed.). Delhi, Aakar Books*
Jamil, Arish, 'Why Mysore? The Idealistic and Materialistic Factors Behind Tipu Sultan's War Rocket Success' (PDF). *Emory Endeavors in World History – Volume 5*. Emory College of Arts and Science
Keys, E., *History of the Madras Army, Government Press. 27 July 1882, via Google Book*
Macquarie University, *Seringapatam 1799: British Regiments*

McCulloch, Ian Macpherson (2006). *Sons of the Mountains, The Highland Regiments in the French & Indian War, 1756–1767, Volume Two*. Purple Mountain Press
Miles, W., (translator), *The history of the Reign of Tipu Sultan*
Mill, James, *A history of British India*, Volume 5
Mysorean Military Commanders and Officials, Seringapatam 1799
Narasimha, Roddam (27 July 2011). 'Rockets in Mysore and Britain, 1750–1850 A.D.' (PDF). National Aeronautical Laboratory and Indian Institute of Science
Naravane, M.S., (2014). *Battles of the Honourable East India Company*, A.P.H. Publishing Corporation
Peers, Douglas M., *India Under Colonial Rule: 1700–1885*, London, 2013
Raugh, Harold E. (2004). *The Victorians at War, 1815–1914: An Encyclopedia of British Military History*
Sil, Narasingha P., 'Tipu Sultan: A Re-Vision,' *Calcutta Historical Journal* (2008) 28#1 pp.1–23
Skelley, Alan Ramsay (1977). *The Victorian army at home: the recruitment and terms and conditions of the British regular, 1859–1899*, London
Sketches of The Character, Manners, and Present State of the Highlanders of Scotland – Seaforth Highlanders
Strandberg, Samuel, *Tipu Sultan: The Tiger of Mysore: or, to fight against the odds*, AB Samuel Travel
Wigington, Robin, *Firearms of Tipu Sultan, 1783–99*, J. Taylor Book Ventures

India and the East India Company
Barua, Pradeep (1994). 'Military developments in India, 1750–1850,' *Journal of Military History*
Bryant, G.J. (2004) 'Asymmetric Warfare: The British Experience in Eighteenth-Century India,' *Journal of Military History*, Vol. 68, No. 2, pp. 431–69
Dalrymple, William (2020). *The Anarchy – The Relentless Rise of the East India Company. London*
——, 'Lessons for capitalism from the East India Company', *Financial Times, 30 August 2019*
Gilbert, Arthur N., 'Recruitment and Reform in the East India Company Army, 1760–1800,' *Journal of British Studies*, 1975
Keay, John (1991), *The Honourable Company: A History of the English East India Company*, London
Roy, Kaushik (2005), 'Military Synthesis in South Asia: Armies, Warfare, and Indian Society, c. 1740--1849,' *Journal of Military History*, Vol. 69, No. 3, pp. 651–90
——, 'The hybrid military establishment of the East India Company in South Asia: 1750–1849', *Journal of Global History*, Vol. 6, Iss. 2, pp. 195–218
Scott, William, *'East India Company, 1817–1827'*, *archiveshub.jisc.ac.uk. Senate House Library Archives, University of London*
Sykes, W.H. (1847). 'Vital Statistics of the East India Company's Armies in India, European and Native', *Journal of the Statistical Society of London*. 10 (2): 100–131

Chapter 2: The 78th Highlanders 1793–1881

Dalrymple, William, 'The Ghosts of Gandamak', *New York Times*, 8 May 2010. sudan
——, *Return of a King; the Battle for Afghanistan*, London 2010
——'The first Anglo-Afghan war: Lessons unlearned'. *The Economist*, 26 January 2013
Germon, Maria, *Journal of the Siege of Lucknow*, London (nd)
Halliday, James, *Scotland: A Concise History* (1990)
——, *1820 Rising: The Radical War* (1993)
Holmes, Richard, *Sahib: The British Soldier in India*, London, 2005

Hopton, Richard (2002), *The Battle of Maida 1806: Fifteen Minutes of Glory*, Barnsley
Howard, Martin R., *Walcheren 1809: The Scandalous Destruction of a British Army*, Barnsley, 2012
Hunt, George Henry (1858), *Outram & Havelock's Persian Campaign*, Routledge & Co
Mac a'Ghobhainn, Seumas, *The Scottish insurrection of 1820, Edinburgh (2001)*
Malalgoda, Kitsiri (1976), *Buddhism in Sinhalese Society, 1750–1900: A Study of Religious Revival and Change*, U. of California Press
Macrory, Patrick (2002). *Retreat from Kabul: The Catastrophic British Defeat in Afghanistan, 1842.* Guilford, Connecticut
Mills, Lennox A. (1933). *Ceylon Under British Rule, 1795–1932.* Oxford
Outram, Lieut General Sir James, *Lieut-General Sir James Outram's Persian Campaign in 1857*, London, 1860
Peebles, Patrick (2006). *The History of Sri Lanka.* Greenwood
Pentland, Gordon, *Spirit of the Union: Popular Politics in Scotland, 1815–1820*, Pickering & Chatto, 2011
Prebble, John, *The King's Jaunt: George IV in Scotland, August 1822 'One and Twenty Daft Days'*, Birlinn Publishers (2000)
Sandes, Lt Col E.W.C., *The Indian Sappers and Miners*, The Institution of Royal Engineers, Chatham, 1948
Schneid, Frederick C., 2002, *Napoleon's Italian Campaigns: 1805–1815.* Westport, Conn
Schrikker, Alicia (2007). *Dutch and British Colonial Intervention in Sri Lanka, 1780–1815: Expansion and Reform.* Leiden
Sivasundaram, Sujit (2010), 'Ethnicity, Indigeneity, and Migration in the Advent of British Rule to Sri Lanka', *The American Historical Review.* 115 (2): pp.428–52
—— (2007), 'Tales of the Land: British Geography and Kandyan Resistance in Sri Lanka, c. 1803–1850, (PDF). *Modern Asian Studies.* 41 (5), pp.925–65
Smith, Digby, *The Napoleonic Wars Data Book,* London
Smout, T.C., *A history of the Scottish people 1560–1830,* London, Fontana (1985)
Spencer, Jonathan (1990), *Sri Lanka: History and the Roots of Conflict,* Psychology Press

Chapter 3: Seaforth Highlanders 1st and 2nd Battalions: 1881–1899

Asher, Michael (2005), *Khartoum: The Ultimate Imperial Adventure,* London
Blunt, Wilfrid Scawen (1907), *the Secret History of the English Occupation of Egypt*, London
Bottomore, Stephen (2007), 'Chapter 4: The Battle of Omdurman (1898) – Moving images of a British victory', *Filming, faking and propaganda: The origins of the war film, 1897–1902* (doctoral), University of Utrecht
Brighton, Terry (1998), *The Last Charge: the 21st Lancers and the Battle of Omdurman*, Marlborough, Crowood
'The Chitral Expedition', *The Lancet* 145, p.1127, 4 May 1895
Clowes, Sir William Laird, *The Royal Navy: A History From the Earliest Times to the Death of Queen Victoria, Volume Seven,* London, Chatham Publishing, 1997.
Daly, E.M., *Empire on the Nile: The Anglo-Egyptian Sudan, 1898–1934*, Cambridge University Press, 1986
Ellis, John (1981), *The Social History of the Machine Gun,* New York
Faught, C. Brad (2016), *Kitchener. Hero and Anti-Hero,* I.B. Tauris
Featherstone, Donald (1993), *Tel El-Kebir 1882,* Osprey Publishing
Green, Dominic, *Three Empires on the Nile: The Victorian Jihad, 1869–1899*, Simon and Schuster, 2007, p.252
Harrington, Peter (1993), *British Artists and War: The Face of Battle in Paintings and Prints, 1700–1914*, Greenhill Books

Harrington, Peter (ed.) (1998), *Omdurman 1898: The Eyewitnesses Speak,* London
Huttenback, Robert A., 'The Siege of Chitral and the "Breach of Faith Controversy"—The Imperial Factor in Late Victorian Party Politics', *Journal of British Studies* 10.1 (1970), pp.126–44
McTiernan, Mick, *A Very Bad Place Indeed For a Soldier. The British involvement in the early stages of the European Intervention in Crete. 1897–1898,* King's College, London, September 2014
Meredith, John (1998), *Omdurman Diaries 1898: Eyewitness Accounts of the Legendary Campaign,* Barnsley
Pakenham, Edward (1992), *The Scramble for Africa,* London
Raugh Jr., Harold E., *British Military Operations in Egypt and the Sudan: A Selected Bibliography,* Scarecrow Press, 2008
Spiers, Edward M. (2004), *The Victorian Soldier in Africa,* Manchester
Wright, William (2009), *A Tidy Little War: The British Invasion of Egypt, 1882,* Spellmount
Zulfo, I.H. (1980), *Karari: The Sudanese Account of the Battle of Omdurman,* Warner

Chapter 4: The 2nd Seaforth Highlanders in the Second Boer War 1899–1902 and After

Barnard, Hennie, 'The Concentration Camps 1899–1902'
Conan Doyle, Arthur (1900), *The Great Boer War*, London
Creswicke, Louis (1900), *South Africa and the Transvaal War.* Vol. 2: From the Commencement of the War to the Battle of Colenso, 15 Dec 1899 (1st ed.), Edinburgh
de Villiers, Professor J.C. (June 1984). 'The Medical Aspect of the Anglo-Boer War, 1899–1902 Part ll'. *South African Military History Journal. 6 (3)*
Fremont-Barnes, Gregory (2003), *The Boer War 1899–1902,* Oxford
Gous, Nico, *'Boer War women, children put in concentration camps 'for own good': British MP sparks outrage'*. See https://www.theguardian.com/world/2001/dec/09/paulharris.theobserver
Hansard, 'SOUTH AFRICAN WAR—CONCENTRATION CAMPS, HC Deb 04 March 1902 vol 104 cc402–67.'
Marais, Martin (2014), *The Battle of Paardeberg: The Lord Roberts' Gambit*, lulu.com
Maurice, Major General Sir Frederick (1998), [1st. pub. 1906], *Maps: Volumes 5–8*, History of the War in South Africa 1899–1902, Naval and Military Press
Pakenham, Thomas (1979), *The Boer War,* New York
Rickard, J. (March 2007), 'Battle of Paardeberg, 18–27 February 1900', *Military History Encyclopedia on the Web*
Scott, John L. (2007), *British Concentration Camps of the Second South African War (The Transvaal, 1900–1902*), FSU Digital Library
Spies, S.B. (1977*), Methods of Barbarism: Roberts and Kitchener and Civilians in the Boer Republics, January 1900-May 1902,* Cape Town
Stirling, John (17 February 2009), 'Gordon Highlanders' (extract), *Our Regiments in South Africa*
Wessels, André (2011), *The Anglo–Boer War 1889–1902: White Man's War, Black Man's War, Traumatic War*. African Sun Media

Chapter 5: The Seaforth Highlanders in the First World War

Battle of Le Cateau 26th August 1914. Tour of the Battlefield, Naval & Military Press London
Beckett, Ian F.W. (2006), *Haig's Generals*, Barnsley
Bird, Antony (2008), *Gentlemen, We Will Stand and Fight: Le Cateau 1914,* Ramsbury
Cave, Nigel (2008). *Le Cateau. Battlefield Europe,* Barnsley

Edmonds, J.E. (1926). *Military Operations France and Belgium, 1914: Mons, the Retreat to the Seine, the Marne and the Aisne August–October 1914. History of the Great War Based on Official Documents by Direction of the Historical Section of the Committee of Imperial Defence. Vol. II (2nd ed.).* London

Gavaghan, Michael (2000), *Illustrated Pocket Guide to Le Cateau, 1914. Forgotten Battles,* Preston

Glanfield, John (2005), *Bravest of the Brave.* Sutton Publishing

Harvey, David (2000), *Monuments to Courage,* Naval & Military Press

Hastings, M. (2013), *Catastrophe: Europe Goes to War 1914,* London

Humphries, M.O. (2013), *Der Weltkrieg: 1914, The Battle of the Frontiers and Pursuit to the Marne. Germany's Western Front: Translations From the German Official History of the Great War, Vol. I. Part 1, Waterloo,* Canada, Wilfrid Laurier University Press

Middlebrook, Martin (1971), *The First Day of the Somme*, London

Chapter 6: The Territorials in the First World War

Beckett, Ian Frederick William (2008), *Territorials: A Century of Service*, Plymouth

—— (2011), *Britain's Part-time Soldiers: The Amateur Military Tradition 1558–1945*, Pen & Sword Military, Barnsley

Bewsher, Frederick William (1921). *The History of the 51st (Highland) Division, 1914–1918.* Edinburgh

Rt. Hon Earl Brownlow (1900), 'The British Volunteer System', *The North American Review*

Campbell, John (2020). *Haldane: The Forgotten Statesman Who Shaped Modern Britain.* London:

Cunningham, Hugh (1975), *The Volunteer Force: A Social and Political History, 1859–1908,* Taylor & Francis

David, Saul, (1994), *After Dunkirk: Churchill's Sacrifice of the Highland Division*, London

Dennis, Peter (1987), *The Territorial Army 1907–1940*, Woodbridge

Fortescue, John (1909), *The county lieutenancies and the army, 1803–1814*, London

Grierson, James Moncrieff (1909). *Records of the Scottish volunteer force, 1859–1908.* Edinburgh: W. Blackwood

Hay, George (2017), *The Yeomanry Cavalry and Military Identities in Rural Britain, 1815–1914*, London

Messenger, Charles (2005), *Call to Arms: the British Army 1914–18*, London

Mileham, Patrick (2003), *The Yeomanry Regiments; Over 200 Years of Tradition*, Staplehurst

Mitchinson, K.W. (2005), *Defending Albion: Britain's Home Army 1908–1919*, London

—— (2008), *England's Last Hope: The Territorial Force, 1908–1914*, London

—— (2014), *The Territorial Force at War, 1914–1916*, London

Pillinger, Dennis (2000), *Victoria Cross Presentations and Locations,* Maidenhead

Ross, Graham (1995), *Scotland's Forgotten Valour*, MacLean Press

The Register of the Victoria Cross (3rd ed.), This England Books, 1997

Simkins, Peter (2007), *Kitchener's Army: The Raising of the New Armies 1914–1916*, Pen & Sword Military, Barnsley

Spiers, Edward (2003), 'The Late Victorian Army 1868–1914', In Chandler, David G. (ed.), *The Oxford History of the British Army*, Oxford, pp.187–210

Steppler, Glenn A. (1992), *Britons, To Arms! The Story of the British Volunteer Soldier*, Stroud

Zuber, Terence (2011), *The Mons Myth,* Stroud

Chapter 8: The Seaforth Highlanders on The North West Frontier

Ahmed, Akbar S., 'Colonial Encounter on the North-West Frontier Province: Myth and Mystification', *Economic and Political Weekly* 14, no. 51/52 (1979): 2092–7

Beattie, Hugh (2019), Chapter 7 – 'British policy in Waziristan and the Razmak base', *Empire and Tribe in the Afghan Frontier Region: Custom, Conflict and British Strategy in Waziristan until 1947*, Bloomsbury Publishing

Collett, Nigel (2006), *The Butcher of Amritsar: General Reginald Dyer*, Hambledon Continuum, London

Digital Library of India 'Part II The Afridi and Red Shirt Rebellion, 1930–31; The Mohmand and Bajaur Operations, 1933', Archive.org, mirror from Digital Library of India

Draper, Alfred (1985). *The Amritsar Massacre: Twilight of the Raj*, Buchan and Enright, London

Dupree, N. (1988), *The Women of Afghanistan*, Islamabad, UNOCHA

Everett, J. (1978), *Women and Social Change in India*, Delhi: Heritage

General Staff, Indian Army Headquarters (2003) [1923]. Operations in Waziristan, 1919–1920

Hiskey, David, 'The Curious Practice of Execution by Golden Shower'. *Today I Found Out* 25 November 2012

Journal of the United Service Institution of India "Two recent actions against Afridis" I-The Night operations against Spintigga 10/11th March 1931; II- The Action in the Gandao Kotal 18th March 1931 (page 73). *Journal of the United Service Institution of India*, Volume 62, 62–86, 1932 Archive.org

Judd, Dennis (1996), 'The Amritsar Massacre of 1919: Gandhi, the Raj and the Growth of Indian Nationalism, 1915–39', in Judd, *Empire: The British Imperial Experience from 1765 to the Present*. Basic Books. Pp.258–72

Kaur, M. (1980), *Role of Women in the Freedom Movement (1857–1947)*, New Delhi

Khattak, Shabana Shamaas Gul, *The Role of North West Frontier Province in the Freedom Struggle for Pakistan (1930–1947)*, National Institute of Historical and Cultural Research, University Islamabad, 2018

Kumar, R. (1998), *Women and the Indian Freedom Struggle*, Jaipur, Pointer Publishers

Lloyd, Nick (2011), *The Amritsar Massacre: The Untold Story of One Fateful Day*, I.B. Tauris, London

Marsh, B. (2015), 'These Infernal Khudai Khidmatgaran: Defining and Repressing Frontier Nationalism, 1930–1931', In *Ramparts of Empire. Britain and the World*. London

Masters, John (1956), *Bugles and a tiger: a volume of autobiography*, Viking Press, p.190

Matthews, Matt M., *An Ever Present Danger A Concise History of British Military Operations on the North-West Frontier, 1849–1947*, Combat Studies Institute Press, US Army Combined Arms Center, Fort Leavenworth KS, 2010

Moreman, Tim (1998). *The Army in India and the Development of Frontier Warfare 1847–1947*, London

Official History of Operations on the North-West Frontier of India 1920–1935 Parts I, II, III [by General Staff Army Headquarters, India], Manager of Publications, Delhi 1945

Roe, Andrew, 'Pink's War – Applying the Principles of Air Control to Waziristan', *Air Power Review* – Volume 13 No.3, 2010

Saiyid, D. (1998) *Muslim Women of the British Punjab, from Seclusion to politics*, London

Soherwordi, Syed Hussain Shaheed 'Punjabisation' in the British Indian Army 1857–1947 and the Advent of Military Rule in Pakistan', *Edinburgh Papers In South Asian Studies* No.24 (2010)

Walters, Wing Commander Dr Andrew 'RAF Inter-War Operations on the North-West Frontier', page 110 (digital page 112) *Air Power Review* Volume 21, No.1 Spring 2018. raf.mod.uk

Chapter 9: Palestine and After

Kabahā, Muṣṭafá (2014), *The Palestinian People: Seeking Sovereignty and State*, Lynne Rienner Publishers Incorporated

Khalidi, Rashid (2006), *The Iron Cage: The Story of the Palestinian Struggle for Statehood*, Beacon Press

'Mandate for Palestine', *Encyclopaedia Judaica*. Vol. 11. Jerusalem, 1972

McCleave, Easterly, William (1998). *The Belgian Rattlesnake: The Lewis Automatic Machine Gun: A Social and Technical Biography of the Gun and Its Inventors*. Collector Grade

——, *The Belgian Rattlesnake: The Lewis Automatic Machine Gun: A Social and Technical Biography of the Gun and Its Inventors*. Collector Grade

Meṣer, Yaʿaqov; Metzer, Jacob (1998),. *The Divided Economy of Mandatory Palestine*. Cambridge

Reynolds, Major E.G.B. (1960), *The Lee-Enfield* (PDF). London, Cox and Wyman Limited

Chapter 10: 2nd Battalion Seaforth Highlanders in the Second World War – The Battle of France

Bond, Brian (2001), *The Battle for France & Flanders: Sixty Years On*, Pen and Sword

David, Saul (1994), *After Dunkirk: Churchill's Sacrifice of the Highland Division, France 1940,* London

Delaforce, Patrick, (2007) *Monty's Highlanders: The Story of the 51st Highland Division*, Pen & Sword

Doherty, Richard, (2006), *None Bolder: The History of 51st Highland Division in the Second World War,* Spellmount

King, Anthony (2017), 'Why did 51st Highland Division Fail? A case-study in command and combat effectiveness', *British Journal for Military History*, Vol. 4 No.1

Linklater, Eric (1942), *The Highland Division*, HMSO

Mitchell, Stewart, *St Valéry and Its Aftermath,* Barnsley, 2017

Salmond, J. B. (1953), *The Story of the 51st Highland Division*, Wm Blackwood & Sons

The Official Website of the 51 Highland Division

The British Army in the Great War: The Long, Long Trail

The Forgotten 51st

The Forgotten Heroes of World War 2 by Robert Beesley

Remember the 51st (Highland) Division at Saint-Valéry-en-Caux

Timeline history of 1940 surrender with photos of the memorial at Veules-les-Roses

https://51hd.co.uk/history

https://51hd.co.uk/history/Valéry_1940

Chapter 11: Sergeant Eric Priest: One Seaforth Highlander's Journey from the Northwest Frontier to Stalag 383, 1925–1945

Chrystal, Paul; Youll, Nina, *Jack Youll VC*, Barnsley 2025

Chrystal, Paul, *Biowarfare and Bioterrorism: Disease as a Weapon of War*, Barnsley, 2023

Chrystal, Paul; Chrystal, David, Major retd, BEM MiD, *Gunners from the Sky: 1st Airlanding Light Regiment RA in Italy and at the Battle of Arnhem, Barnsley*, 2023

——, *A History of the World in 100 Pandemics, Plagues & Epidemics*, Barnsley, 2022

——, *Old Hartlepool and West Hartlepool,* Catrine, 2019

——, *British Army of the Rhine: The BAOR 1945–1993*, Barnsley, 2018

Chapter 12: 1st Battalion Seaforth Highlanders in the Second World War and After

Christopher, Paul (2013*)*. 'Malaya, 1948–1955: Case Outcome: COIN Win', *Paths to Victory: Detailed Insurgency Case Studies*, pp.51–63

Deery, Phillip, 'Malaya: Britain's Asian Cold War?', *Journal of Cold War Studies*, Vol. 9, issue 1, 1948

Denoon, B., *1st Battalion Seaforth Highlanders – India and Burma 1941–1944*

Fussell, Paul (1990). *Wartime: Understanding and Behavior in the Second World War*. New York

George, Kenneth (1996), *Showing Signs of Violence: The Cultural Politics of a Twentieth-Century Headhunting Ritual*, Berkeley, University of California Press

Hack, Karl (1999). 'Iron claws on Malaya': the historiography of the Malayan Emergency', *Journal of Southeast Asian Studies*. 30 (1): pp.99–125

Hack, Karl (1999), 'Corpses, Prisoners of War and Captured Documents: British and Communist Narratives of the Malayan Emergency, and the Dynamics of Intelligence Transformation', *Intelligence and National Security*, 14 (4): 211–41

Hack, Karl,(2000) *Defence and Decolonisation in South-East Asia: Britain, Malaya and Singapore 1941–1967,* London

Hack, Karl (28 September 2012). 'Everyone Lived in fear: Malaya and the British way of counter-insurgency'. *Small Wars & Counterinsurgencies*. 23 (4–5): 682–4

Hack, Karl (2018). 'Devils that suck the blood of the Malayan People: The Case for Post-Revisionist Analysis of Counter-insurgency Violence', *War in History*, 25 (2): 202–26

Hack, Karl (2022), *The Malayan Emergency: Revolution and Counterinsurgency at the End of Empire.* Cambridge

Harrison, Simon (2012), *Dark Trophies: Hunting and the Enemy Body in Modern War*. Oxford, Berghahn

Hay, Alastair *(1982),* 'The Chemical Scythe: Lessons of 2, 4, 5-T, and dioxin', *Springer Nature. pp. 149–50*

Holland, James, (2016) *Burma '44, The Battle that Turned Britain's War in the East*, London

Hughes, Matthew (October 2012), 'Introduction: British ways of counter-insurgency', *Small Wars & Insurgencies*. London, Taylor & Francis. 23 (4–5), 580–90

Jacob, Claus; Walters, Adam (2021). 'Risk and Responsibility in Chemical Research: The Case of Agent Orange', in Schummer, Joachim; Børsen, Tom (eds.). *Ethics Of Chemistry: From Poison Gas to Climate Engineering, Singapore,* World Scientific pp.169–94

Keo, Bernard Z. (March 2019), 'A small, distant war? Historiographical reflections on the Malayan Emergency', *History Compass*,17 (3)

Komer, R.W. (February 1972). *The Malayan Emergency in Retrospect: Organisation of a Successful Counterinsurgency Effort* (PDF). Rand Corporation

McLynn, Frank (2011), *The Burma Campaign: Disaster into Triumph 1942–1945*, London

Mitchell, David F. (2016), 'The Malayan Emergency: How to Fight a Counterinsurgency War', *Warfare History Network*

Newsinger, John (2013), *The Blood Never Dried: A People's History of the British Empire* (2nd ed.), London

Newsinger, John (2015), *British Counterinsurgency* (2nd ed.), Basingstoke

Roadnight, A., 'Sleeping with the Enemy: Britain, Japanese Troops and the Netherlands East Indies, 1945–1946', *History*, 87 (286), 245–68 (2002)

Siver, Christi L., 'The Other Forgotten War: Understanding Atrocities During the Malayan Emergency' (2009). APSA 2009 Toronto Meeting Paper, Available at SSRN: https://ssrn.com/abstract=1451517

Stubbs, Richard (2004), *Hearts and Minds in Guerilla Warfare: The Malayan Emergency 1948–1960,* Eastern University

Taber, Robert (2002), *War of the flea: the classic study of guerrilla warfare*, Brassey's

Thompson, Julian (2010), *Forgotten Voices of Burma*, London

Ucko, David H. (2019), 'Counterinsurgency as armed reform: The political history of the Malayan Emergency', *Journal of Strategic Studies*, 42 (3–4): 448–79

Weingartner, James J. (1992). 'Trophies of War: U.S. Troops and the Mutilation of Japanese War Dead, 1941–1945', *Pacific Historical Review*. 61 (1): 53–67

https://www.facebook.com/thehighlandersmuseum/photos/1st-battalion-seaforth-highlanders-india-and-burma-1941-1944-written-and-compile/1851149078283352

Chapter 13: 2nd Battalion Seaforth Highlanders after St Valéry

Buffetaut, Yves (1995). *Operation Supercharge-La seconde bataille d'El Alamein*, Les grandes batailles de la Seconde Guerre mondiale: Collection hors-série Militaria, Paris: Histoire et Collections

Churchill, W. (1950), *The Hinge of Fate. The Second World War,* New York

Doherty, Richard (2020), *A Noble Crusade: The History of Eighth Army, 1941 to 1945*, Pen & Sword Military, Barnsley

Doherty, Richard (2006), *None Bolder: The History of 51st (Highland) Division in the Second World War*, Spellmount

Doherty, Richard (1994), *Only the Enemy in Front (Every Other Beggar Behind): The Recce Corps at War, 1940–1946*, Spellmount

Doherty, Richard (2002), *The Sound of History: El Alamein – 1942*, Spellmount

Doherty, Richard (2007), *The British Reconnaissance Corps in World War II*, Osprey, Oxford

Lucas, James Sydney (1983). *War in the Desert: The Eighth Army at El Alamein*. New York

Chapter 14: The Territorials in the Second World War

Jackson, Ashley (2018), *An Overview of Persian Command: A History of the Second World War in Iran and Iraq*, Yale

Chapter 15: 1945 and beyond

Lesley-Dixon, Kenneth, (201), *Northern Ireland: The Troubles, from the Provos to the Det,* Barnsley

Chrystal, Paul, (2018), *British Army of the Rhine 1945–1993*, Barnsley

The Highlander. The Regimental Journal of The Highlanders (Seaforth, Gordons and Camerons)

Jackson, Robert (2008), *The Malayan Emergency and Indonesian Confrontation: The Commonwealth's Wars 1948–1966,* Barnsley

King, Hannah, '4 SCOTS Return to Work in Catterick after Afghanistan Deployment', *Forces News*, 3 December 2020

Museum of the Royal Scots and the Royal Regiment of Scotland. The Royal Scots

Paul, James, (2008). 'Index of the Borneo–Malay Peninsula Confrontation, *Britain's Small Wars*

Queen's Own Highlanders: A Short History, Regimental HQ QO Hldrs

'The Royal Regiment of Scotland 2006, *Scottish Military Article*

'Shinty in the Armed Forces, *Shinty*, 20 March 2014

'Yesterday, soldiers from 4th Battalion @The_SCOTS spoke with Defence Secretary @BWallaceMP on his visit to Catterick Garrison', *British Army – Twitter, 20 February 2021*

Index